Raising,
and Losing,
My Remarkable
Teenage Mother

Published 2021
Printed in the United States of America
Hardcover ISBN: 978-1-7364605-0-4
Paperback ISBN: 978-1-7364605-3-5
E-ISBN: 978-1-7364605-2-8
Library of Congress Control Number: 2021904143

Astoria Books
Seattle, WA
info@astoriabooks.com

Names and identifying characteristics have been changed to protect the privacy of certain individuals.

Book design by Stacey Aaronson
Printed in the USA

Raising, and Losing, My Remarkable Teenage Mother

A Memoir

by

Stacey Aaronson

ASTORIA BOOKS

For Bree,
of course

remarkable

adjective

worthy of attention; striking

synonyms:

extraordinary, wonderful, stunning, out of the ordinary, uncommon, unique, quirky, surprising

My Mom

My Mom is nice and sweet and kind
My Mom is one that's hard to find
She's really great in special ways
When I'm with her there are happy days
We like the same things, like the weather
And we sure do like to be together.

Taken from the Mother's Day
"Super Mom" Booklet I made when I was ten
May 11, 1979

Introduction

I entertained the notion for many years of writing the story of my mom and me, simply because our nontraditional, decidedly quirky, lifelong role-reversal friendship was unlike any mother-daughter relationship either of us had ever heard of (until *Gilmore Girls*, but that will come later in the book). I imagined a kind of collaboration between us at some point, where I would do the actual writing, but I'd verify certain facts with her that only she might know. The reminiscing would be a hoot, we'd laugh like we always did, and it would be fun to see what each of us remembered about those years of growing up together.

But that's not the way it happened.

My mom, who was only sixteen years older than me and therefore someone I was certain I would have in my life much longer than most daughters had their mothers, got sick. And then we went on a pilgrimage to get her well naturally, and it seemed she got better. And then, in what felt like the cruelest twist, the better was only temporary. And then, in a whirlwind of disbelief and heartbreak and grace, she left me at only sixty-eight.

To be honest, I still can't believe she is physically gone. We talked or texted nearly every day, sometimes multiple times a day. I smile easily when I think of her, but I tear up easily too. I shared both my exciting and seemingly mundane news with her, and she shared hers with me. We seamlessly rolled any of a number of favorite movie lines into almost every conversation, were as at ease with witty banter as we were with genuinely listening to one another and sharing opinions, and never ceased to crack each other up, be elated for each other's triumphs, or offer empathy in the face of laments, whether significant or petty. Her physical absence is palpable, to say the least.

But in the writing of this book, she has remained particularly close to me. I've spent countless hours recalling the details of the fifty-one years we shared, which has meant bringing to the surface hilarity and heartache, disappointment and pride, separation and reunion, embarrassments and evolutions, all of which comprised the tapestry of our half century together. Mostly, though, I have felt immense gratitude that I was brilliant enough to choose her as my mother in this lifetime, and that I willingly accepted, from my earliest days, being her touchstone.

Though most of my memories are pretty solid from the time I was old enough to walk, I admit that I may not have gotten every detail right from her perspective. Some things I simply couldn't know for sure without having her here to confirm. But I think what matters is my recollection of the uniqueness of what we shared, of what people have told us over and over was a one-of-a-kind relationship they wished they'd had with their own mothers or daughters.

And I believe that's what she has influenced as her stardust has surrounded, and indeed suffused, the writing of this book.

When I told a dear friend the title I had chosen for this memoir, she told me that she imagined other young mothers deriving hope when they saw it, that perhaps their unexpected little bundle was going to turn out just fine, even if they felt completely unprepared to raise a child. That was something I hadn't thought of, but certainly something I hope is true. Though there are parts of my childhood that will likely shock you and make you wonder what my mom was thinking at times —and how I didn't turn out completely different than I did—there are also numerous gems in my mom's offbeat parenting style that are worth absorbing and embracing.

Yes, a lot of factors are involved in how a child turns out because of, or in spite of, the environments into which they are born—and there is no doubt that I had some of the greatest factors in my favor. My sincere hope is that you will be glad you got a peek into a truly special and uncommon relationship, no matter which parts resonate with you. And I hope, too, that if you shed a few tears along the way, the wacky repartee will balance them out.

My mom was a beautiful, hilarious, sarcastic, wounded, accepting, sincere, resilient, generous, loving ray of light.

I can't wait for you to meet her.

∞

First Time's the Charm

It was May 1, 1968. She was fifteen; he was nineteen. They had been dating for several months when he found out he had been drafted. Vietnam was raging, and there was every reason to believe he would be called overseas after boot camp. Sex seemed the next natural step in the relationship. After all, what if he died and never had another chance?

Six weeks later she turned sixteen. Her period never came that month. Neither did the next. They had broken up soon after he left, and she had no idea what to do, so she wrote him a letter.

Not long after he started reading, "Oh, shit" tumbled out of his mouth.

His bunkmates immediately gathered around.

"Something wrong at home?" one of them asked.

"Yeah, my girlfriend . . . actually, *ex*-girlfriend . . . is pregnant."

"Ooh . . . you're in for it now, Ralph," they razzed. "Better send her money for an abortion, and quick."

But Ralph had no intention of encouraging Cindy to end the pregnancy. He may have been young, and he may have been facing an uncertain future as a Marine, but he just wasn't the type of guy to bail on a child he had created, even if he and the girl had called things off.

The first weekend possible, Cindy drove down to Camp Pendleton in Oceanside, CA, about an hour from her home in Lakewood. She wasn't showing yet, so no one at the base was the wiser. Someone snapped a happy-looking photo of them that day, and they looked like a typical teenage couple having a long-awaited visit. But behind Cindy's smile was a growing panic.

"What are we going to do?" she wanted to know.

"Have you told your parents yet?"

"God, no."

"Well, you're going to have to tell them at some point."

"And then what? We're not even together anymore."

"I know . . . but we could get back together."

Cindy sighed. "You don't even know when you'll be back. *If* you'll be back." She didn't want to sound maudlin about his chances of making it home alive, but she already knew about hometown kids who had died in Vietnam.

Ralph nodded. "I know. But if I do, I want to be this baby's father, even if we decide to call it quits for good."

∞

Together Again

She was about six weeks along, so it was time: my chance to re-unite with the person who was currently Cynthia Hays, daughter of Darrell and Lucille. We had a soul contract to live multiple lifetimes together, and this was going to be our next. So, once her little fetus's heart was formed enough, I slipped my soul into that baby in Cynthia's tummy, sparked the heartbeat, and waited.

For the next three months, my mom held me in the best she could. She wore blousy tops and fastened her pants underneath with a rubber band hugging the buttons. Finally, when she was nearly five months along, she confessed to her parents she had something to tell them.

"I know," was my grandma's response upon hearing the news.

My mom's heart leapt. "You do? How?"

"I could tell something wasn't right with you. The baggy clothes, your mood."

My mom was perplexed. "Why didn't you say anything?"

"I've been waiting for you to come to me."

Tears streamed down my mom's cheeks. Clearly, this wasn't the dream her parents had for her, and she hated disappointing them.

"So now what?" she said between sobs.

"Well," my grandma said calmly and with resolve, "what's done is done."

Her typically easy-going father quietly agreed. Then, he abruptly rose, made his way to his thirteen-year-old son's room, threw open the door and announced, "Your sister's pregnant!" Then, before closing the door he added for emphasis, "Goddammit!"

Teenager Unraveled

*I*n 1968, a discussion around a teenage pregnancy usually involved three things: abortion, adoption, and being sent to an unwed mothers home.

To my grandparents' credit, none of these things came up in that initial conversation when the hopes for their daughter's bright future as a writer (she had a gift for it), or a seamstress (she had a gift for that too), or even a college graduate were seemingly dashed.

For one, she was five months along—too late for an abortion. But even if she hadn't been that far along, none of them would have entertained the idea. Giving me up for adoption? Curiously, it never came up either. And though my grandparents were indeed embarrassed by the situation and cringed at what their wide social circle would think, they never suggested my mom be secreted away for that last trimester, or give birth in a place filled with sneering nuns shaking disapproving fingers at her.

My grandparents did, however, insist on one thing: that my parents get married. Immediately. And so, despite their broken-up status, on October 1st they were whisked with both sets of parents to Las Vegas to make the whole thing somewhat respectable in everyone's eyes. My mom may have been knocked up, but at least she was *married* and knocked up.

But that was only step one.

The Vegas wedding, though official, wasn't quite enough for my grandparents. For an added bonus, they thought a follow-up church wedding was in order too. My poor mom couldn't have been more mortified. So, just two weeks later, on October 13th, the slapdash yet lovely wedding was held—complete with attendants on both sides donning the usual attire—so that these two youngsters who were no longer in love could profess a fictitious commitment to each other before God. The groom wore his Marine uniform and had a clean-shaven head. The bride wore a pale pink, just-above-the-knee A-line dress and held a sweet bouquet that hid me perfectly.

Although they were now married, because my dad was living at the base down in Oceanside, my mom continued to live at home. They saw each other on certain weekends, but my mom's biggest priority was not spending time with her new husband. It was something much more pressing. She could be forced to marry—twice—and endure a teen pregnancy. She could even manage the humiliation of having to drop out of school only two months into her junior year, as no student more than five months pregnant could attend high school back then. But she simply couldn't bear the idea of having a baby while she had braces on her teeth. The problem was, she was nowhere near ready for her orthodontic journey to end, and she knew my grandparents would never allow her braces to be removed prematurely. She had been saddled with a horrible overbite, and while that was mostly corrected, her teeth weren't yet straight. No matter. Ensconcing herself in the bathroom one night, my mom, by what means I still don't understand, pulled out the wires and scraped off those brackets by hand until not a single one remained.

"I refuse to give birth with braces on," she declared to my grandparents. "So I took them off myself."

I can only imagine how they thought about what it had taken to save up the money for orthodontia, and how they were now seeing their efforts end up crooked, literally.

I can also imagine them trying to figure out which was worse: an interrupted dental plan, or their first grandchild on the way in their mid-forties.

By the Grace of God

*M*y dad lived in a rather private and primo bachelor pad: a three-hundred-square-foot room off the back patio of his parents' house that boasted a kitchenette, a postage stamp–sized bathroom with a skinny shower in the corner and a pull-up bar in the doorway, and a closet covering half of one wall. The rest was open space that was suitable for one person, a stretch for two, and crazy-making for three. But my dad was already envisioning his little family in that room, even if my mom couldn't imagine it at all. The truth was, despite his young age and unsure future, he was all in. He just didn't know how soon his number would be called to go to Vietnam.

No young man enlisted in the military in the late sixties expected to escape going overseas. But by an incredible stroke of luck, my dad met a guy who told him how to strategically do poorly on certain tests and well on others, and therefore remain in the military but be ineligible for deployment. Now, my dad was a smart guy and wasn't the type to make himself look bad—or to ditch his obligation to his country—but he had a child on the way he sincerely wanted to raise, so he followed his buddy's lead. The result was that my dad, by absolute miracle, performed his duty in the Marines for his conscription, but he never went to Vietnam.

On January 12, 1969, my dad turned twenty, just a few weeks before I was due on February 2nd. He was still living at the base, but around this time, my mom officially moved into my dad's cozy abode to get ready for my impending arrival. This meant some serious redecorating: squeezing my stylish olive green crib onto one wall, a bath/changing table combo on another, and a wind-up baby swing in the middle.

Feeling fat, miserable, and scared out of her wits, my mom wasn't up for much. But my dad did get occasional weekends home, and they needed to decide on a name for me. So one night, while playing a rousing game of Yahtzee, my mom flipped over the lid of the box and wrote "Stacey" inside.

"What do you think of this name for a girl?" she asked my dad. "I like it with the 'e.'"

"I like it. But what about if it's a boy?"

My mom shrugged. Truth be told, she couldn't imagine having anything but a girl.

"I like Grant," my dad said.

Our last name was "Hill," and while there's now a famous basketball player with that name (so no offense to him), my mom wasn't thrilled with the plain-sounding "Grant Hill." But she agreed to it, secretly praying I would be a girl and that she wouldn't have to battle over a boy's name when the time came.

She was also secretly grateful that, even under the awkward circumstances of their relationship, she wouldn't have to raise the dependent little human growing in her belly all by herself.

∞

Asserting Myself

I may have been due on February 2nd. And my mom may have certainly been ready to get the birth part out of the way by that date. But I had other plans.

Back then, doctors didn't induce women who went past their due date. Babies just came when they were ready. In my case, I wasn't ready until the 18th. I felt bad putting my mom through the extra sixteen days of misery, but for various reasons that will be apparent later, I *wanted* to be born on this date. So, I waited until Monday night to get labor underway, knowing I would be born sometime on Tuesday.

Unfortunately, there were several unsavory elements about the birth process for my mom:

1. They didn't do epidurals yet, and a spinal block couldn't be done early enough to get her through the hours of contractions without pain.

2. My dad, striving to be the responsible husband, insisted on keeping my grandma out of the delivery room (her not being my dad's biggest fan was likely a factor in that insistence), even though my mom kept asking for her.

3. She contended, even fifty years later, that it was the worst pain of her life and that she never forgot it.

At 8:47 a.m., I entered the world and was placed in my mom's arms. I don't think she knew quite what to think. She probably looked at my squinty eyes and red face and thought, *I can't believe I just went through the worst pain of my life for this*. But I had a plan. And soon enough, she would know about it.

Adjusting to Motherhood

*I*n the earliest pictures of us, my mom looks exhausted, less than happy to be photographed, and gobsmacked as to how this is now her life. I can't blame her. I wasn't the best sleeper, and I had colic from the outset. Fortunately, it wasn't long before my dad was able to come home as a new father and help out.

Lucky for both my mom and me, my dad was up for doing all the parent duties: bathing me, feeding me, changing me, dressing me. Unfortunately, he seemed to be harboring an unspoken fantasy of having a little boy. There are a few photos of me in a one-piece coverall number with my hair combed over to the side. But mostly, my dad seemed tickled blue to have a daughter.

The problem was, this whole marriage and baby thing was way too much for my mom. She wasn't equipped to be a wife *and* a mother, especially considering she was really still just a child herself. So, only months into marital non-bliss, she told my dad she wanted a divorce. He would have stayed in it and done his best to make it work, but he conceded.

So, without a whole lot of fuss, my grandparents felt they could do nothing but support the decision, and before I was a year old, my parents were no longer a legal item. As was custom, my mom received full custody, and my dad received every-other-weekend visitation and the obligation of monthly child support, both of which he accepted with an open heart and an open wallet.

And, lickety-split, we moved back into my mom's old bedroom in my grandparents' house.

"Where's Stacey?" my grandma asked, seeing my mom enter the den with empty arms and my crib not having arrived yet.

"She's sleeping on my bed."

I was already walking at nine months, so my grandma said, "But she could wake up and try to get down herself. You can't just leave her there like that."

At that, my grandma came to retrieve me, lest I end up on the hardwood floor with a concussion.

The truth was, my mom had no idea what to do with me. She had grown up adoring her baby dolls, and I was basically her most extraordinary one yet, being live and all. She dressed me in the cutest matching outfits and booties, but beyond that, she was at a loss.

She wasn't thrilled about having to move back home, either. But she was grateful that my grandma stepped in and took care of me—a lot. With my grandma home all the time, my mom was able to get a part-time job with the phone company and go to night school to get her GED. I was okay with her being gone because I was crazy about my grandma. But it wasn't long before my mom wanted to stretch her wings. She had lost the majority of her high school friends once she got pregnant and had to drop out of school, so she started making some new friends—and those friends wanted her to go out with them.

Let's face it: she deserved to have some fun.

Before the age of eighteen, she had gotten pregnant the first time she had sex, been forced to endure two weddings to a man she was no longer in love with, been pushed out of high school when things were just starting to get fun, moved out of her home, given birth (the worst pain of her life), become a mother, gotten divorced, and moved back home into her childhood bedroom, which now had a crib across from her bed where her near one-year-old made a delightful alarm clock.

I understood her desire to go out sometimes after work. I adored my grandparents, and I loved being with my dad on weekends, so I wasn't suffering in any way. But my grandma didn't like the way she was shirking her responsibilities as a mother. It was a good thing she didn't realize my mom was doing other things that would have appalled her too. Like, once I started talking, my mom thought it was hilarious to try to get me to say bad words.

"Stacey, say 'shit,'" she'd beg.

"No."

"Come on. Say 'shit.'"

"No."

"Just once? For Mommy?"

"No."

She would even do it when she took me with her to see friends.

"Watch what happens when I try to get Stacey to say a bad word," she'd say. She would substitute "shit" with various other expletives, but I always shook my head with resolve and refused. Then they would crack up. How I knew these were words I shouldn't say, I don't know. Most kids will repeat whatever comes out of their parents' mouths, with or without permission. But I had my mom's number from the start. And I'm pretty sure she knew it.

Becoming Buddies

I was keenly aware of what I was getting myself into when I swooped into that fetus growing inside of Cindy and made that little body mine. I knew she was young, immature, and would sometimes be a bit careless, like letting me stand in the front passenger seat of her super cool pale yellow Datsun 240Z, instead of sitting in the seat like a normal kid, wherever we drove. (But hey, it was the early '70s, and car seats that accommodated toddlers weren't really a thing yet, nor was wearing those optional safety devices called seat belts.) But I also knew she would give me incomparable freedom and acceptance to be who I was, which was a gift beyond measure. I knew, too, that we would be great friends.

From the time I could carry on conversations, which was around age two, my mom talked to me about all kinds of stuff. For example, from as far back as I can remember, I knew my mom was only sixteen when she had me, that my dad was twenty, and that my grandma and grandpa on my mom's side were forty-five and forty-six, respectively. I also knew everyone's birthdays, that my mom was adopted, and that my grandma had had something called a hysterectomy at age 26 and couldn't have children of her own. Basically, I knew some facts most two-year-olds wouldn't be privy to, care about, or perhaps even understand. But that was our relationship. My mom was no longer a biologically unconnected entity in the world. She now had me. And she was open and forthcoming with me about everything, as if we existed on the same level in pretty much every way.

So it maybe wasn't such a bizarre occurrence that I came to my mom one morning, when I was three or so, with a fascinating news flash.

"I had a dream about your birth mother," I said. "She was in a hospital bed, and I saw her right after you were born. She had red hair and green eyes."

"Really?" she said, wide-eyed. "She had red hair?"

"Uh huh."

(Mind you, she seemed more perplexed by her mother's hair color, perhaps because we were both blond as blond could be, than the fact that her toddler had a dream about the day she was born.)

"Did you see anything else?" she wanted to know.

"Just that she was in a bed, and nobody else was in the room."

"Was she holding me?"

"No. You weren't there. Just her."

"So how did you know who she was and that she had just given birth to me?"

I shrugged. "I just knew."

At the time, although my mom was starting to become fascinated with astrology, the works of Edgar Cayce, and the mysteries of the Universe, she wasn't yet aware that time didn't really exist, and that all quantum arrows point to the theory that we essentially live multiple parallel lives that we think of as past, present, and future.

For the record, I wasn't consciously aware of that either at age three.

But she took my dream as seriously as I did. In fact, she thought it was pretty darn cool. She did remain perplexed about the red hair, though.

Moving Up . . .
or At Least, Out

I became my grandma's "ever-lovin' doll" from the beginning, and she willingly took care of me on a regular basis, which fostered a profound, unbreakable bond between us. But the truth was that she thought my mom should be with me more. My mom, however, felt somewhat confined by the turn her life had taken. She wanted desperately to find herself, to be part of the dawn of the '70s and all the peace, love, and freedom it carried with it. Part of that was allowing herself to bloom as a young woman—and part of it was earning enough so that we could get a place of our own.

It didn't take much for me to observe that my mom's relationship with my grandma wasn't the same one my grandma had with me. There was always a sense of tension, or exasperation, or guardedness between them. For a multitude of reasons, they sadly just didn't click. My mom struggled with feeling like both a disappointment and a burden to my grandma, and it was clear that she felt a degree of suffocation living under the same roof.

So, after two years plus of raising me at home with her parents, my mom found us an apartment in Long Beach, twenty minutes or so from my grandparents' house. It was a modest one bedroom, one bath place with a big "3" on the door. I remember it was three because I was three years old, and I thought that number was for me. The door opened right into the modest kitchen, where my mom set up a cute dining table for two, and beyond that was an even more modest living room. I suppose it made sense that my mom got the bedroom, but there was no room for another bed for me in there, so I slept on the couch. She kept my clothes in her drawers and closet, and I kept my books and toys in various baskets in the living room.

Of course my mom had to work, which meant that she had to schlep me all the way to my grandparents' house on weekday mornings. But this minuscule dwelling with the "3" on the door was the first place my mom could call her own. She decorated it as cute as her salary would allow, in the oranges and greens and popular daisy florals of the day, and she cobbled together hand-me-down furnishings to make it as homey as she could.

To be honest, I recall spending more time at my dad's bachelor pad and my grandparents' house than I did in that apartment, but I also remember that my mom seemed happy there. She was such a free spirit, and she finally had the space to be the independent young woman she wanted so much to be.

Becoming a Hippie

*N*ow that we no longer lived with my grandparents, my mom didn't want to rely on them to babysit at night more than she had to. She also didn't want them knowing how she was spending her free time, or questioning where she was going. So there were times when she took me with her to the fun gatherings she was invited to.

It was around this time I received a moniker from my mom that would be mine from that day forward: *Doobie.*

Let's take a moment to examine that.

It was 1972. Marijuana was the recreation of choice, and being my mom's buddy and all, I witnessed all kinds of people getting high. We'd show up at someone's apartment, filled with beanbags, doorway beads, and a bunch of *very* happy people, and all eyes would turn to me.

"Aww," the men with their long hair and bearded faces, and the women with their flowy, straight hair and big, clanky bracelets, would say. "Look how cute she is."

The room would smell funny to me, but I got used to it pretty quickly. I also got used to being the only kid at these parties. I supposed no one else there had kids yet, since my mom had me so young. I also had an innate feeling it wasn't really a party for kids, and that what was making the adults so happy was something they probably shouldn't be doing.

But being an only child with a vivid imagination and no problem entertaining myself, I would either go into another room to play, or hang out with all the adults. I didn't like the smoking, though, and I was surprised my mom was okay with it. My grandma smoked, and while I adored her, my mom and I both despised the cigarettes she was addicted to. But these cigarettes were different. They didn't come out of a white and gold Marlboro Lights package. These had a pointy shape, and the people at the parties sat around and made their own, using dried-up little pieces of brownish-green stuff rolled in delicate white paper. And they puffed on them differently too. For one, they held them between their thumb and index finger, not the way my grandma did, between her index and middle fingers. Two, they would inhale, then inhale again, then sometimes again. Then they would hold the smoke purposely before blowing it out slowly, sometimes with a bit of a cough.

I wasn't necessarily keen on attending these parties, but I didn't put up much of a fuss. I was always a night owl, and if I got tired, there was usually a bedroom where I could crash. And whatever made the guests so mellow and blissful and ravenous didn't have the same effect on me at all. I guessed it was because they inhaled the "grass" or "pot," as they called it, from the "joint" they rolled up and passed around, and I never did. Plus, everyone was always super welcoming and nice to me, and no one ever made any inappropriate overtures toward me. If they had, I would have told my mom, and I'm certain she would have believed me and reverted to dropping me off at my grandparents'.

Luckily, nothing untoward ever happened, which was good on two accounts: one, I wasn't potentially scarred emotionally for life; and two, my grandparents had no idea of my mom's nightlife that included me.

I was curious, however, about the nickname she started calling me. I had heard someone at one of these occasional parties refer to their stubby cigarette thing as a "doobie." Everyone seemed to think they were the most delightful little things, even if they were awfully short sometimes and had to be held with a feathery clip.

"Why are you calling me the same name as that little cigarette you smoke at the parties?" I wanted to know.

"It's not a cigarette," she insisted. "I would never smoke a cigarette."

"So what is it?"

"It's an herb."

I suspected she might be trying to justify this fun little habit, so I pushed.

"But I thought you didn't like smoking."

"Well, this is different. It's not like what Grandma smokes. Hers are bad for you. Mine are good for you."

Hmm.

To be honest, I didn't buy it.

Then she tossed out the *real* source of my new nickname. "The Doobie Brothers are one of my favorite bands. I named you after them."

It was a funny-sounding name to me, but she loved it and there was no going back.

My mom now had her apartment, her relative freedom, and a side-kick to share it with. She also had a daughter who was beginning to see she needed to look out for her little wild child of a mother.

Preschool Begins,
Preschool Ends

One of my extraordinary blessings was the brain my parents' merging produced, though both of them marveled at how I came by it. No one on either side of my family was a genius, or even a college graduate (not that that is an indication of intelligence), except for my great-grandpa Hays, who was a chemical engineer and had taught community college. My mom was bright and showed a lot of potential in grade school but got dinged on report cards for talking too much, and my dad was mechanically adept but had skidded by with Cs most of the time. But somehow, I arrived with some truly astonishing skills that my mom chalked up to my "not being from here," alluding to her assertion that I was a bit otherworldly. She also felt proud of the fact that she had been an "untainted host," meaning that being so young, she'd had no opportunity yet to mess up her body with alcohol or drugs, or God forbid, smoking. The worst I got in-vitro was the second-hand smoke from my grandma (whom, as you'll recall, my mom did her best to avoid during the first two trimesters of her pregnancy). That, and the energy of my poor mom being scared and stressed and humiliated instead of being excited about the prom or being chosen for the cheer squad.

As a result of whatever forces came together to form my brain, my mom says no one actually taught me how to read, that I "just knew how." (My family did read to me a lot, and I had a photographic memory, so I must have just had the ability to match their words with those on the page, then memorize them.) The same was true of my ability to count, recall, and calculate numbers. I actually remember lying in my mom's bed at night when we lived with my grandparents, when my mom might be at school and I had the room to myself, counting up to a thousand. No doubt, I received some *ultra*-cool gifts.

Nonetheless, my grandparents thought I would benefit from going to preschool. So, my mom signed me up and dropped me off for my first three-hour session.

When she picked me up and asked how my day went, I told her I didn't like it.

"They made us take a nap," I said.

I was never really a nap-taker, so this was a veritable assault on me.

"Oh," she said, with a drop in tone, totally getting why I was bent out of shape.

"And the teacher gave us these colors to learn, but I already know these." I handed her a three-by-three packet of construction-paper squares with a big paper clip.

She glanced at the colored squares, then her eyes returned to mine. "Do you want to go back?"

"No."

"Okay," she said matter-of-factly, "you don't have to."

We drove to my grandparents' house that afternoon, where my grandma was poised to hear all about my first day.

"She's not going to preschool," my mom told her.

My grandma was taken aback, having expected me to love it. "Why not?"

"Because she didn't like it."

And that about sums up my mom's mothering philosophy: If I was really opposed to something—a food, an outing, a chore, a choice of outfit—I was off the hook. She didn't believe in forcing me to do anything I didn't want to, so my first day of preschool was, with no argument from her, my last.

∞

Moving Up for Real

My grandma's mother, my great-grandma Leslie, had been sick for several months, and my grandma was doing her best to balance checking in on her while taking care of me. Her father had died the year I was born, so I only had a relationship with her mom. That relationship was mostly about hugging her plump body and kissing her kind face, and running to the compact den that had two built-in drawers in the wall, just above the floor. That was where she kept little gifts just for me. Every time my grandma and I visited her, I was allowed to choose one wrapped item from one of the drawers. It would be some kind of cute toy, and I thought she was the sweetest person to have those drawers expressly for me.

But one day, on one of our visits, I ran to the drawers to discover that neither had anything in it. My grandma explained that Leslie had been too ill to go out and get any more gifts for me. I was sad about the gifts, but sadder to know that my great-grandma was that sick.

Not long after that, Leslie passed away. My grandma and her sister inherited her house, and instead of selling it, they decided to let my mom and me live in it. I was overjoyed! Not only would I have my own room for the first time, but I would have an amazing backyard to play in, complete with a massive fig tree perfect for climbing.

The house was on Gundry Avenue in Long Beach, not too far from our apartment, but in a much nicer neighborhood called California Heights, adjacent to Signal Hill. It was one of those signature Spanish-style houses that populated the area, and my great-grandparents had built it in 1920. My grandma and her sister had grown up there, and now their old room was going to be mine.

My mom went straight to work making it cute for me. I'm sure my grandparents chipped in, because that was always their way, but however the funds were pooled, I now had my very own twin bed with a Holly Hobbie bedspread, a nightstand, a bookshelf, a toy box, and even a desk with my own black-and-white TV that sat atop. That TV must have been someone's extra, because I can't imagine my mom would buy a four-year-old a TV with her meager income, but I had one nonetheless.

The house itself wasn't large, but we each had a bedroom, one bathroom to share, a beautiful living room with a fireplace and windows that faced the front yard, a dining room, the den with the special drawers, and the envy of every neighbor on the block: a vibrant orange and yellow kitchen, complete with a breakfast nook.

Around that time, my mom got a job at an imports store called Akron, which was a California-based store akin to Pier 1. She was a salesperson and cashier who had a nice employee discount, so little by little, our house became populated with cool knickknacks, scented candles, and art from the store.

One day, my mom came home from work with a present for me: a set of four t-shirts, each a different pastel shade—lime, lavender, sky blue, and pink—with an adorable cupie-like image screen printed on the front and a saying, such as "Hello, nice friend." The shirts were actually much too big for me, but my mom thought they would be cute for me to wear as nightshirts. This was a decision she would quickly come to regret.

In our new house, I had a tall, narrow, walk-in closet in my room that almost felt like a secret portal to a fantasy world. It had a tall clothing bar on the right that I needed a chair to reach, and a dresser on the left. Every night I would go inside to my pajama drawer and pull out one of my shirts. Then I'd call out, "Guess what color!" The idea, of course, was to see if my mom was clairvoyant enough to guess which color shirt I'd chosen for that night. I'd give her three chances to get it right, which I thought was generous, considering there were only four choices. The reward for getting the color right, particularly on the first try, was me being completely impressed and tickled by it (which for her was hardly the claim to fame it was in my eyes).

The ritual was cute at first. But after several weeks, Guess What Color's novelty wore off—not for me, mind you, but for her. That's actually putting it sweetly. My mom *hated* Guess What Color. She thought it was the most annoying game. She began rattling all the colors off in one breath, or yelling back, "Who cares?!" She even threatened to get rid of those shirts if I didn't knock off that nightly lightning round of irritation. Eventually, I conceded. After all, she took all the fun out of it by not *really* thinking about it and playing it correctly.

Come to think of it, maybe my concession to cease Guess What Color was when she procured me the television.

Finding Our Bliss

*A*s much as preschool hadn't been my cup of tea, I was elated to start kindergarten. First, there were no naps in kindergarten. Second, I *loved* books and reading and math, and I couldn't wait to be in a real classroom. My mom had bought me a light pink, just-past-the-underwear dress to wear my first day (the trend then was the shorter, the better), parted my shoulder-length, downy-like hair on the side, and finished off my outfit with white knee socks and my favorite shoes: black patent leather Mary Janes. What more could I have needed for my academic career to begin?

When my mom picked me up that day, she was hoping for a much more favorable report than the one she'd received from my preschool endeavor. And she got it—sort of.

"I *love* my teacher, Mrs. Chamberlain," I told her. "And I *love* my classroom."

"That's great!" She probably inhaled at that point, feeling a "but" coming on.

"But it's so weird," I said. "Mrs. Chamberlain gave all of us a booklet with the letters of the alphabet in it. I thought it was a coloring book, but then she said she was going to be *teaching* us the letters. Can you believe it? No one in my class knows how to read!"

To me, this was completely astonishing. How could anyone start school and not already know how to read? It never crossed my mind that my fellow students would be so far behind in life.

"Well," my mom tried to explain, "a lot of kids don't learn to read until they start school. You're kind of unusual."

Until then, because I'd never been in a classroom environment, it never occurred to me how different—or how fortunate—I was in that arena. I was over the moon when I received books as gifts, and I read my books over and over, every day. But these poor saps in my classroom? They were still learning their letters, for Pete's sake! They'd been missing out on *so* much.

I wanted to know what I should do. I didn't want to pretend I couldn't read, but I didn't want the other kids to feel bad when they found out they'd been screwed out of at least two precious years of enjoyment without their knowledge.

"Just tell your teacher you already know how to read," my mom said. "Maybe there's something else you can do while she's teaching the other kids."

So, the next day, I went up to Mrs. Chamberlain and delicately told her the shocking news in a low voice. "Um, I just wanted you to know that I already know how to read."

"You do? That's wonderful!" she said.

"So . . . I don't really need you to teach me how."

She became thoughtful then. "How about this," she offered. "Since the other kids haven't had a chance to learn yet, maybe you could help some of them if they're having a hard time."

Me? My teacher's helper? As a lifelong pleaser and perfectionist, I was all over it.

When I told my mom, I could see how filled with pride she was.

But the pride didn't end there. I had another piece of scintillating news.

"And then, at recess today, the boys chose me to be the kissy girl."

"The kissy girl? What's that?"

"During recess, the boys run around the playground and try to kiss me."

"That's really a thing?"

"Yeah. They pick a girl they think is pretty, and they picked *me.*"

Forget how chauvinistic, demeaning, and ridiculous this was, or who in God's name started it and how these five-year-old boys even knew that was part of their coming-of-age ritual. In a sea of, I'm sure, many attractive little girls in my class, I had been singled out as pretty and my mom thought that was pretty cool. As a child, her lovely blond curls, sparkling eyes, and adorable figure hadn't outweighed her unfortunate overbite, so being picked as anything akin to the kissy girl never entered her radar. But her daughter being chosen? She was elated.

That next month was Back to School Night, when all the parents and their kids came to their classrooms one evening to get to know the teacher and see some of the projects we'd done so far.

"Is *that* your mom?" several kids wanted to know.

"Uh huh," I said smiling.

The compliments flowed.

"She's so young!"

"She's so pretty!"

"I love her hair."

"I love her clothes."

Looking around at the other parents, I could see why my mom stood out in a way I hadn't noticed before. A lot of the moms had hairdos from beauty shops and wore polyester pantsuits with sensible shoes, while my mom had long, golden blond hair and sported a flowy off-the-shoulder dress that hugged her tiny waist, and a pair of side-zip boots. Some of the moms were plump; mine looked like a fashion model. Many of them were already ancient in their thirties, while *my* mom was a mere twenty-one. I think every boy, girl, and husband in the room stared at my mom more than they listened to the teacher discuss her plans for the school year. And I think the mothers probably both envied and hated that my mom received so much attention.

Me? I was beaming inside and out to have such a young, beautiful mother everyone fawned over as if she was a celebrity.

And my mom? Her days of being self-conscious, or the kid who was teased about her beaver teeth, or the one who felt she didn't belong because she didn't look like anyone in her family, were decidedly over.

Putting My Foot Down

While it was flattering at first, being the kissy girl really started cramping my style. First off, running around the playground squealing while boys chased me and tried to kiss me got annoying. I had no time to play on the swings or the slide or to chat with my friends. Plus, there were some boys I did *not* want to kiss me, even on the cheek. So, I announced to them one day that I didn't want to be the kissy girl anymore and that they needed to choose someone else. A couple of boys actually put up a fuss about it, which stroked my ego, but in the end, they conceded and picked some other poor little girl to demean.

And I wasn't the only one whose style was cramped.

Not long into my kindergarten career, when it was time to leave for school one morning, my mom put on a dejected face.

"Please don't go to school today," she whined.

"What? I have to."

"No, you don't."

"*Yes*, I do."

"But I want you to stay home and play with me."

I sighed. "I can't stay home and play with you. I have school. And I *want* to go."

My mom deflated even further. "But I won't have anyone to play with."

"Well, you're just going to have to find something to do. I don't want to stay home. I love school."

I might as well have just told her she couldn't get a fudgsicle today from the ice cream man because I didn't have any cash.

"But it's boring without you."

"I'm sorry," I tried to console, "but we have to leave now or I'll be late."

This would not be the last time my mom begged me to stay home from school and play with her. I refused repeatedly until I finally couldn't take her pitiful pleading anymore and agreed to stay home with her, but *just this once*. My surrender elicited a veritable triple-scoop smile from her with a dollop of giddiness, complete with clapping and jumping up and down. I could only shake my head as I caved.

That day, I sat in front of her big wooden box of albums and pulled out all our favorites: *Goodbye Yellow Brick Road* by Elton John; *Tapestry* by Carole King; *The Best of Carly Simon*; *What's Going On* by Marvin Gaye; *Chicago IX: Chicago's Greatest Hits*. We danced around that day for hours, twirling each other and singing "Bennie and the Jets" and "I Feel the Earth Move" and "You're so Vain" and "Mercy, Mercy Me" and "Saturday in the Park" and all the other songs I loved most from that soundtrack of my childhood—the ones that would remind me of that heaven-kissed time my mom and I shared for all the days that followed.

Inner Knowing

*I*n the mid 1970s, there were three ways to see a movie, in this order: the drive-in, the walk-in, and on TV. To anchor you in the time, movies weren't shown on TV nearly the way they are today. They played *The Wizard of Oz* around Easter, and of course the fuzzy-mation Christmas classics were played every year. But up to that point, I had only gone to see movies at the drive-in, curled up under a big blanket with the sound pumped into the car through crackly speakers. On this day, though, my mom was taking me to the *walk-in* theater to see a movie, and I thought it was the most exciting thing.

They were showing *The Blue Bird*, the 1940 classic that starred Shirley Temple. At the time, I didn't know it was an old movie. It was made in Technicolor and resembled *The Wizard of Oz* in some ways, but this movie was decidedly different. From the beginning, I was mesmerized by the magic and visual impact of the film. But what struck me most viscerally, and what I never forgot about it, was the scene near the end where the children are up in heaven waiting to be called to their lives on Earth. Once called, they scurry onto a magical swan boat propelled by the angelic voices of their mothers, as if being pulled by a mystical connection the child's soul understands as the right match in that lifetime.

Now, I'll be honest. As precocious as I was, I didn't suddenly turn to my mom and say, "That's how it was when I came to you!"

But what I *can* say is that it made perfect sense to me that that's how it all worked.

Which brings me to my earlier assertion that I *chose* my mother.

I realize there are religious and cultural traditions that don't entertain such a belief, so this may sound like a bizarre or even incomprehensible concept to you. And I agree that it's hard to swallow why some children would willingly choose a family that is filled with pain and hardship. The only explanation that makes sense to me is that we can't always understand on a purely human level what the soul is seeking to learn on a particular life journey. And I will say that from a parental standpoint, viewing your child as having chosen *you* can most definitely shed a whole new perspective on your relationship. But whatever your personal take on it may be, there are spiritual circles that proclaim, with no doubt, that we indeed choose our parents for each leg of our soul's evolution, and this is the camp that has come to resonate most truthfully with me.

Before I was even aware that these beliefs existed, I *felt* on a profound level that I was exactly where I was supposed to be, with precisely the family I was supposed to have. I can't explain it outside of feeling, because as a child, I didn't possess that level of awareness in my conscious mind. But in my unconscious mind, all the lifetimes I'd lived were seemingly present and wrapped up in a bundle of wisdom I carried inside of me. And part of that wisdom was understanding that I was meant to be my mother's daughter, and at times, my mother's mother.

Sometime after seeing *The Blue Bird*, and always keeping it close to me as a favorite, my mom's new friend Becci (a creative spelling of Becky) came over to our house. While she was engaging in conversation with me, she turned to my mom with an amazed expression and said, "Stacey is such an old soul."

I had never heard that term before, but I can honestly say that a little light went on inside me, as if someone had just cracked a code.

Little (Manic) Mommy

Of all the things I loved most—books, puzzles, and games being at the top—there was nothing I loved more than my baby dolls. Only let's get it straight right now that no one, and I mean *no one*, was allowed to call them "dolls." They were *real* babies, and nobody could convince me otherwise (and believe me, after a single dramatic meltdown over a reference to one as a "doll," no one who knew me dared cross that line again).

During my toddlerhood, one thing was perfectly clear: I came to this planet with some serious maternal instinct. I loved every one of my babies. I named them, fed them, rocked them, played with them. Receiving a miniature stroller about put me over the top. I tended to and talked to those babies as if they truly breathed oxygen and were alive on some level, even if it didn't appear that way on the outside.

In the first grade, our first "field trip" was to the local library, which was about a half-mile walk from my school. My beloved teacher, Mrs. Garrison, gently ushered us inside where the librarian explained in a soft voice how we would each be getting a library card, and that we could choose two books to check out. Then she directed us toward the children's section. Only I didn't follow my classmates to the picture and chapter books.

Branching off on my own, I sought out the Parenting section. If I was going to raise my babies well, I needed a book about ways to accomplish that. No one noticed I went off to another section until I walked up to the librarian with my book: *Dr. Spock's Baby and Child Care.*

"Is it okay if I check this book out?" I asked.

The librarian took one look at my tome and got a decidedly odd look on her face. "*This* is the book you want to check out? Not something from the children's section?"

"No," I said matter-of-factly. "I want to check out this one."

She motioned to another library worker, as if to say, *Get a load of this kid*, then directed me to the counter to check it out.

When I brought the book home from school that day, I couldn't wait to show it to my mom.

"Wow," she said. "That's the book you picked out?"

"Yep. I'm going to find out everything I need to know about being a mother," I said confidently.

She didn't say it then, and I didn't have the insight yet to articulate it, but I think we both knew I wasn't seeking advice on how to care for my babies. I was trying to figure out how best to raise my mom.

Messing with My Head

_D_espite taking my reference manual for parenting very seriously, which I read as if I was sixteen not six, my mom still managed to put a few things over on me. The coup de grâce was the Big Black Button.

But before we get to that, let's take a look at her chosen method of discipline: scaring the crap out of me in a way that was hilarious to her.

Overall, I was a pretty good kid. I was a pleaser on steroids, addicted to school, exceedingly affectionate, and happy by nature (and nurture). I was also stubborn, strong-willed, opinionated, and hated being wrong about _anything, ever_. So, while my mom was incredibly lenient and let me be me the majority of the time, she sometimes felt the need to curtail some assertion on my part, particularly if I told her she was mean for the way she was responding to my whims. She did this by threatening me with the worst possible punishment: calling the Mean Mothers Association.

My best friend, Christi, was two years younger than me and lived two doors down from my grandparents, and her mom, Lynne, and my mom were best friends too. Christi was pretty much a little angel child, but Lynne had dreamed up this Mean Mothers thing to keep Christi in line when the necessity arose. Neither one believed in hitting children, thank God, and both were exceptionally happy-go-lucky when it came to parenting. But all bets were off on threats that worked. In this case, both Christi and I were major suckers.

If I pushed my mom too far on something, all she had to do was reach for the phone.

"Do I have to call the Mean Mothers Association to come pick you up, so you can find out what a mean mother really is?"

"NO!" I would howl. "NOOOOOO!"

"Well, then," she would say as her hand hovered menacingly over the receiver, trying not to burst out laughing and blow the one threat I fell for.

You see, what I imagined, if she ever actually called the Mean Mothers Association, was that the person who answered the phone would look around a room full of beefy, seething, scary-looking women who were held for heinous crimes, and she would point to one, summon her over, and give her our address to come pick me up. *Nothing* freaked me out more than this possibility. It was the one thing my mom could use to fully control me if she wanted to (and to her credit, she used it sparingly). But it did take several years before I realized the whole thing had been a ruse. (Don't think I didn't voice my opinion about *that*.) I never let her live that one down, but did she ever get a kick out of reenacting how paranoid I would get when she threatened me with it. Eventually (and I mean, *eventually*), I found it pretty funny.

But it was not long after we moved into our new house that she really messed with my head.

Just inside the door that led to the backyard, high up on the wall (well, for me at that age anyway) was a round black button about the size of a quarter that stuck out a smidge.

"What's that button for?" I wanted to know one day.

"You can never push that button," she told me.

"Why not?"

"Because it will blow up the house."

My eyes widened. "Why would we have a button that would do that?"

"Some houses have one. I guess it's for some kind of emergency."

I looked at her askance. That made absolutely no sense to me. *Why would anyone have occasion to blow up their own house?*

I was still hooked into believing there really was a Mean Mothers Association, so even though the Big Black Button theory was clearly nonsensical, I bought it ... for a while.

As you might imagine, every time I came in or out the back door, that button seemed to mock me. I would stare up at it and hope that my mom, in some moment of absentmindedness, wouldn't lean up against it by accident and blow us all to smithereens.

Then, after several months, or maybe even a year or more, had gone by, I just couldn't take it anymore. I had pondered and pondered this house-destruction button, and I just didn't see why anyone would have such a thing. My grandparents didn't have one. My dad didn't have one. I grew more and more certain that my mom was messing with me, and I *had* to find out.

I hung out in my climbing tree for a while, knowing it might be my last time. Then, I walked across the back door threshold and met the eye of the Big Black Button. I knew the next thing I saw might be an explosion, but the curiosity was just too great to let it go any longer. I reached up, put my index finger on the button, squeezed my eyes shut, and pushed.

A light came on above my head.

A light!

The Big Black Button was a *light switch*? No wonder that had never occurred to me. I had never, *anywhere*, seen a light switch like that.

But oh, ho, ho, the jig was up.

I walked up to my mom and threw my hands on my hips.

"You lied to me."

"About what?"

"The Big Black Button. It doesn't blow up the house. It's a light."

"How do you know it's a light?"

"Because I pushed it and found out!"

Her mouth dropped open. "You mean you actually pushed it, knowing you might blow up the house?"

I nodded. "I haven't believed you about it for a long time. I *had* to know the truth."

The look that crossed her face was some combination of *That's my girl, What a pistol,* and *Uh oh, she's fully on to me now.*

She was right on all three counts.

The library had stopped letting me check out *Dr. Spock's Baby and Child Care* by that point. But no matter. It was now abundantly clear that I was going to need a stiffer drink than that to raise this mother of mine.

✆

Coitus Interruptus

When it came to men, my mom was a veritable heartbreaker. They were drawn to her like hummingbirds to sugar water, and she readily soaked up the attention and how desirable it made her feel.

Now that we had our own house, and I wasn't sleeping on the couch in the living room anymore, she could be a little more discreet about having a man spend the night. Don't get me wrong: my mom didn't have a turnstile at the entrance, or a ticket machine next to her bed with a line out the door. But she did enjoy an activity that was about to no longer be a complete mystery to me.

One night, she took me to her current boyfriend's house, where we were going to spend the night. I was relegated to a bedroom, and eventually I fell asleep. At some point, I woke up and wanted water, so I opened the door and walked into the living room. There was my mom on the couch, on top of the boyfriend, with no clothes on. She turned her head abruptly toward me.

"I just want a drink of water," I said, not giving the awkward moment a second thought.

"Oh," my mom said. "Okay."

I went into the kitchen, filled a glass, then walked past the naked duo and into the bedroom, shutting the door with only a brief peek at them.

I lay there for a little bit. *What were they doing?* I could tell my mom was surprised when I caught them doing it, but she didn't seem to be hurt by the couch game, so I figured she was fine.

The next day, on our way home, my mom asked if I was okay after walking in on her and her boyfriend the night before.

"Yeah," I said nonchalantly.

"Because if you want to talk about it . . ."

"No, not really."

The truth was, I hadn't seen much at all in terms of action. But I did hope that what she was doing was a good idea. I was already questioning the pot smoking, which I had somehow determined was a "drug" and therefore bad for her, and now this.

I feared I might have to keep a closer eye on her choices and told her so.

"You don't have to worry about me," she said. "I'm okay."

It was hard to tell if her tone conveyed that she resented having me monitor her social encounters, or if she secretly appreciated having a daughter who was protective of her like a mother.

∽

Trifecta

*Y*ou may be wondering how my dad and grandparents fit into this orbit of my mom's and mine, now that we were on our own. Well, here's how that glorious trifecta played out.

One of my truly remarkable blessings was that my parents got divorced while I was still a baby. I know that sounds weird, but for me, this family dynamic made me supremely fortunate.

For one, I never knew my parents as a married couple, so I never had to lament them breaking up. I also recognized from a very early age that my parents were *not* couple material because they were so different. They were amicable for the most part, and it certainly helped that my dad held up his responsibilities as a father and then some, but I could just tell that the two of them didn't belong together. That was fine with me, though. In place of having two unhappy parents as a duo, I had a life with each one separately that had its own special flavor. On top of that, I had a wonderful life with my grandparents that had its own flavor too.

To give you an abbreviated glimpse:

The world of my mom was unstructured, free-spirited, playful, mischievous, silly, irreverent, and full of music.

The world of my dad was structured, responsible, practical, fun, and filled with educational activities, sports, and games of all kinds.

The world of my grandparents was stability, manners, appreciation of fine things, comfort foods, soap operas, and game shows.

As you can imagine, each of these environments influenced me in their own significant way, and I treasured my time in all of them. But there were also some things that crossed over all three that truly shaped the person I became.

Without exception:

I was adored.

I was respected.

I was listened to.

I was given a voice.

I was valued.

I was treated with dignity.

I was showered with affection.

I was encouraged in my gifts and passions.

I was provided for generously.

I was accepted as exactly who I was.

I was loved unconditionally.

And, despite the circumstances, I was never, and I mean *never*, made to feel anything but completely wanted.

This is why I call these three angel entities my trifecta.

Hand Made for
My Special Little Girl

While I undoubtedly felt like the parent a lot of the time in our relationship, and I did worry about my mom and some of the choices she made, I was also, without question, her little girl, and so there was a balance of sorts for me between being the mother and the daughter in this wacky partnership.

One of the things we did where I was absolutely the kid was our regular trips to a wonderful corner of the world not far from our house called Cherry Avenue Park. We would take a nice stroll there together from our house and talk about all kinds of things on the way. My mom always found my opinions interesting, so she never hesitated to ask me what I thought about any number of topics. Once we arrived, I would romp around on the usual playground staples: swings, slide, merry-go-round, jungle gym, while my mom sat on a bench and watched, or hung out nearby and took pictures of me having fun. I loved that park, and I loved going there with my mom.

Another thing my mom did for me was make me the most adorable clothes—mostly dresses, but short sets and rompers too, as well as my Halloween costumes. As I mentioned earlier, she had a gift for sewing, and at that age, I loved that my mom made outfits for me. If you're old enough to remember when department stores had a fabric section, usually on the basement level, you'll recall the tables and tables of enormous pattern books from Butterick, McCalls, Simplicity, and others. Of course, fabric stores had these same books too. Going to one of these stores with my mom, and poring over these books to look for patterns, was one of our most enjoyable outings. When I found something I liked, she'd go to one of the giant drawers that held the patterns, fan through to find the number, and then see if they had it in my size range. If they did, she'd see what kind of material we needed, and then we'd look for fabric to find a cute print in the right weight and texture, along with all the notions the outfit needed. I often got to choose fun-shaped or colored buttons for my little numbers, and I thought that was the coolest thing.

But perhaps the sweetest part of all the fashionable ensembles my mom made for me was the embroidered label she sewed at the neck of each one. It read: Hand Made for My Special Little Girl. She had found these sweet pink labels early in her Mommy Seamstress stage, and she loved putting her stamp on my clothing creations this way. That label meant so much to me. In seven little words, I felt all the love that went into her making those items every time I put one on.

Though I outgrew those clothes long ago, one romper remains, with that label of love perfectly intact.

Serious Boyfriends

I was used to my mom dating, but it wasn't until she met Bobby that she seemed to be truly head over heels about someone.

I don't recall how they met, but Bobby was a tall, dark, handsome Italian who fell hard in love with my mom. He didn't move in to our house, but he did spend a lot of time with us, which included spending the night.

By that point, I had absorbed that the attention of men made my mom happy, and now that Bobby was around a lot, that whatever they did that made sounds come from her bedroom late at night seemed to be part of it (not that I heard anything unless I happened to wake up for an ill-timed trip to the bathroom). I had the gist of what that was from the couch encounter, and frankly, that was enough for me.

I continued to observe my mom from a maternal standpoint of wanting her to be safe and cared for (and I kept a watchful eye on Bobby to make sure he didn't make any false moves), but I also found myself emulating her a bit too.

After my stint as the kissy girl and snubbing the title of my own volition, I reconsidered the attention of boys in the first grade. How could I not when red-haired and freckled twins Philip and Freddy both took a liking to me? Truth be told, although they were identical, Freddy was the slightly cuter twin, and I could only choose one, so I chose him. I felt bad about Philip, though. So I let Freddy be my boyfriend for a while, and then I told him I was switching to his brother to be fair. I imagined that's what my mom might do, and it seemed like the right decision, especially after Philip declared his love for me and gave me my first kiss on the mouth (a quickie) in the hall one day.

By the time I was in second grade, Bobby was still a fixture in our lives, and I had moved on from the twins. (Full disclosure: I had crushes on other cute boys, as well as on a girl in my class named Vanessa.) But sometime during that school year, my mom and Bobby broke up, and though they always remained friends, a new man came into our world.

His name was Josh and he was a musician. He, like Bobby, was nice to me and was flipped over my mom. The intensity of their relationship grew quickly, and after several months, my mom decided we were going to move up to Northern California where Josh was from, and where his music career, he was certain, was going to take off. He also had two children around my age from a previous marriage who lived there, and he wanted to be close to them again, which meant that our free-wheeling lives in our storybook house were coming to an end once school got out for the summer.

I didn't want to move. I was used to bouncing between relatives after school, on weekends, and on holidays, but I craved the stability of a home and hated the idea of change. Plus, moving with her meant moving away from my dad, my grandparents, and my beloved school, and I couldn't imagine that either. But, after what I picture being heated discussions about rashness and unfairness between my parents and between my mom and grandparents, my dad reluctantly conceded (with stipulations) and my grandparents didn't have much of a choice. My mom loved Josh, saw an exciting future with him, and was taking me on this joyride with her.

∞

Santa Cruz

 A gainst all of my wishes, and with a lot of tears, we packed up our beloved Gundry house and moved five and a half hours away to Aptos, a quaint town in Santa Cruz County. My mom had promised me that Josh was going to rent us a nice house, and when we arrived, he didn't disappoint. Although I missed my dad and grandparents already, we weren't *so* far away that we couldn't visit, and our new house definitely perked up my spirits.

I had never seen an upside-down house before, but Josh said they were common there. Our bedrooms and bathrooms were on the ground floor, and the living room, kitchen, and a half bathroom were upstairs. My dad had bought a two-story condo a couple years prior, and his place was flipped the opposite way, like all the other two-story houses I'd ever seen on TV. This house, though, wasn't only unique in its structure, it had some seriously cool features.

To begin with, my bedroom was enormous. Even completely furnished, I could do a full cartwheel in there and not worry about knocking into anything. One whole wall was a closet, so not only could I hang my clothes where I could reach them, but I had room for shoes, games, and toys too—way more room than I needed. And just around the corner from my room was my own full-size bathroom, complete with a long counter for the sink and a shower/bathtub combo, where I promptly displayed my Mr. Bubble, my bath paints, and my No More Tears shampoo right on the ledge.

My mom and Josh had a huge bedroom too, on the opposite side of the first floor from mine, with a bathroom in their room. Basically, the house was designed for two roommates, or two couples, or kids and parents to have their own space, which was nice because I wouldn't be able to hear a thing coming from their bedroom.

But that wasn't all.

Our rust-colored, shag-carpeted slatted stairwell went up, stopped at a landing, then turned and continued to the second floor. A floor-to-ceiling window backed the far side of it, so lots of natural light poured into both the upper and lower levels. But the coolest part was that there was a little door that opened into an ample light-filled space *under* the stairs.

"That's yours too," my mom beamed. I could tell how badly she wanted to soothe my broken heart and show me how nice it was going to be in our new pad. "You get to keep whatever you want under there and use it as a playroom."

I was elated. I had loved my Gundry house bedroom and our whole house too, but this was more than I could have imagined. The under-stair space was also carpeted, so it was going to be a perfect place to play. I immediately pictured my Sunshine Family and their furniture under there, where I could create a whole community just for them.

I gave her a huge hug. When she let go, she squatted down in front of me. "Do you think you're going to like it here?"

For a moment, missing my dad and grandparents, and my school and my friends, competed with the excitement of this new abode. But I nodded nonetheless. "I think so," I said.

"I hope so." Her face opened up into her dazzling smile, then she suggested that while she and Josh unpacked, I go check out the neighborhood to see if any other kids my age lived nearby.

I thought that sounded like a good idea, so off I went exploring on my own.

Behind our house was a bit of a slope that met another row of houses on the street below. Just as I made my way down, a girl ambled up the side of her house.

"Hi," I said. "My name's Stacey. We just moved in up there." I turned and pointed to our house.

"Really? I'm Tricia. I live right below you!"

Tricia appeared to be my age exactly. "Are you going to be in third grade next year?" I asked.

"Uh huh. You too?"

"Yep."

"We'll probably be in the same class, then," she said smiling. "Come on, I'll show you the beach."

I followed her across the street, where the sand stretched out just on the other side. It was a cool, overcast day in June, and hardly anyone was there. And it wasn't the same kind of beach I was used to in Southern California. It was filled with big and small chunks of wood, which was something I'd never seen on a beach.

"My brother and I collect driftwood," she told me. "Pieces that are neat looking."

"Oh," I said, trudging through the sand with her, observing how many different sizes of wood there were. "How old is your brother?"

"He's eleven. And he's a real pain. His name is Warren."

I couldn't imagine having an older brother. I loved being an only child. And I loved that my parents and my mom's parents had only me to lavish their love on. I thought I had the greatest deal. "I don't have any brothers or sisters," I told her. "It's just me."

"You're *sooo* lucky," she said.

After getting to know each other a bit more, she had to go in for dinner, and I couldn't wait to tell my mom that I had already met my new best friend.

She couldn't have sparkled more brightly when I told her.

Rude Awakening

$\mathcal{B}$y the time I started third grade at my new school, Tricia and I had indeed become best friends, and she was in my class, just like we hoped. The problem was, Rio Del Mar Elementary was nothing like my old school.

Both of my parents and I had the immense gift to attend one of the top grade schools in Long Beach: Mark Twain Elementary. What made it so special was its gifted program. Each grade had one class reserved for the students who scored highest on certain exams and showed the most skill in reading, math, and language, and the teachers of those classes not only taught above the actual grade level, but were given abundant freedom to be creative with how they taught all the subjects. I was fortunate to be accepted into the gifted program in first and second grade, and that, coupled with all the workbooks I lapped up that my dad bought for me, had put me beyond the third grade in several academic areas.

This may sound like a wonderful advantage, and it was, but my new teacher, Mrs. Kelly, didn't like my academic prowess one bit.

One day, early in the school year, she passed out a timed math test of single- and double-column addition and subtraction problems, then set a timer for ten minutes. Being blessed with a mind for numbers, and having done these types of problems dozens of times before, I was able to blaze through all of them in just barely a minute. When I was finished, I walked up to Mrs. Kelly's desk to turn it in.

"You can't possibly be done with this test," she sneered.

"Yes, I am," I said politely, handing it to her.

Seeing that all the answers were indeed written in, she whispered snidely, "Well, there's no way you got all of them right. You did them much too fast to be accurate. Go back to your desk and check your answers."

I didn't want to sound arrogant, but I insisted, "I don't need to. I know they're all right. I'm used to doing these kinds of problems at my old school."

With that, she gave me a huff and asserted once again that there was no way my answers could all be correct, and that if I was going to be that stubborn about it, she'd prove it to me by correcting my paper right there in front of her.

"That's fine," I said, completely confident.

She grabbed her red pen and started hovering it over each problem, expecting to find a mistake. But she got all the way to the bottom and discovered I was right: I had gotten all of the answers correct.

"See?" I said.

She saw all right. And she didn't like it one bit. She pointed to the door and told me I had to sit outside until the rest of the class was done with the test.

I couldn't believe it. I never got in trouble at school, and being smart was typically a positive thing. Now I was being punished for it?

Under the long row of windows that looked into our classroom was a cement wall. I sat down hard against it and crossed my arms. *She can't do this to me,* I fumed. *How dare she make me feel bad for being ahead of my grade.*

It was then that I hatched a plan. If I kept low enough, I could squat and walk the length of our classroom without being seen out the windows, and then I would hightail it home. It was a long walk to our house, but I was willing to do it to get away from this horrible woman in this lame-o school.

I crouched low, then I scurried down the walkway. When I reached the end of the windows, I stood up and bolted.

Only I stood up sooner than I realized. Mrs. Kelly caught a flash of my blond hair and dashed to the classroom door, throwing it open.

"Where are you going?" she bellowed down the corridor.

Being my mother's daughter, I wanted to say *shit*, but I still refused to swear. Instead, I had to think fast. I couldn't tell Mrs. Kelly I was escaping from this inferior school.

"I have to go to the bathroom," I yelled back.

"Why were you running?" she wanted to know.

"Because I have to go really bad!"

She stood there for a minute, looking annoyed as all get out, deciding if she believed me or not.

As much as I hated to, I resorted to magic words. "Pleeeaaase," I said. "I reeeaaally have to go." I even held my crotch for emphasis.

"Fine," she conceded. "But you come right back."

At that, I turned and dashed to the bathroom. *What now?* I did *not* want to go back. Being a big-time pleaser, I was agreeable about most things, especially when it came to school. But since my mom almost never made me do anything I didn't truly want to, I figured if my teacher was mean and didn't appreciate my brain, I was sure my mom would insist I have a better teacher, a nicer teacher, like I was used to. *I can still go home*, I reasoned. *From here, I can run off campus and Mrs. Kelly will be too far away to know it. By the time she goes looking for me in the bathroom, I'll be long gone. And I'll have my mom on my side. That stupid teacher won't be able to do anything when my mom tells her she can't treat her little girl that way.*

Poised to carry out my plan, I suddenly got scared. What if my mom wasn't home when I got there? I might have to sit outside all day waiting for her. And what if I really did have to use the bathroom and couldn't get into my house? It was still early, and though my mom didn't have a job, she could have gone anywhere for the day, and it seemed like a big chance to take. So, with my tail *very* resentfully between my legs, I returned to my classroom.

When I got home from school, I told my mom all about the test, how Mrs. Kelly treated me, and my brilliant but unfulfilled plan.

"What would you have done if I left school and walked home?" I wanted to know. "Would you have made me go back?"

"No," she said, matter-of-factly. "You had every right to leave."

I smiled. *I knew it.*

"Can you find me another school, maybe?"

She shook her head with a grimace. "I don't know what other school you could go to. This is the only one close enough to our house in the district."

I was bummed but understood the dilemma. "Well, can you at least get me a different teacher?"

Her forehead creased. "I can try. But we had to enroll you late as it was. There may not be room in any other third grade class."

I was crestfallen. I could not imagine spending a whole year with a teacher who was mean to me, and who gave assignments for work I'd already mastered. I loved the challenge of school and learning new things, and I feared I'd learn nothing at all at Rio Del Mar.

My mom could see how upset I was. And she knew this wouldn't be happening if she hadn't dragged me away from the school I loved.

"I'll try," she assured me.

And she did try.

But she was right. The other classes *were* full. Which meant I was stuck in that witchy woman's class for the entire school year.

❧

Third Grade Highlights

This is a perfect time for a quiz:

Mrs. Kelly:

A. grew fond of me over time

B. learned to appreciate my intelligence and enlisted me as a teacher's helper

C. loved how my mom looked out for my best interest

D. started giving me assignments more suited to my knowledge level, like my teachers at Twain had done

E. was happy when I made lots of friends with my classmates

F. all of the above

G. none of the above

If you answered G, I hope you can hear the bells going off and see the confetti floating down, because Mrs. Kelly *never* took a liking to me, my mom, or the things I'd "already learned at my old school." As a result, it was pretty much a "wash" year academically. (Though we did learn to dance The Hustle at school, which was supremely cool.) We also had to eventually move out of our awesome house with the stadium-sized bedroom and playspace under the stairs and into a smaller apartment because Josh couldn't afford the rent anymore. But before that happened, there were some decidedly blue-ribbon moments living in Santa Cruz.

For one, I got to start taking the one-hour flight down to Long Beach every month to visit my dad. I had never been on an airplane before, and I quickly found out that children flying alone got special treatment. I received an airline coloring book for each trip, they put a sticker on me that alerted the flight crew I was flying by myself, and the stewardesses, as they were called back then, paid particular attention to me. One time I even got to meet the pilot—*in* the cockpit! It was kind of a lot to pack up and fly down just for weekends, but it was worth it to see my dad.

Another amazing event that occurred was on my ninth birthday, which fell perfectly on a Saturday. My mom had planned a typical party for me and four friends, with favors, musical chairs, Pin the Tail on the Donkey, hot potato, and prizes for the winners. But there were two elements of my birthday I didn't see coming.

As I was getting ready for my special day, the doorbell rang. My mom rushed down to get the door while I was upstairs helping to set up my games. When I turned toward the stairwell and saw who was coming up the steps, I about lost it. It was my grandparents! I had missed them terribly, and so along with planning my party and my gifts, my mom arranged with them to drive up for my party to surprise me. I rushed into my grandma's arms and smothered her with kisses, then did the same with my grandpa. Then I turned to my mom with another squeal and hugged her too. I had no idea they were coming, so it was truly the best surprise she could have given me.

This was the first time my grandparents had seen our house, so they got a tour before all my friends arrived. (Of course, all traces of pot and its attendant accessories were safely stowed away for this occasion.) Once the festivities began, my grandparents had ringside seats—and even danced with my friends and me to the *Saturday Night Fever* soundtrack. My mom took a bunch of pictures of all of us having fun together. Then she disappeared into the kitchen, cued the singing of the guests, and walked out with the most magical cake I'd ever seen: a carousel cake she created with Mother's pink and white frosted animal cookies "moving up and down" around the sides, with multicolored toothpicks for the poles, and a triangular flag waving from the center candle on top.

"Oh my gosh! This is *the* best birthday cake ever," I gushed.

That day—with my best friends, my beloved grandparents, and my beautiful mom surrounding me—almost, but not quite, surpassed the biggest highlight of our time living in that house: the Christmas just eight weeks prior.

We never had an abundance of money, but whenever my mom could, she found a way to buy me things she knew I really wanted. It probably helped that I wasn't a spoiled brat; in fact, receiving a new baby, or a piece of clothing I longed for, or anything really, sent me into a spiral of giddiness and professions of my love and happiness for it. Just the prior year, for example, I had seen a beautiful dress at our favorite high-end children's shop in the mall called Tot Toggery. It had a $35 price tag, which was a lot in 1977 for a dress I might grow out of in a year. But my mom saw how much I loved that dress, and she bought it for me for my birthday. Even at eight, I understood what a big deal it was that my mom made a way to buy me that expensive dress, and I was over the moon wearing it at my birthday party.

But even with her generosity when she could swing it, I could never have anticipated what awaited me that same year on Christmas morning.

Josh's kids spent the holiday with us that year, and all of us were having a ball opening our gifts. But then, after I thought we had opened them all, my mom presented me with a large box. She was smiling so big, I knew that this present she had saved all morning must be something special. I carefully unwrapped the paper to reveal a fancy box. I slowly lifted the lid, and lying inside was the most beautiful, unbelievable, *life-like* baby I had ever seen. I'm not exaggerating . . . the moment I saw that cherubic little face framed in her pink bonnet, wearing her delicate blush-colored dress and matching coat, with her tiny white socks and shoes, I felt like I had just given birth to the most precious baby ever born. My eyes couldn't have been wider, my mouth couldn't have dropped more in awe as I carefully untied the satin ribbons that held her arms, legs, and body in place, then lifted her out. Tears streamed down my cheeks as I held her gently in my arms.

"She's a Madame Alexander," my mom said sweetly. "She's called a Pussy Cat." (Note here that she never said the word "doll.")

"Oh my gosh," I cried. "I've never seen anything like her. I can't believe you got her for me."

With the most heartfelt smile, she said, "I saw her in a store one day, and I just knew I had to get her for you."

In that pocket of time, where the minutes seemed to magically stand still, Josh and his kids faded into the periphery, and it felt like no one existed in that room besides my mom, me, and this baby of all babies I was cradling. And I could tell that as overjoyed as I was, my mom was equally elated to have been able to give me this gift she knew I would treasure beyond words. I had nearly twenty babies already, of all types and sizes, but this one was unlike any of them, and I knew she had to cost way more than we could easily afford. All of my babies to that point had come from toy stores in boxes with clear plastic fronts and had been advertised on television. But this one had come from a place more akin to heaven.

I promptly named my new baby Natasha Marie, and from that day forward, she was the primary object of my affection, slept (very carefully) with me every night, accompanied me on every flight home to see my dad, and was my joy and constant companion every year that marched by. And, because she was the size of an actual newborn, I got to buy real baby dresses and shoes for her with the money I saved, which the mommy in me delighted in to no end.

Even with all the times I would move in the future, Natasha was never packed away, or relegated to a box of keepsakes from my childhood. She always had a place on my bed, or in a special spot of her own, and the sight of her never failed to bring back that moment when I first laid eyes on her, when my mom had surprised and touched me with the most thoughtful gift of all time.

To this day, Natasha sits on a love seat in our living room. I still delight in buying her real baby clothes whenever I find something I love.

And she is still the most meaningful gift I have ever received.

A Life-Changing Decision

When the school year ended in Santa Cruz, I packed my red Samsonite to the brim, placed Natasha on my hip, and climbed into the car for the ride to the airport. My parents had agreed on me spending the whole summer with my dad, instead of only six weeks, and while I always had a hard time leaving my mom, I was excited to have so much uninterrupted time with my dad. Plus, even though it was long distance, I'd be able to call my mom every week.

I already had my own room at my dad's condo, with my favorite colored blocks I built houses with for hours, my Fisher Price house and people, my Lite-Brite, Viewmaster, and plenty of books. I had a vivid imagination and, being an only child, I was used to playing by myself. I had a penchant for language and loved to write too, and I had even started writing a novel the year before. (Okay, it amounted to several pages in a notebook that I never finished, but I did actually have the *intention* of writing a novel.)

Since my dad had to work four weekdays and most Saturdays as a mail carrier, and because it was summer, he found some fun kids' programs to enroll me in at the local community college: a cooking class, an art class, and a theater class that put on *Snow White and the Seven Dwarfs* on a real stage (I had the riveting role of Sleepy, which my mom flew down to see). On those days, my dad dropped me off at a friend's house who took me to the college; on the other days, I went to my grandma Hill's house, who was monumentally crafty and taught me how to do simple hand sewing, needlepoint, cross-stitch, and latch-hook rugs. In other words, I was flooded with learning new things and doing creative projects.

During the evenings and weekends with my dad, we had a ball going miniature golfing and bowling, attending his park league baseball games, doing advanced workbooks he bought me at the teachers supply store, and playing all kinds of board games, card games, and strategy games. He even bought me an electronics set where we built something that actually lit up.

Although Grandma Hill and my grandparents only lived a few minutes apart, my dad favored me having time with *his* mom, since I had spent much more time with my grandparents in my early years than with my grandma. I loved Grandma Hill and appreciated all the fun things she did with me, but I did miss seeing my grandparents. I told my mom that on the phone one week, and she asked to talk to my dad. Next thing I knew, I had more frequent visits with my grandparents too.

In an envelope postmarked August 30, 1978, I wrote my mom the following letter:

Dear Mommy,

I got all of your letters. I miss you. I'm at Grandma's house today and Christi got to have lunch with me. We had Spaghettios and Grandma's famous grilled cheese sandwiches.

Grandma got me some school clothes. Two pairs of shorts, a pair of light blue Dittos, and a blue top with another checkered top. For school I would like to have some pretty dresses (you pick out some pretty ones) and underwear with turtles on them.

Sorry that's all!

Lots of love, Doobie

(For the record: Dittos were highly fashionable pants, with a horseshoe shape on the butt and bell bottoms, that both my mom and I sported proudly; my mom *did* buy me a few dresses that awaited me in Santa Cruz; and my grandma came through with the underwear with turtles on them.)

During that summer, it became clear to me how much I missed living in Southern California. Yes, my dad and all my grandparents were there, but so was my beloved school. After my bizarre-o year in Mrs. Kelly's class, I longed to be back at Twain, where school days were the light of my life. I couldn't imagine another year of repeating the same things I already knew and being made to feel somehow bad that I knew them.

Though it seemed impossible to me not to return to my mom, as the summer neared its end, I decided to ask my dad a big question: did he think it was possible for me to stay and live with him for the fourth grade.

One thing I'd known since I was little was that the decision of where I lived was always mine. My mom had official custody, but both my parents wanted the choice to be up to me. Until then, I never imagined not living with my mom, but we had already moved three (yes, three) times in one year, and I was worried about her free-spirited, vagabond existence becoming our new way of life.

With my dad, I knew I would have stability, which I craved. We had already navigated the routine of early-morning drop-offs and late-afternoon pickups at my grandma's house, and since she lived only blocks from my school, I thought maybe she could take me and pick me up. Right away, my dad was open to it. He loved having me with him, and he was willing to do whatever he had to to make it work. My grandma agreed to be my ride to and from school most days, and my grandparents loved the idea of me being close by again. What made my heart ache, though, was the idea of telling my mom.

My heart pounded as I dialed her number. We talked for a few minutes, during which the topic of me coming home soon came up.

"Actually," I began, "I decided I want to stay with my dad and go back to my school. Would that be okay with you?"

There was a slight hesitation, and then she said, "Of course. If that's what you want. You know it's always been up to you where you live."

I felt relieved that she supported my decision, yet heartbroken that she hadn't objected, not even a little.

"But I can still fly up and see you, right? And you'll come to visit me?" I asked.

"Yes, of course," she promised. "As often as we can."

"Okay, then, as long as you're okay with it."

"I'm fine," she assured me.

Then my dad took the phone for a few minutes, and that was it.

I didn't find out until years later that my mom hung up the phone and cried her eyes out.

Dad Drops a Bomb

As much as I loved living with my dad, in my mind, my plan to stay with him was a temporary one. I adored being back in the gifted program with my former friends, but my tie to my mom pulled hard on my heartstrings. I needed her, and at the same time, I believed she needed *me*. But her seemingly easy acquiescence to let me live with my dad, and the fact that she never asked me to change my mind, made me wonder if she needed me as much as I'd thought.

For about five months, my dad and I were a perfectly happy twosome. And then one evening he said he had something he wanted to discuss with me. He had joined the Long Beach Ski Club some months prior, and at a recent meeting, he had met a new member he was interested in dating. Her name was Leah, and she had just turned twenty. (For anchoring purposes here, my dad was just shy of thirty and I just shy of ten.) My dad had rarely gone on dates I knew about, and he hadn't had a steady girlfriend my whole childhood up to then. But from then on out, he and Leah began seeing each other regularly.

About six months in, they sat me down and announced that they were engaged. I acted happy for them, but inside, I didn't quite understand the match. My dad and I were tight, and I sensed that Leah didn't genuinely like me. She pretended to on the surface, but she had been raised very differently than I had, and it seemed she wasn't particularly comfortable with the open, easy friendship I possessed with my dad, or with the freedom I was accustomed to. That, and the fact that we were only ten years apart in age, made it hard for me to imagine her as my stepmom.

What I knew without a doubt, however, was she was *not* going to be my mom. I had a mother I loved, and even though she wasn't nearby at the time, *no one* was going to try to step into her place. I protected her fiercely—her decisions, her character, her carefree way of living life—and I wouldn't let anyone criticize her even a smidge without jumping to her defense.

When I told my mom that my dad was engaged, she was happy for him, but surprised about his fiancée being so young. To her credit, she made a valiant and honest effort to be positive about it with me, and encouraged me to see how things went before I decided I didn't like the idea of having a stepmom. But it was too late. I already didn't like it.

Once Leah started occasionally spending the night with us and dropping me off at school sometimes, she became adamant about not letting me leave in the morning without a barrette in my hair. I had worn my hair long and straight for a while now, which was how my mom liked it, but Leah didn't think it flattered me, so she insisted on a change. In my eyes, though, she didn't really like *anything* about me, not just my hair. And I wasn't used to any kind of authoritarian parenting, only easy-going and respectful parenting, so her insistence on something so petty rubbed me the wrong way, and then some. I'd begrudgingly slide a barrette into my hair for the ride to school, then promptly remove it the moment she drove away.

But despite this assault I thought worthy of my dad breaking up with her, the wedding took place in September of 1979, with me as a junior bridesmaid. My grandparents were invited as a courtesy because of me, and they sat at the very back of the church. When the ceremony was over, being the odd bridesmaid with no groomsman, I was last and relegated to walk back down the aisle with the minister. I had held my emotion in throughout the nuptials, but it was bubbling up big time by the time they ended. All I wanted was to get out of that church. But instead of meeting me on the altar and swiftly escorting me down and out, the minister linked my arm and then stopped to address the congregation. As he thanked everyone for coming and babbled about where the reception would be, I was a veritable dam about to burst—

with everyone looking right at me. Finally, he began the stroll. My grandparents had slipped out and I could see them standing outside in the distance. I walked with the minister as far as I could, then I pulled my arm away and bolted down the rest of the aisle, out the doors, and straight into the arms of my grandma. I clung to her and broke into sobs. Eventually, she held me at arm's length, wanting to know exactly why I was crying.

But without saying a word, she already knew why.

I felt like I had just lost my dad, in the way we had been together for the last ten and a half years, for good.

＠

Ch-Ch-Ch-Ch-Changes

s if we had all lived in the small town of Mayberry, it turned out that Leah had grown up only four blocks away from my grandparents in Lakewood. So, after my dad sold his condo, while he and Leah were doing a bunch of work on their new house in Long Beach, we lived temporarily with her parents. They were nice people with good hearts, and they even called themselves my grandparents, but I felt like a total fish out of water living with them. The best thing about the two months we were there was how close I was to my grandparents's house, and I found every excuse possible to be there.

My mom and Josh had split up by this point, but my mom had continued to live up north for a while in Santa Cruz. It was around this time, in 1979, that she decided to do something she'd wanted to do for years: change her name. She hadn't minded her formal name of Cynthia, which was after my grandma's grandma and also my grandma's middle name, but she had always been called "Cindy," and she didn't like having such a common name of her generation. She also wanted to drop "Hill," which made total sense. She had been married to my dad for eleven minutes, yet she'd carried his name (mainly because it was mine) for eleven years. Neither suited her independent, free-spirited persona at all. So, she bought baby name books and pored over options, searching for an uncommon name that would reflect her uniqueness. Finally, she landed on a first name she felt was perfect for her: Briana (pronounced bree-AH-nah). That name, and derivations of it, have been popular for a couple decades now, but in the late 1970s, hardly anyone had heard of it. (My grandparents actually thought it was an "ethnic" name, and why would she choose that when she was lily white?) For her last name, she turned to Hollywood. Suzanne Somers was exceedingly popular at the time on *Three's Company*, and not only did my mom love the name "Somers," it sounded pretty with "Briana." And so, to my grandparents' puzzlement and a bit of sadness, and to my complete acceptance and delight, my mom officially became Briana Somers, and was soon nicknamed by friends as Bree.

But that wasn't the only name that changed.

As our relationship evolved, and because we had always been more like friends than mother and daughter, I felt less and less inclined to call her "Mommy" and to call her some kind of nickname. She was totally open to that, so at one point, I coined the oddly similar "Mohni" (pronounced "MOCH-ni" with a whispery, throaty "ch"), whose novelty wore off after a while (gosh, I wonder why). No other appropriate nickname came to mind after that, so I settled on calling her "Bree" too, which was so cute and perfect for her, only I often added "Mommie" to it. From then on, she was either Mommie Bree, or just Bree, but I never directly called her "Mommy" again, or even "Mom," except for addressing her in letters when I was young. (The "choosing our own name" thing was big for us, and as you'll see, became a recurring theme.)

Just when I thought my mom might be returning to Southern California to be near me, she moved south to San Diego to live in the home of a wealthy disabled man named Beau as his assistant. She explained to me that she needed the money and that she couldn't afford to live on her own anymore, but I was still crestfallen. Like before, though, I traveled on my own to see her—this time by train, which I found to be a grand adventure—and wrote her frequent letters.

By this time, I lived with my dad and Leah in their new house in Long Beach, which wasn't a hop and a skip from my school anymore. Instead of a five-or-so-minute drive, it was more like a fifteen-to-twenty-minute drive, so either Leah took me to school, or I was dropped off at my grandparents' or grandma Hill's house and one of them took me. I had an extraordinary fifth-grade teacher, and I loved school more than ever, but adjusting to having a stepmother, and a slightly different dynamic with my dad, was admittedly tough. I would sometimes, out of the blue, be sitting in class and feel overcome with emotion. When this happened, I would lift the lid of my desk and stick my head inside, pretending to look for something so my classmates wouldn't see my tears. I didn't know how to articulate what I was feeling; I only knew there was a sadness that resided in me that would pop up without my permission. Nonetheless, I found solace in writing creative letters to my mom in my progressively rounded, fancy handwriting, complemented by an abundance of Hello Kitty and Little Twin Stars stickers.

> April 18, 1980
> Dear Mommy,
> I miss ["U" sticker] very much!
> Here the [sun sticker] is out every day and our [flowers sticker] are blooming very pretty. Here is the sticker you liked [round, red Hello Kitty sticker]. Pretty soon I will send you a tape (with my voice talking to you).
> Well, goodbye is too hard to say so I'll say [big adorable elephant sticker that says "hello"].
> [bright pink Hello Kitty sticker]
> I love you.
> Anastasia

(Anastasia was my new formal name of choice after I discovered in one of my mom's baby name books that "Stacey" was derived from it. My full theatrical name was Anastasia Briana Somers.)

Around this time, near the end of fifth grade, my dad caught me privately in our driveway.

"Uh, Stace," he began, "the time has come where you're going to have to start wearing a bra."

Now, my dad and I had always talked openly and honestly about things, but this was admittedly awkward. Apparently, when I wasn't sporting my Mork from Ork rainbow suspenders with all the cool buttons pinned to them (come on, *everyone* who was cool in the late '70s had a pair), or my blousy softball uniform top (I played on a Bobby Sox team), or a puffy sweater of some kind (even with a camisole underneath, which I always wore because my grandma told me it was ladylike to do so and I loved them), my breast buds poked out just a little too far. Before I could even respond, he added, "So I'm going to have Leah take you shopping to get one."

"NO!" I blurted out in a panic. "No! I'll call my mom and have her send me one."

My dad pulled back slightly, probably from the sheer force of my refusal. "Okay, fine. But if she doesn't send it within a week, I'm having Leah take you."

"No!" I repeated, my panic rising. "If my mom can't get one that fast for some reason, I'll have my grandma take me."

"Well, whatever . . . that's fine, as long as you have one within the week."

I promptly called my mom and told her of my dire situation.

Five days later, a padded mailer arrived with a note of love and my first training bra.

Soon after the bra crisis was averted, my dad dropped another bomb: he insisted I learn how to swim.

I know. I grew up in Southern California, in *Long Beach* for heaven's sake. I went to the beach my whole childhood. I was willing to wade in the shallow tide, or even play in the sprinklers on a hot day. And taking baths and washing my hair was okay. But I absolutely despised the idea of being immersed in a pool, or having water sprayed in my face, or God forbid, going *under* the water. So, of course, my mom had never made me.

But my dad was worried about my inability to swim. "Everyone should know how for safety reasons," he told me. So he enrolled me in swimming lessons at the local park. Days later, my mom received this letter written on my light pink stationery adorned with the usual variety of stickers.

June 18, 1980

Dear Mommie,

I think I'm gonna die!

Swimming lessons are the pits! They're 2 weeks long. I think I might have to go to the next session. Please don't let my Dad put me in it again. I Positively Hate It!

Oh well, drop the subject.

Can you believe I'm going to be in 6th grade?

Oh! I wrote an article for this paper (The Ski Breeze from the ski club my Dad's in. It's not a public paper. It just goes to the people in the ski club) about the ski club's Family Picnic Softball Game. I won't get paid, but who cares? I've got some bucks (about $2.50). I'm going to get a velcro wallet this Saturday. I also got two more lip glosses, strawberry and green apple.

Well, PLEASE call me when you get this letter. I want you to know ...

[here I placed a sticker of a sad koala that says "Sure do miss you"]

Love, Anastasia

P.S. I love you

P.S.P.S. I cry every night 'cause I miss you so much

Whether this letter was the catalyst, or the job with Beau came to an end, my mom called to tell me that she was coming back. The last thing she wanted to do as an adult was move back in with her parents, but she needed time to get on her feet and save up some money, so in their typical supportive and generous way, my grandparents welcomed her with open arms.

The moment, and I mean *the* moment, I found out my mom was moving back in with my grandparents, I asked if I could move there too. My grandparents didn't hesitate to say yes, and my mom was thrilled, but my dad, well, he wasn't so thrilled. He was worried about my stability, and how long my mom might be around. But once again, the decision was left to me, and it was an easy one.

My red Samsonite had never been packed so fast.

Reunited
(and It Feels So Good)

 ow that my mom and I were back together after our two years apart, all seemed right with the world. And it wasn't just that the golden thread that bound us was pulled physically tight again, but living with my grandparents meant I would be close to my school, which was wonderful because it was my last year at Twain and I wanted to live closer to my friends.

That summer, my mom not only enrolled in a couple classes at Long Beach City College, she quickly got a job at a high-end steak-house-type restaurant called Clinkerdagger's as a cocktail waitress in the bar. I imagine she didn't even have to interview; the manager probably took one look at her and she was in. The cocktail servers had to wear a navy blue Danskin tank leotard up top, and a mid-thigh-length Danskin wraparound skirt with high heels below. And being a classy bar in a classy restaurant, and my mom being a knockout and having a naturally warm and winning personality, she was perfect for the job. As you might surmise, she also made some pretty nice tips.

The thing about my mom and me was that our relationship had always been open and close. You'll recall she talked to me candidly from the time I could talk (and probably even before that), so that was the dynamic I'd always been used to. True to that, she held nothing back when I asked about her financial situation, or what her plans were for the future. Yes, my mom's life had been what you might call cobbled together for the last two years—multiple living arrangements, various jobs, a couple of hand-me-down cars after her prized Datsun 240Z was stolen—and now she was living at home yet again. But her positivity, resilience, and desire to move up were clear. She was bright, healthy, and completely determined to find her way. Plus, if she had to live at home for a spell, at least her little girl was at long last with her.

Another thing that was admirable—and progressive—about my mom was her understanding that love was love.

When I was four, she had taken me to meet her dear friends, Peter and Brian, at their apartment. After having a wonderful time with them, we walked to our car hand-in-hand.

"Are Peter and Brian brothers?" I asked.

"No," she said without hesitation. "They're a couple."

"Oh," I said, with a comprehending nod.

And that was all the conversation we needed.

Now, my mom was back in the dating scene again, and this time she started dating Everett, who happened to be black. I thought Everett was supremely cool, and he made me feel the same. My grandparents, though quite accepting for their generation, were a bit taken aback by the pairing—but I wasn't. My mom saw people for their character, not their color, sexual orientation, or any other label, and she instilled the same in me, by beautiful example.

Being in my mom's everyday life again meant that I knew where she was most of the time, and I liked it. Being apart the prior two years, I worried about her, and I derived some level of comfort knowing her general whereabouts, not to mention when her whereabouts included me.

After our escapades in her VW Rabbit ended with its premature demise, my mom had the chance to get a new car. Well, not exactly a *new* car, but after resorting to borrowing my grandparents' classic white Barracuda every day, it was newish enough. This enviable showpiece was a blue second-hand Dodge my aunt gave to my mom (or sold to her for cheap, I'm not sure). Either way, that car was a bomb. It was old, made funny noises, and bounced when we stopped at lights. We promptly made up a song to commemorate the heap:

We are riding in the Dodge, doo dah, doo dah,
We are riding in the Dodge, oh doo dah day.
Ridin' in the Dodge all night,
Ridin' in the Dodge all day,
Ridin' in the dumb ol' dirty Dodge, oh da doo dah day.

We would sing this song every time we drove somewhere, and we would laugh and laugh.

Which was undeniably better than all the weeping I had done every time I had to leave her after a visit, or the nights I had cried because I didn't know how long it would be before I'd see her again.

Falling in Love Again

My mom and Everett didn't end up being much more than a passing fling, but sometime during sixth grade, she did meet someone new—someone I adored.

Some months after my mom started working at Clinkerdagger's—or "Clink's," as everyone called it—she met Danny King. He was a witty, wacky sweetheart of a guy who regularly came with his work buddies to happy hour in the bar. After getting to know each other a bit, he and my mom began dating, and I felt like she had finally found the perfect person for her. As protective of her as I was, and as much as I never quite pictured her marrying again, when Danny eventually proposed, he received my full stamp of approval.

The combination of my mom being in a wonderful partnership, and that Danny and I clicked as buds from the start, meant that I took to the idea of my mom's getting married again more than I took to my dad's, probably because Leah and I simply weren't what you'd call simpatico. It wasn't her fault—she was young and walked into a solid, uncommon relationship between my dad and me, and she wasn't prepared at all to be my stepmother, let alone my friend. So we were basically thrown together with the hope we'd get along. We were civil, mind you, just never close.

So as my mom delighted in planning her wedding, which she shared with me right down to her dress—and mine—I imagined living with her and Danny, somewhere near my grandparents, where I could go to junior high with most of my friends. The group of kids in the gifted program had mostly been the same tight-knit bunch for multiple grades, and I could not imagine having to break away from them after all these years.

But unfortunately, the three of us—my mom, Danny, and I—falling in love with each other wasn't going to work out quite the way I envisioned.

Boomerang

*A*fter my elementary school career came to a close, with a festive class picnic and all my friends signing the Little Twin Stars autograph book my grandma bought for me, my mom and Danny made plans to move in together. My mom was admittedly happy to no longer be beholden to her parents, but I couldn't help but feel a whoosh of abandonment. Soon enough, I found out that my mom and Danny had no plans to live in Lakewood, or even nearby in Long Beach; in fact, they had their eye on a lovely new housing development in Phillips Ranch, thirty-five miles away, where they could afford to buy a beautiful, brand-new house. I hated that they were moving so far away, but I *wanted* my mom to have a beautiful new house after going through such a rough time of it, so I tried my best to be happy for her.

Once my dad got wind that my mom was moving to an area that took three traffic-laden SoCal freeways to get to, he beckoned me back to live with him, where I could attend an excellent junior high school near their house and not have to worry about moving anytime soon.

"But I don't want to go to Stanford Junior High," I pleaded. "I want to go to Bancroft where a lot of my friends are going. *None* of my friends from Twain are going to Stanford. I won't know anyone!"

"But we don't live in the district for Bancroft," my dad countered. "Plus, Stanford has a reputation of being an exceptional school."

I didn't give a hoot about their reputation. "Then I'll stay with my grandparents. They said I could."

My dad calmly, yet solidly, put his foot down. "There's no reason for you to live with your grandparents when you have two parents . . . plus, you already have a home here with us."

I didn't like his reasoning at all, but the truth was, as much as I wanted to live with my mom and Danny—and I was welcome to do so —I didn't want to move that far away. The dilemma of it all weighed on me like a thousand boulders. I wanted my mom to be happy, and I wanted to be part of it, but it took over an hour to get to their new house. At the same time, I did *not* want to move back in with my dad and Leah and go to a school where I'd be starting completely over, in *junior high* at that. (Of course, this would have been the scenario had I moved with my mom too, but my poor dad received the brunt of that drama.) Since my dad wouldn't allow me to live with my grandparents, though, that really only left me with one choice.

My boomerang had spun for a glorious year with two elements of my trifecta in one place, and now it was returning to where it had started.

A Match Made at Birth

*I*t turned out that one boy from my class at Twain was going to Stanford after all. Big whoop. I'd know *one* person. Oh, and the younger sister of one of Leah's dear friends was going there too. Zip-a-dee-doo-dah. That made *two* whole people I'd know. Well, it was more than I knew when we moved to Santa Cruz. But this was *junior high*, the biggest transition of my life yet. At least it felt that major to me.

The good news is that I fell in love with Stanford Junior High pretty quickly. The bad news is that I had P.E. *first* period. Seriously. What was the point of getting all dolled up for school when I'd get trashed first period? I couldn't believe my stupid luck. But then, some good news even came out of that.

One day early in the school year, when we were in the locker room changing for P.E., a few girls were asking when each other's birthdays were. I turned to my new friend, Lisa.

"When's your birthday?"

"February."

"Really? Mine too! February what?"

"18th."

"What??!! Mine too!!"

"Really? That's amazing!"

"It is!" I took a beat. "What hospital were you born in?"

"Long Beach Community."

"NO WAY. *I* was born at Long Beach Community!"

"NO WAY!"

We both stared at each other in awe for a moment.

"You know what that means?" I said. "It means we were in the hospital nursery together, maybe even *right* next to each other. And then, all these years later, we meet in junior high!"

"Whoa," she said. "You're right. Too bad there's no way to find out."

"Whatever," I said. "Just knowing we were there together is a pretty big deal, don't you think?"

"For sure."

When I called and told my mom this news, she thought it was pretty amazing too.

"See, I was supposed to be born on the 18th," I reminded her, "so that I could go to a new school and have a best friend with my exact same birthday."

"I guess that's one good reason," she conceded. (She still hadn't completely forgiven me for being sixteen days late, or for putting her through the worst pain of her life.)

Not long after, my mom bought me a cream sweater with pastel patterned stitching across the shoulders. The first time I wore it to school, I about keeled over when I met Lisa at her locker. She was wearing the identical sweater!

When I told my mom *this* incredible news, she said, "I know it wasn't what you wanted, but maybe it really was the best decision for you to move back with your dad and go to Stanford. It sounds like things are really going well for you."

I hated to admit it, but with my new best friend, our matching birthdays and sweaters, and classes I loved, maybe I could manage seeing my mom only occasionally yet again.

Absence and Adolescence

Though I knew it made sense to live with my dad at this point, and to have the stability of home and school, being a twelve-year-old girl without the consistent presence of my mom created a gaping hole in my heart. Leah and I just didn't mesh that well at all. We never did anything together, and I didn't feel comfortable talking to her about any subject, especially something sensitive.

The blessing for me, though, was that I never took it personally that we didn't share a closeness. I neither craved nor wished for a mother's love from her, and I never sought her approval to boost my self-esteem. I considered this a godsend because if I *had* craved these things from her, and it simply wasn't in her heart to offer them, I might have felt a sense of rejection. But because we were simply too different to have much of a bond, we existed with (mostly) polite tolerance under the same roof, with no real animosity but rarely an exchange of love or affection either.

So you can imagine my dilemma when I arrived home from school on February 15th, 1982, just three days shy of my thirteenth birthday, went straight to the bathroom as usual, and discovered a brownish spot in my underwear.

Oh my God, I thought, *I think I just got my first period.*

I hadn't felt anything, not a cramp or a funny leak or even a twinge. But most every girl my age had read *Are You There God? It's Me, Margaret*, so even if we didn't have *that* talk with a parent, we had some idea that this monthly visitor was coming and could show up at any time.

Right away, I panicked. Even though she wasn't there, I *had* to tell my mom first. That's the way it was supposed to be. A girl told her *mom* these things, not her dad, not her stepmom. I could have called my grandma, but I desperately wanted my mom to be the first to know. Plus, I needed to know how to keep the rest from flowing out. I had witnessed my mom insert her O.B. non-applicator tampons any number of times, but that seemed disgusting and painful, so I guessed I needed the maxi pads they advertised during soap operas.

In our house, we had one centrally located phone in the open dining room, which meant it was difficult to have a private conversation without your voice projecting everywhere. On that day, my dad happened to be home already and was out in the garage, and Leah was in their bedroom, folding laundry. So, I quietly crept out to the dining room and dialed my mom's number, praying she would be there and answer. When she did, I whispered, "I'm so glad you're home!"

"Doob?" she said. "Are you okay? Why are you talking so low?"

"Because something happened, and I don't want Leah to hear."

"What happened?" She sounded worried.

"I just got my first period, and I'm not sure what to do."

"You did?" she exclaimed. "Well, welcome to the club!"

I laughed, but only slightly. "Yeah, welcome to adolescence. What a thirteenth birthday gift."

"Have you told your dad?"

"No!" I whispered louder than I meant to, my mortification at the thought making my belly contract. "I wanted to tell you first."

"Well, I'm glad I was here so you could. This is wonderful news, honey. But . . . you need to tell your dad."

"I don't want to. I feel weird about it."

"You don't have to feel weird. You know your dad will be understanding."

I flashed to the scene on the driveway when he tried to discretely tell me my breast buds were making him uncomfortable, and therefore the world uncomfortable, and it was high time we did something about it.

"I guess," I conceded. "I just *don't* want to have to tell Leah."

"I know you two don't have that kind of relationship, but she'll probably be the one to get you what you need."

I wanted to cry. Why couldn't my *mom* be the one to get me what I needed? My grandma was my designated bra-shopping companion, which had worked out beautifully since taking me to buy a second and third AAA for when the one my mom mailed me needed washing, then my AAs, and now my fashionable set of As. But maxi pads? And maybe even tampons? That was a decidedly *mom* job, and my mom wasn't going to be able to do it for me, at least not this first time.

My silence alerted my mom to my tears. "I'm sorry I'm not there," she said with regret in her voice. "But do go tell your dad, okay? He deserves to be part of this news too."

I hung up feeling like my world was crumbling. I was glad I was able to tell my mom first—she could have very easily not been home when I called—but what lay ahead felt like walking through honey in lead shoes.

I trudged out to the garage.

"Hey, Stace," my dad said, with his usual cheerful self.

"Hey, Dad," I said, glancing downward.

"What's goin' on?"

"Um . . . I have something to tell you."

"Okay. What is it?"

"I . . . I just got my first period."

With utter empathy and poise, he said, "Oh great. Now there are two women under this roof."

Mind you, I do believe this was his nervous reaction to something he wasn't expecting. He actually didn't say it in a mean way, but rather in a lighthearted way. But to me it sounded like I had just ruined his life, and I wasn't sure how to respond. No matter, he followed up his pronouncement with a chuckle and a "Well, I guess Leah has something for that."

This, of course, meant *me* telling Leah. Not my dad delicately telling her so I could avoid the awkward moment.

So, I returned to the house and approached Leah. With as little pomp and circumstance as I could emit, I said, "I just got my period and my dad said you would have something."

I could immediately tell that she felt as awkward as I did. "Oh. Okay." She disappeared into the bathroom and returned with a box of maxis. "I'll get more at the store next time I go," she said.

Before she could say anything else, I thanked her and rushed back to my bathroom. Then I realized I needed a clean pair of underwear, so I dashed to my room, then back to the bathroom, where I promptly locked the door. After changing, I pulled out a pad and peeled off the plastic strip to expose the adhesive, then centered and pressed the behemoth into my panties. When I pulled them up, I couldn't believe how it felt. I might as well as have been wearing a diaper, for God's sake. *No wonder my mom wears tampons*, I thought. *This sucks!*

But I couldn't imagine pushing a stubby tampon up inside me like my mom did, and I had no idea there was any alternative. So, for the next year and half, I sucked it up and prayed every month that those cotton wads between my legs wouldn't overflow during class and make me the laughing stock of Stanford Junior High.

Teenage Blues and Pinks

The summer after seventh grade ended, on August 1, 1982, my mom and Danny had a sweet, intimate wedding in someone's lovely home, with my grandparents, Danny's mom and sister, a group of their closest friends, and me as a bridesmaid. Unlike at my dad's wedding, I didn't bolt into my grandma's arms in tears after the "I do's." I did hover around her as I usually did at functions where we were both present, but this was a decidedly happy day, and all the photos reflect that. My grandparents loved Danny, Danny's mom and sister loved my mom and me, and the two of them made a beautiful pair.

Not long after the wedding, my mom became pregnant. I don't know why, but I had never considered her having more children. We had such a unique bond, and I assumed it would always be just the two of us on our little biological twig of the family tree. So, it was with mixed feelings on my end when my mom discovered it was an ectopic pregnancy and thankfully, for her sake, had a miscarriage.

Several months later, my mom once again took a pregnancy test that came out positive. She and Danny were ecstatic. But after a couple months, when she started having pain, Danny took her to the doctor. My mom's crotchety old physician said she was fine and sent her home with some meds. But when the pain became excruciating, she was rushed to the hospital. An ultrasound showed that my mom was in grave danger with yet another ectopic pregnancy, one perilously close to bursting. They rushed her into emergency surgery, where the surgeon opened her up just as the pregnancy was giving way in her fallopian tube. Had the surgery taken place even a minute after, the doctor said, my mom would have died.

It took a while for my mom to recover, and when she and Danny went to a new doctor to find out why she was having ectopic pregnancies, they were told that she was essentially "cobwebs down there," meaning she simply didn't have the functioning mechanics of her ovaries or fallopian tubes anymore for pregnancy, even though she was only thirty and still menstruating.

This was devastating news for both of them. The letdown of not being able to have a biological child together, along with other unfortunate events, made them mutually decide to go their separate ways after only two years of marriage. I was deeply shocked and saddened by the news. I had loved spending time with them at their house, and I loved them as a couple. I couldn't fathom that their union was ending so soon, and that what had seemed like my mom's fairy tale was already coming to an end.

Though Danny hadn't been my stepdad for long, he and I shared a sweet friendship, and luckily, he and my mom stayed friends too. In fact, he and my mom never really lost touch, which at least made a happier ending to the story.

While I was admittedly, and selfishly, relieved that it appeared I was going to be my mom's one and only for all time, I was elated when my dad told me that Leah was pregnant. I was fourteen, and I was over the moon that we were going to have a baby in the house. I was way beyond any worry of attention diverted away from me; in fact, I had become less and less talkative at home and welcomed a shift of focus.

So, on July 13, 1983, the summer before my ninth grade year, when my baby sister, Lindsay, was born, I felt as if *I* had just given birth to the baby girl I always wanted (only without going through the worst pain of my life). Natasha was still a permanent fixture, even in my teenage world, but a real baby obviously took things to a whole new level.

From the moment Lindsay was born, I wanted to claim her as mine. And in as many ways as I could at that age, I did.

My mom was thrilled for me that I had a baby sister.

And I was thrilled that I got her through my dad, and not through having to give up a single treasured piece I had of my mom.

∞

Sophomore Kitten

When junior high came to a close, I wept as if I was attending a funeral for all of my friends at once. My mom had lent me a grownup-looking suit to wear for the ceremony (I had shot up five inches since seventh grade and we were now the same height), and in every photo, it's clear that I'm crying through my smile. That exceptional school my dad had wanted me to go to, the one I had so forcefully rejected a few years before and not cared a flying leap what its reputation was, had become one of the most memorable experiences of my life.

Though some of my friends were going on to my high school, others were going to different schools in our district because of where they lived (including my dear friend, Michelle, who, after listening to my laments of wearing giant panty pillows every month, had graciously relieved me of my maxi-pad blues by bringing a remainder box of her junior-size applicator tampons to school one day—complete with the written instructions—and graphically explained to me how to use them. I don't know what I was more thankful for: a candid, caring friend, or discovering there was a feminine hygiene product that didn't involve impaling myself with my finger).

Just like at the end of sixth grade, I was devastated to lose some of my most beloved pals. But as I was reading some of the signatures in my yearbook, something momentarily quelled my sadness with curiosity. My friend, Grace, had written "Stacey for Sophomore Princess" under her signature and drawn a cute little face wearing a crown. I had no idea what Sophomore Princess was, but I thought it was an awfully sweet thing to write to me.

Then, my first or second week of high school, something miraculous happened: an office aide came to the doorway of my third-period dance class with a folded paper addressed to me. When I opened it, it read:

Congratulations! You have received votes by your peers that placed you in the top five to run for Millikan High School's Sophomore Princess at this year's Homecoming.

It was followed by instructions on where to post my chosen 5x7 photo on campus, along with a write-up I was required to pen to describe myself.

I was gobsmacked. How had I missed this? I didn't recall having the chance to nominate anyone, and here *I* was nominated? Who had been so kind to vote for me? And I made the top five students?

When I called my mom to tell her, she was overjoyed for me. She had never had any real opportunities in high school to be popular or to shine, and she was so proud that her daughter had been nominated.

"So what does it mean that you're in the top five?" she wanted to know.

"Apparently, although it seems weird, the five of us put our photos and descriptions of ourselves in this big glass case at school. And then all the students decide who they think merits the vote the most and submit a marked ballot. Whoever gets the most votes wins and gets to be in the homecoming court."

"So you could actually be named Sophomore Kitten!" she said with glee.

"Sophomore Kitten?" I laughed. "No, it's Sophomore Princess."

"I know," she said. "But on the TV show *Father Knows Best*, the two daughters were Princess and Kitten. I just think you being Sophomore Kitten sounds cuter."

I laughed again. "Hmm. I like it. But honestly, I don't even know if I have a real chance. The other girls are really pretty."

"And what are you, chopped liver?" she teased.

"Well, you know what I mean. And I know it's not just about looks . . . it's supposed to be about character and achievements too . . . but it seems like a beauty pageant the way they set it up. It's actually kind of embarrassing."

"But people voted for you to be in the running, so I think you should be happy and enjoy it. I don't think I even went to my sophomore homecoming. And I wasn't there to go to my junior or senior, *as you know*."

I felt bad being reminded. The reason for that was because of me. Not that it was *my* fault, and she certainly didn't blame me (except to tease me) but, you know.

"Yeah, I know. Well, okay . . . I'll let you know when I find out. They're going to announce the winner next week."

"Fingers crossed for you, honey!"

For all of her quirks and teasing me at times, one thing my mom did brilliantly and seamlessly was to, without fail, display genuine joy and pride in my achievements. Sure, most parents want better for their children than they might have had, but others, in their immaturity or insecurity, aim to keep their children down so that they can feel superior. But my mom, despite how young she was, and despite the emotional wounds she carried deep within, never resented that I had opportunities she never had, or excelled in areas she didn't. In fact, I was often the one to compare myself to *her*, wanting to be as radiant, winning, and attractive as she was. As dissimilar as we were in many ways, and as solid as I was in my own convictions and personal choices that differed from hers, I was proud of the ways we were alike, and she was still that glowing presence to me that all the kids had oohed and aahed over whenever she came to my school.

The following week, Millikan held a pep rally to announce the homecoming court. I really did feel special just to be nominated, but you can imagine my surprise when I was announced as the winner.

"Doob, I'm so happy for you!" my mom bubbled when I called her. "I can't wait to be there."

Yes, we had been apart for a few years now, with only sporadic visits at times. But in a few short weeks, Briana's little girl was indeed going to be Sophomore Kitten, and there was no way she was going to miss it.

On Homecoming night, my date (a boyfriend I dropped right after the big event because he was cramping my style wanting to spend too much time with me) rented his uncle's very cool classic convertible, I borrowed a dear friend's blue-and-white Cinderella-style dress, and my mom lent me her cropped white faux-fur jacket to wear over it while I sat on the football field on my big red throne.

It was an undeniably exciting night. My entire family was there to cheer me on—my dad, Leah, and her parents; my grandparents; my grandma Hill; my uncle and aunt; my mom; and even my childhood best friend, Christi, and her parents—all sitting together, all perfectly amicable as they always had been. When my name was announced and our driver slowly brought us around the field toward the stands, I could hear my posse all shouting my name with enthusiasm. I beamed as I waved like a good little kitten, and shining radiantly through the hundreds of people in the stands, was my mom, with the brightest smile of all.

Fighting Demons

s I headed toward my senior year, I'd had some pretty exciting things happen. After being crowned Sophomore Kitten, I was exceedingly fortunate to make some superb new friends I adored, along with my friends from junior high who went to Millikan too. School itself was just okay, but it perked up when I made the drill team as a Kidette my junior year (we were the Millikan Rams, hence Kidettes. Get it? *Kid-ettes*. Baby rams. Ha ha). Then, at the end of my junior year, I really hit the big time.

At my high school, there were twenty-four spots that were considered elite for a senior girl: the twelve on the Varsity Cheer squad, the six on the (short) Flag squad, and the six on the Song squad (the latter two making up the collective Pepsters). Well, I had zippo skill in gymnastics, so Cheer was out. And though I gave it a whirl, I could *not* master the twirling and flipping of the short flags. But Song was something I could definitely try out for, as it was more focused on dance ability with some Cheer elements thrown in. Plus, my year as a Kidette gave me an advantage. So, I threw myself in with my hilarious, ultra-talented best friend Wendi (who became hilarious, ultra-talented Wendi McLendon-Covey of TV and movie fame) and started choreographing my tryout routine.

After several weeks of practice, I was ready as I could be—and my audition went well, I thought. A few days later, as if akin to announcing Oscar winners, the current group of Song and Flag Girls made a spectacle of proclaiming who their successors would be. Gathered around the giant circle of cement that held the flag pole, facing each other, they yelled in a slow cadence:

"The first '86–'87 Song girl is . . ." Then they swiveled to face the crowd and paused for drama. "[insert name]!"

This went on, one by one, until all the Song and Flag girls were announced.

With intense anticipation, I stood in the quad after four Song girls had been named, including Wendi, as I held my breath on number five.

"The fifth '86–'87 Song Girl is . . ." [swivel and pause] "Stacey Hill!"

I erupted into squeals and jumped up and down with Wendi. "We both made it! We both made it!" we echoed.

And I really did feel like I had made it.

But something that lurked beneath the surface was soon to shake my seeming outward confidence to the core.

When our senior year began, being on Song wasn't only an honor, it was a boatload of work. We had to be at school for zero *and* first periods to choreograph a new routine for the rallies every week of football and basketball season, as well as to create and perfect other routines to perform at the games. Truth be told, as much as I loved being on the squad, I tended to feel like the least talented in terms of dance ability, which caused a bitter memory to bubble to the surface.

When I was seven years old, my mom enrolled me in a ballet and tap class, and I couldn't have been more in my element. I *loved* both styles of dance and instantly thought I had found my path in life. I had the long, trim build of a dancer and had inherited my mom's shapely legs, and I got the moves so quickly, and spent so much time perfecting each one at home, that my teachers put me up front in our performance of *The Nutcracker* to lead the rest of my class in our segment as tin soldiers.

Being on a real stage, in my sequin-covered red, white, and blue leotard, was the absolute highlight of my young life. I wanted nothing more than to keep going to dance class and become the prima ballerina I was surely meant to be. But when the next session was due to begin, my mom told me she couldn't drive me there anymore. My studio was about fifteen minutes from our house, and for some reason, it had become inconvenient. Tears filled my eyes.

"But I *love* ballet. Maybe Grandma can take me."

But she didn't want to ask my grandma, and I couldn't understand why. I was *good* at dance, so she couldn't have been trying to save me from making a fool of myself. I had just been singled out as a star performer in my recital, for goodness' sake. It just didn't make sense. But, unable to strike a deal with her (possibly because the cost of my classes was the issue, and in this case for some reason, she didn't want me to know), my dance career was over only a year after it started, and I had lamented what I might have become ever since.

Now, in the rehearsal room with five other girls who had *all* taken dance practically their entire lives, I felt like a sorry sixth member. Clearly, my front-and-center-stage abilities when I was seven had shriveled up to a sadly inferior level compared with my teammates. I was good enough to make the squad out of many girls who tried out, so I didn't suck by any means. But I often had to work a lot harder to perfect a routine than the other girls did. Wendi was especially brilliant at choreography and often created the best parts of our routines, so while I admired her and was incredibly proud of her abilities, having my best friend regularly outshine me—at least in *my* mind—bummed me out too.

Over time, my inner feelings of inferiority, though not apparent to others at all on the outside, were joined by something altogether new.

Though I was used to being at school by 7:00 a.m. and spending two straight hours working hard on routines, I started feeling more and more tired by second-period Physics class. I had no interest at all in Physics; it was one of those ridiculous graduation prerequisites that most of us would never use. So my disinterest, coupled with my lack of ability in grasping the subject, fueled my fatigue. Sometimes, it was such a struggle to keep my eyes open that I actually fell asleep in class, something I had *never* done before. Ever since my sophomore year, my usual As and Bs had been slipping too, and I had actually become satisfied sliding by with a mere C in this class, as well as a few others, which was glaringly uncharacteristic of me.

My next period was a class called Effective Living, which was a brilliant course about how to live in the real world. We had to "marry" another class member and plan an entire wedding based on our appointed career's average income, have and care 24/7 for a "baby" (an egg stamped with our teacher's name on the bottom so that if we broke our baby, we couldn't replace it without his knowledge), and other real-world tasks. I bring this up because this class was everyone's favorite. Our teacher was a gregarious, caring man, and most of the class sessions were highly interactive. But some days, I would feel such an intense depression in this class that I couldn't enjoy it at all. I even had to fight tears I couldn't explain at times. Often, this sadness and fatigue would carry over from Physics class; other times, I would perk up after Physics and have a blast in Effective Living with my friends. The problem was, I felt like I couldn't control my varying emotions at all. And it wasn't PMS; it felt like something serious.

I had heard of manic depression, now more commonly called being bipolar, where people's moods swung from high to low without reason or warning. I was certain I had this, and I was scared. Not being in control of when I felt happy or overcome with sadness seemed like something that needed professional intervention. Plus, I'd been having intermittent thoughts of suicide, which scared me even more.

One of my close friend's dads was a psychologist, so I confided in her about what I was going through, and she completely understood. She herself had seen a therapist colleague of her dad's, a woman named Bonnie, and she gave me her business card. That evening, I called this therapist and explained my situation and that I wanted to get help.

"It's highly unusual to receive a call like this from a teenager," she told me. "I normally receive these kinds of calls from a concerned parent. Does your mom or dad know you're contacting me?"

"No." I hadn't wanted to bring my dad into it, but someone was going to have to pay for this therapy, so I realized he had to know. "And it's my dad I live with."

"I see. Well, can I speak to him directly? Is he there?"

"Do you have to?"

"I do. I can't see a minor without parental consent." She paused. "I can hold if you like."

I wished I could have her talk to my mom, but this was urgent, and I already had her on the phone, so I went to my dad and explained that there was a therapist I wanted to see and that she was on the phone. You might imagine the befuddled reaction he gave to that. He had no idea I was anything but an ebullient Song leader and gushing big sister, with a heaping side of typical teenage moodiness.

"If something's going on with you, Stace, why can't you just talk to me?" he wanted to know.

"Because I *can't*."

"Why not?"

"I just *can't*. I need to talk to someone who doesn't know me."

He didn't like having this news dumped on him, with a therapist holding the line for him, but he talked to her anyway. When he hung up, he told me he would let me go if I *really* believed I needed to, but she was going to cost $80 an hour, which he was only willing to fork out if my mom split the cost.

I honestly didn't know if she could swing that on a weekly basis, but I felt certain she'd do it for me if she could.

"I still don't understand why you can't just talk to me for free," my dad said, shaking his head.

But there was no getting him to understand something I didn't understand myself. So I thanked him for letting me make my first appointment, secured my mom's supportive agreement on the cost, and promptly wrangled my grandma to pick me up from school to drive me.

After a few sessions of working to get to the bottom of my unexplained mood jumps, it started becoming apparent that there were several contributing factors, one of which was that the complex relationship I had with my mom was affecting me in a way I wasn't aware of.

Over the past five years, my mom had stayed local, and we saw each other whenever we could. She came to some of my softball games on Saturdays and to see me cheer at occasional football games. We went to movies, hung out, and went shopping together. She even took me out to a fancy lunch on my sixteenth birthday and told me something no one had ever confided in me before: that my grandparents had wanted to adopt a third child, another girl, but that they couldn't afford it back then. And then I came along when they were still young—and what a miracle it was, despite the circumstances, that they got the third child, and second daughter, they'd always wanted. Indeed, they had loved me as their own, but I wondered if my mom had felt somehow "used" in that deal. She assured me she didn't feel that way at all, that she was happy for so many reasons that she had been the vessel through which I came into the world.

But while I knew she was being genuine, and that she loved me without a doubt, I was battling the fact that she routinely canceled on me whenever we had plans. Sometimes it was because she had been invited to some event, or that she "wasn't going to be able to make it after all" because something had come up. Every time this happened, another layer of self-doubt built within me, wondering why I wasn't important enough to her to keep our dates.

I knew that for my dad, being my consistently steady parent in the face of these disappointments wasn't easy. He hated seeing me hurt. But something equally unsettling had recently happened with him, too—something that at the time, he wasn't aware had shaken my sense of self-worth on the level that it did.

The summer after I made Song, one of the requirements to prep for the year was attending Cheer Camp. I knew this before I tried out, and my dad knew it too. He agreed that if I made it, he would pay $400 toward the $1,200 projected expenses to be on the squad for the year, which included Cheer Camp—but that was *it*. The rest I'd have to earn by getting a job. The problem was, I refused to work in a fast food restaurant (I know that sounds snobby, but that's where my head was at the time), and after applying at the nearby grocery store, Hallmark store, and other places without scoring an interview or being chosen for a position, I wasn't sure what to do.

"Well," my dad insisted, "if you don't have a job by the time you leave for Cheer Camp, you can't live here. You'll have to move out."

I was dumbstruck. I was seventeen, I was about to be a senior in high school, I had no car, and I helped out all the time at home between cleaning, cooking, and caring for Lindsay, and now a new baby brother too. And I would have to move out if I didn't get a job in a few weeks?

I really did try, but places just weren't hiring. "You haven't applied at McDonald's or Jack-in-the-Box yet," my dad reminded me.

"I'm *not* working at a fast food place," I persisted.

But the date for my departure to Cheer Camp arrived, and I still didn't have a job. So, I spent the five days that were supposed to be one of the most fun experiences of my teen life trying to figure out where I was going to live. My mom couldn't afford to have me with her at the time, and I knew how my dad felt about me living with my grandparents. But whichever way it panned out, I was going to have to leave my beloved baby sister, and my barely born little brother. I cried in my bunk at night in disbelief that I was getting kicked out of my house.

"Geez, you don't even drink or go to parties," one of my teammates said. "That's messed up. You're, like, as square as they come. *And* you babysit!"

But none of that seemed to matter.

When I got dropped off at home after Cheer Camp ended, I ambled up the walkway feeling incredibly depressed. As soon as I opened the screen door, three-year-old Lindsay ran up to me and threw her arms around my legs. "Sissy! Sissy! I misssssed you!"

I squatted down and held her to me as a dam broke behind my eyes. My dad said hi, and I kept my face hidden as I muttered a "hi" back, picked up Lindsay, and carried her into my room.

My dad didn't follow me right away, but a little while later, he came to my doorway. "I know I said you had to move out when you got back, but Lindsay really missed you while you were gone. And seeing her with you when you came home . . . well . . . I'm willing to give you some more time to find a job."

"Thanks," I said flatly.

What I really wanted to say was, *Wow, how generous. My time at Cheer Camp was basically ruined with this hanging over me. If it weren't for Lindsay, you'd still be pushing me out, hoping my mom would take care of me for a while, huh? I'm shocked you're still willing to be stuck with me. I guess you don't want to lose your babysitter after all.*

My dad had never made me feel like he was "stuck" with me, but the incident had addled me, and these feelings of acrimony came pouring out in my sessions with Bonnie.

I had been affected right away by my dad's threat to boot jobless, disappointing me out. But I hadn't thought about my mom's actions in such a deep way until Bonnie coaxed it out of me and the dots started to connect. All of it, though, had added up to these bouts of manic depression I was experiencing and hadn't understood.

"It's no wonder you've been questioning your self-worth," she said, siding with me. She tapped her pencil on her notebook. "Do you think your parents would be willing to be part of a session, separately of course, so that you could explain what you've shared with me? And I would be a neutral third party to support you?"

I shrugged. "I guess so."

Picturing a session with my mom and Bonnie felt weird. I did *not* want to hurt my mom by telling her how much her cancellations had affected me. Then I pictured sitting there with my dad and Leah, and having Bonnie as a buffer. That *did* feel good. I wanted to get my feelings out about a few things that felt out of balance to me, even if I was admittedly lucky in a lot of ways too.

"Good," Bonnie said. "It doesn't matter which order they come, as long as you get to express yourself to each one."

"Okay," I said, feeling nervous and vindicated all at once.

Figuring I'd warm up with my dad, I came home and told him that Bonnie wanted him and Leah to come to my next session. To be honest, I could tell he was uncomfortable with the idea. And I knew it was the last place Leah wanted to be. But they conceded nonetheless.

During the session, Bonnie was the neutral third party she promised she'd be, but I did feel she was on *my* side, which was nice. I felt empowered and entitled to share my feelings, and after I spilled all my upset about the whole moving thing, and how I'd felt underappreciated at home, my dad admitted that he had only used the threat as motivation, that he never really intended to toss my sorry ass (my words, not his) out at seventeen.

I really did have a wonderful father. And I know that raising a teenage daughter, even under the best of circumstances, isn't always a walk in the park. But this "motivational" tactic decidedly hadn't been his finest parental hour. In the end, though, my dad apologized for causing me so much undue stress, and I felt like we had a bit of a fresh start.

When my mom came to the following session, the air felt completely different. I was so reticent to tell her she had done anything to cause me pain that I wept as I admitted it. In response, my mom put her hand on her heart as her eyes filled with tears.

"Oh honey," she said, "I had no idea I was doing that to you. I guess I just never thought about how much our time together meant to you. You have such a full life with school and your friends . . . I should have never assumed you wouldn't mind if I couldn't make it sometimes."

"It's okay," I said, wiping a tear. "You didn't realize."

"I would *never* want you to think you weren't the most important thing to me."

I nodded. "I know."

"How can I make it up to you?"

"Just . . . don't make plans with me if you don't think you can keep them. And don't cancel on me unless it's an emergency. I understand it might happen sometimes. But . . . I need you."

I realized during that hour that my mom had grown to think I was more fine without her consistent presence than I was. And I had grown to think my mom didn't care as much about being in my life as she did.

After that session, where these dormant truths were finally awakened and released, we became closer than ever. I admired so much that she made no excuses and was completely willing to be accountable, and she admired that I was brave enough to be honest with her when she knew how difficult it was for me to potentially bruise her heart.

From that day forward, she stayed true to her word—striving to only make plans with me when she knew for certain she could keep them.

A Time to Stay,
and a Time to Leave

$\mathcal{A}$fter I graduated from high school—and not having made plans or submitted applications for college like some of my friends did—I enrolled in community college, though by then I had lost all my motivation to pursue academics. I got a job as a waitress in a small family restaurant near school and my grandparents' house, which allowed me to buy (with a co-sign on the loan from my dad) my first car: a brand-new Honda CRX. But within a few short months, I simply didn't have the focus for or interest in school, so I not only dropped out of college but I decided waitressing just wasn't for me.

At the time, my mom was dating a guy named Tom who owned a company in Century City. He was looking for an assistant for his two main employees, and while I knew nothing about his industry, I interviewed well and he gave me the job. Though it was a maddening, traffic-heavy drive from Long Beach to LA every day, I made much better money than I had at the restaurant, and I became good friends with the women I worked for. Also, it was exciting working in Century City. The three of us girls went out to lunch every day at the sprawling, open-air food Disneyland across the street, and it wasn't uncommon to see star sightings (I even saw Dick Van Dyke once!).

But it wasn't long before two big things occurred: one, the time came to move out of my dad's and in with my grandparents yet again; and two, I got wise to Tom's debauchery. In short, I was certain he was cheating on my mom. This presented me with all kinds of awkward. I needed this job to pay for my car, yet I couldn't *not* tell my mom that her boyfriend was being unfaithful. What made it worse was that the ladies I worked for knew the situation and felt equally uncomfortable. At the same time, neither of them wanted me to leave.

My loyalty to my mom won out, though. As much as I didn't want to deliver such shattering news, I told her what I had observed about Tom when I was at work. She was glad I told her, but she didn't want me losing my job over their breakup. I, however, refused to continue working for someone with character I didn't admire. Lucky for me, I applied at the Nordstrom store near my grandparents' house and promptly got hired, which meant I could quit the Century City job and my mom and I could both move on.

Celebrity Connection

*A*t Nordstrom, I worked a lot of closing shifts, and when I got home I was usually wired. Old reruns of *The Honeymooners* came on at 11:00, and though I had never watched the show before, I was drawn to watching it now, mainly because I felt an inexplicable connection to its female star, Audrey Meadows.

As I had done in the past when I loved a celebrity, I found a way to write her a fan letter. To my elation and shock, Audrey wrote me back immediately. So I wrote her back to thank her, and then she wrote me back again, and before I knew it, I had cultivated an epistolary friendship with an icon of classic television. The letters were typed on her personal stationery with her handwritten signature at the bottom, so there was no reason to believe they weren't legitimate. Still, it was an unusual gesture for such a big star, even if her career had certainly died down since the 1950s, to write to a nineteen-year-old fan on a regular basis.

One day, while I was at work, I had an unmistakable feeling come over me. I sensed that my mom had had some kind of encounter with Audrey. My mom now had a great job working as a rep for a stationery company, and her territory was in LA. I couldn't explain the feeling, but I didn't have to think about it for long. Within thirty minutes, my mom called me at work.

"Doob, you're not going to believe who I just ran into at one of my accounts."

"Was it Audrey?"

"Yes! How did you know?"

My heart was pounding. "I don't know. I just had this feeling about it! How did it happen? Tell me everything!"

She related how she had been standing at the counter, showing samples to the buyer, when a woman at the front of the store, wearing a big hat and glasses, asked if she could get a price on something. Now, if you've ever heard Audrey Meadows speak, you may recall she had a distinct-sounding voice—and it became more distinct as she aged because she was a smoker. Right away, my mom looked over at the woman, struck by her voice. She approached her then said, "You *are* Audrey Meadows."

"Yes, I am," Audrey said with a smile.

"You have a little penpal named Stacey . . ."

At this, Audrey tilted her head in surprise with a definite air of curiosity. "Yes, I do."

"Well," my mom said, "she's my daughter."

Audrey threw her head back with her mouth agape. "Well, what do you know about that?"

They had a brief, friendly conversation, and then Audrey finished her shopping and left.

"I can't believe *you* met Audrey," I squealed. "What are the chances of that?"

"I know! I couldn't believe it either. If only you'd been with me today . . . that would have really been something."

"She must have flipped when you brought up my name."

"She *was* shocked by it, but very pleasantly surprised when I told her you were my daughter."

The next letter I received from Audrey, she noted at the bottom to give her best to my mom. In fact, a common sign-off from Audrey became, "My best to you and to your beautiful mom."

Digging Up Secrets

As mothers go, my mom had been saddled with—or rather, chose for *her* soul's journey—a double whammy: she was adopted, which left her feeling unwanted and rejected by her birth mother; and she had always felt disconnected from and like a burden to my grandma. To my grandparents' credit, they had told my mom and uncle at an early age that they were adopted and made a big deal out of them being "chosen." They even bought a box set called *The Adopted Family: Book I: You and Your Child, A Guide for Adoptive Parents* that also included a sweet picture book to read to the adoptive child called *The Family That Grew.*

But while my grandpa was quite open about the kids being adopted, my grandma was sensitive about it. Feeling somehow threatened, she would quickly change the subject if questions about birth mothers came up. Hence, my mom didn't know much about how she came into the world or through whom. She only knew that my grandparents had answered an ad in the newspaper about a baby girl being available to adopt, with a lawyer's name to contact. From that, she assumed her birth mother was probably young like she herself had been when she had me. She knew the hospital and city she was born in, but that was the extent of it. All her life, she had longed to know more, but she knew the topic wasn't a comfortable one to bring up with my grandma, and she also knew that her adoption was closed, which meant that all records were sealed for the protection of the birth mother.

Unable to bear the secrets any longer, on January 29, 1990, my mom wrote a letter to the Department of Social Services, Adoption Branch, to request all non-identifying information about her birth family. She included a few facts she knew for verification, then sent it off and waited.

Six weeks later, in a response dated March 9, 1990, my mom received a letter with the following enclosure:

Person Requesting Background Information: Adoptee

Adoptee's Name: Cynthia A. King

Birth Date: June 14, 1952

BIRTH MOTHER (SOURCE: Birth Mother)

Descent - Race: Caucasian/English-Irish

Place of Birth: California

Age at Birth of Child: 26

Religion: Protestant

Education: She completed two years of high school.

Occupation: She was employed as a sales clerk.

Physical Description: She was 5 feet, 6 inches tall, weighed 130 pounds, and had reddish-brown hair, blue-green eyes, and a fair complexion. She was described as an attractive, poised young woman.

Special Interests: None stated

Were Birth Parents Married to Each Other?   No

Extended Family:

Parents of Birth Mother: Both of her parents were killed in an automobile accident when she was twelve years old. She lived with various relatives and friends until she was sixteen years old and had completed two years of high school. She then got a job and remained independent and self-supporting.

Siblings of Birth Mother: She had one brother (age not specified) who was killed in action in World War II.

Marriages of Birth Mother: None

Siblings of Adoptee: None

<u>Health</u>:   She was reported to be in good physical and mental health.

<u>Birth Mother's Health at Birth of the Child</u>:   Her general health and physical condition were described as excellent. Her mental level was described as above average. Her pregnancy was full term. There were no complications of pregnancy or delivery. There was no known history or evidence of organic or functional disorders. There was no known history of hereditary diseases or abnormalities.

<u>Child's Health at Birth</u>:   Your health was good at birth and at discharge from the hospital. Your birth weight was 7 pounds, 3 1/2 ounces.

<u>Circumstances of Placement</u>:   Your birth mother was single when she became pregnant. Your birth father was in the military and went overseas. Your mother did not tell him about her pregnancy. She stated that he had already gone overseas by the time she was sure she was pregnant, and that she did not think it was fair to disturb him with the news, especially since he could not do anything about it and she was not sure if she wanted to marry him. She learned about your adoptive parents through a mutual friend. Your birth mother appeared to have difficulty giving you up, but decided that it was the best thing to do for your long-term welfare. She felt that she would never be able to give you the kind of life the adopting parents could provide. She felt strongly about it due to her own difficult and insecure childhood. She wanted to do everything she could to insure that you would have a normal, happy life.

<u>BIRTH FATHER</u> (<u>SOURCE</u>: <u>Birth Mother</u>)

Your birth father was 30 years old, of Anglo-Saxon ethnic descent, and the Protestant faith. He was single and in good health. He served in the U.S. Army and was overseas at the time of the adoption. He was 6 feet, 2 inches tall, of slender build, and had blue eyes and dark hair. He was interested in sports.

Almost immediately upon receiving this, my mom called me.

"Doob, you're not going to believe it. I just received some information about my birth mother."

"You did? Oh my gosh! What does it say? Tell me everything!"

She read me the enclosure verbatim, after which she zeroed in on the two points that stood out most for her: that her birth mother was 26 and not near a child at all when she had her; and that the information stated her birth mother appeared to have difficulty giving her up. One created a new layer of mystery, and the other was a balm for her soul.

"And can you believe she had red hair?" she added. "What a trip."

I smiled to myself. "You don't remember, do you?"

"Remember what?"

"The dream I had when I was a toddler, the one where I saw your birth mother in the hospital just after you were born. I told you your mom had red hair."

"Oh my God," she said. "You did."

"And I said she had green eyes too."

"That's right," she said, remembering now. "It's as if your soul was present at my birth."

We had both always believed we'd been together before in a past life, or in more than one. Our connection was too atypical and exceptional to believe otherwise, and we both sensed our long-time connection on a visceral level.

"I wouldn't doubt it," I said.

And now, at long last, we had some more information about the branch of our little tree. The problem was, the birth records themselves were sealed, which meant the names of her birth parents were sealed forever too.

Or so we thought.

Becoming Roomies

L ater in 1990, after two wonderful years of being welcomed with open arms back into my grandparents' house, and being completely ensconced in the ethos of Nordstrom, an opportunity arose that I hadn't expected.

With my mom having her best job to date and a healthy, steady income, she asked me what I thought about us living together. She had a one-bedroom apartment in a nice complex in Long Beach, and she said that if I could chip in for the rent difference, she was willing to leave her place so we could move into a two-bedroom in the same complex. It was a farther drive to work for me, but I couldn't resist the proposal of being back together at long last and happily agreed.

This move was a monumental one for both of us—mainly because we hadn't lived together since I was twelve, and I was now twenty-one. During those nine years, we had remained friends as we'd always been, and we had grown in our relationship, but now we would be getting to know each other on a whole new level, as adults. My mom had been used to me being a little adult throughout my childhood, but now I actually *had* grown up, and I think we were both curious what it would be like for us to exist in a new dynamic.

From the beginning, we loved living together. We each had our own space and independence, but when we were home at the same time, we relished hanging out, watching favorite movies, and fostering what would become our signature witty banter.

Over the next four years, we moved on up like The Jeffersons a little more with each progressive move—first to a bigger apartment closer to my store, and then buying a townhouse together not far from our second abode. I also got promoted—twice—first into management in my store, and then eight months later to a bigger store in Santa Ana. My mom got scooped up by a more prestigious fine paper company as a sales rep, so both of us were doing well personally as well as professionally. But before I jump ahead too far, I have to rewind a little to something special that happened in September of 1991.

In one of my letters from Audrey, she told me she was going to be playing the grandmother on a new sitcom based on the movie *Uncle Buck*, and "could I please send her my phone number in case she was able to get tickets for my mom and me to come to a taping because a letter might not reach me quickly enough."

What??!!

We had been writing to each other on a fairly regular basis for two years by this point, and I had sent her a few pictures of me with the many photos I had of her on my wall at my grandparents' house (yes, I was a major fan; no, I wasn't a creepy stalker). She had even admired some of the photos I'd acquired that were hard to find, and I had sent her one as a gift that she particularly loved and didn't have.

I promptly wrote her back and sent our home number, affirming that *of course* we would be delighted to come to a taping and meet her.

Not long after, I came home from work to find my mom with a peculiar look on her face. She led me to the answering machine and pushed the play button.

"I'm calling for Stacey and it's Audrey Meadows, to see if she wants to come Friday night for the taping. It will be, I'm sure, the same time as it always is, but I can call back and leave a message tomorrow on this service . . . or . . . she could call Norma tonight at [phone number]. Thank you . . . bye-bye."

I was in awe. Audrey said she wanted my phone number, but I never imagined *she* would actually call me herself. And now both my mom and I would be VIP guests at the soundstage at Universal Studios? I was over the moon with excitement.

When the evening arrived, my mom drove up to the booth and told the man we were there for the *Uncle Buck* taping. But before my mom could say anything else, the young man said, "Oh yes, you're here with Audrey Meadows! She said you were coming tonight." We just looked at each other in shock, feeling like celebrities ourselves.

Once inside the studio, we were escorted to reserved seats fairly close to the set. Growing up near Hollywood, I'd been to a few TV show tapings before, but this one was undeniably the most exciting of all. When it ended, we were allowed to go down on the set to meet Audrey. I had brought her a big bouquet of flowers, and when I walked up to her, we had the most surreal moment of meeting in person. My mom hung back, but as Audrey hugged me, she noticed my mom, who of course she already knew so well from their encounter months before. She called her over and we shared about fifteen minutes of chatting and taking pictures, then Audrey needed to change and get home.

I existed on a dreamlike cloud as we drove back to Long Beach. I had just met a famous actress with whom I had fostered a sweet and highly uncommon friendship, and my mom, who had missed some of the coming-of-age days of my teen years, had been there to be a wonderful part of it.

∞

Mother Lode

$\mathcal{T}$he little bit of information my mom had received about her birth parents had been gnawing at her for over a year. There was no Internet then, and certainly nothing close to Ancestry.com or 23andMe. So, desperate to find out if she could unearth her birth mother's name and possibly reach out to her, she engaged a woman named Joy who specialized in helping children petition the court to unseal adoption records and to find their birth parents. When my mom shared everything with her that she had received from the Department of Social Services, she added that she herself had had a daughter when she was only sixteen.

"I'm not surprised," Joy said. "I work with a lot of women who were adopted and had children young. Whether it's subconscious or deliberate, the longing to be biologically connected to someone is so strong that teenage pregnancy among adopted girls isn't uncommon at all."

She asked my mom if she had the support of her adoptive parents in finding her birth mother.

"My dad would be fine with it, but my mom . . . she's always been threatened by the idea and would be upset by it. So for now, I'm not telling either of them. But my daughter and I are very close, and she knows how this has weighed on me all my life. She's sharing this journey with me and is 100 percent supportive."

It took some months for the court order to come through, but one day Joy called my mom to give her the news that she had essentially exhumed the name of my mom's biological mother. It was a highly unusual name, both first (Aletha) and last, and she was certain this woman was my mom's birth mother. Based on the Russian last name, it seemed her mother had married after giving my mom up for adoption, as she hadn't mentioned anything about being from Russian descent.

"So what now?" my mom wanted to know.

"Well, you can do some digging if you want to. I would go to the library and start looking in phone books for that name."

From there, my mom and I became detectives, on a mission to uncover the whereabouts of her birth mother, who at that point could have lived anywhere. But since my mom had been adopted in Southern California, it was possible her birth mother was still local. Even with the unusual name, however, we couldn't find anything, so she re-engaged Joy.

Shortly afterward, Joy called my mom to tell her she had found a phone number for Aletha in Auburn, CA, which was about 440 miles north of us. She instructed her on precisely what to say when she called, so as not to upset or shock Aletha, which let's face it, was nearly impossible to avoid. She also warned her that many adoptive parents from that generation, having expected the records to remain sealed forever, aren't happy to be found. Some deny that they're the parent, and others lash out. Still others are thrilled to be reunited, having always wished it could somehow happen against the odds.

"As you know," Joy told my mom, "if both parties contact the Department of Social Services expressing the wish to be reunited, they will sometimes help arrange that. But in your case, there's no record of Aletha contacting them, so it's difficult to know what her reaction to you might be."

"I understand."

"I know you have high hopes for this . . . I just want you to have realistic expectations. I've seen it all, and the outcome isn't always a favorable one is all."

My mom repeated that she understood and thanked her for all her guidance.

My mom waited a few days to gather her courage, and then she sat down late one morning and dialed Aletha's number. When she answered, my mom used the words Joy had given her.

"Hi . . . you don't know me . . . but does the date June 14, 1952, have meaning for you?"

"No," Aletha said directly.

"Okay . . . well . . . my name is Briana King, and I was adopted." Slight pause. "I have reason to believe that you're my birth mother."

Aletha didn't even take a beat. "You have the wrong person. I never gave up a child for adoption."

Joy had warned my mom about this reaction and cautioned her not to push too hard the first call.

"I see," my mom said. "Well, I'm sorry to have bothered you."

"Okay," Aletha said. "Good luck." Then she hung up.

Flooded with rejection all over again, my mom called Joy and told her about the failed call. "Are you *sure* she's my birth mother?" my mom asked her. "She sounded pretty definite that she wasn't."

"I'm sure," Joy promised. "There's no one else in this country with that first and last name. It has to be her. She just can't believe she was found. This is her way of keeping her secret."

"But I don't want to upset her. If she doesn't want to connect with me, I don't want to push it."

"I know. But this is common. You just dropped a major bomb on her. She denied it as a reflex, but she knows who you are. She needs time to process it, though. So wait a few days, and then call her back. On some level, it's rare for a birth mother not to at least want to know what happened to her child . . . or to be assured she's okay."

Joy gave her a new script, and my mom did as she said.

Only when she called Aletha back, the denial continued. She flat out told my mom that she couldn't be who she thought she was, even after my mom had told Aletha that she didn't want anything from her, only to let her know that she was okay.

Riddled with dejection, and feeling it was best to give up, my mom called Joy again.

"Don't give up yet, Briana. Let's give her a couple days and then try one more time. Trust me, I've seen this happen before."

With a heavy heart, my mom once again relayed to me what had happened, and I couldn't believe that after all she'd carried and all she'd hoped for, Aletha could flat out deny that Bree was hers. It seemed so heartless to me, no matter what this woman's situation was.

When my mom called the third time, reiterating that she didn't want to upset her life, or want anything from her, Aletha finally admitted she was her birth mother. But it wasn't a sweet, tearful reunion kind of call after that. Instead, Aletha lashed out in anger.

"Those birth records were supposed to be kept sealed forever," she insisted. "You shouldn't have been able to find me."

But my mom's understanding, kindness, and genuineness finally cracked Aletha, a little. Once that occurred, they talked for a bit, but it was clear that baby steps were in order. Aletha admitted that she hadn't held my mom after she was born, which reflected the dream I'd had as a toddler. She even had the nerve to say that she gave my mom up and never looked back or thought about her after that, which was certainly hard to believe. But she did express that she was glad my mom was adopted by good people, and that she'd had a good life. And she was mildly interested in the fact that my mom had a daughter when she was young, but she wasn't too forthcoming yet about her side of the story.

This news settled my heart a bit for my mom, but I had so wished she'd had the happy reunion she craved. She'd waited so many years to find this woman who gave her life, and then she'd put my mom through an agonizing week of rejection and hurt. The only saving grace was that Aletha agreed they could talk on the phone again soon, and over time, the cement block she was encased in—though always on Aletha's terms —began to crumble and morph into something that actually bloomed into a candid, if not somewhat guarded, friendship.

Introspection

𝒮 ometime in 1993, we moved into our townhome. There, I had my own suite downstairs, and my mom had hers upstairs where the living space was (similar to our upside-down house in Santa Cruz), which was great for our privacy but perfect for sharing our lives too.

I had been invited to two more tapings to see Audrey, and of course my mom was invited too. But my mom didn't want to intrude on what she knew was a special connection Audrey and I shared, so she bowed out each subsequent time. No matter what brand of closeness I might share with someone—and I had a lot of older women friends over the years—my mom never projected even a shred of jealousy. Rather, she would embrace these women as significant in my life and love them as much as I did.

The truth was, I was comfortable being friends with women of all ages, not only because my own mother had always been more of a friend than a traditional mom, but also because I had grown up around so many adults and had easy conversations with them, no matter how young I was. I was the only child my age at all the family functions, and I was the youngest person in my department at Nordstrom, even as the manager. At a certain point I recognized that some of my close female friends were also like mother figures to me, something I had missed out on to a degree, even with my grandma so present in my life. I didn't directly think of them as mothers, but certain ones adopted a nurturing role with me that I appreciated in a way I didn't consciously realize I needed.

To my mom's credit, even if she saw me drawn to women friends who were old enough to be my mother, she never took it as an affront to her—and in fairness, I never touted them as stand-ins for her either. What my mom and I had was unique, and I never wanted her to be anyone other than who she was. But I had missed her over the years, which was why finally being together as adults meant so much to me, and so much to her too.

One day, something occurred that I couldn't help but view as remarkable.

Our phone rang and I answered it.

"Is this you, Briana?"

Believing I recognized the unmistakable voice, I said, "No, it's Stacey. Is this you, Audrey?"

"No," the woman said with a throaty laugh. "It's Aletha."

I had never spoken to Aletha or heard her voice, so the encounter shocked us both. "Oh my gosh," I said, taken aback. "I could have sworn you were Audrey Meadows."

"The actress?"

"Yes, she and I are friends. It's a long story."

"Oh. Well, your mother will have to tell me about that sometime. Is she there?"

At that, I retrieved my mom. When I came back to my room, I couldn't get over the resemblance. Aletha and Audrey were nearly the same age. They both had red hair. And they both had resonant and distinct smokers' voices that sounded eerily alike. What was that connection about?

For years, people had asked me why I was so drawn to Audrey Meadows.

"I don't know," I always said. "I just feel a connection to her I can't explain."

My mom had found it curious too but chalked it up to universal magic (and me being a chronically unusual child who always "danced to my own drummer," as my mom liked to say). Did I connect Audrey to Aletha because of the dream I'd had when I was three? Anything was possible, I supposed. I had always believed that Audrey and I might have known each other in another life, and that I simply recognized that and was drawn to her soul. But why had Audrey not only taken the time to write back to me that first time, but continued to nurture an epistolary friendship between us for years? I reasoned that perhaps not a lot of people were able to find her home address the way I did (I had connections . . . wink), and so maybe fan letters were few and far between in the twilight of her career.

Sometime after that, Audrey wrote a memoir called *Love, Alice: My Life as a Honeymooner*. She mailed me a signed copy of the book, which she also signed on a separate page to me, with a handwritten note inside.

Dear Stacey,

You will receive an invitation for a champagne reception and booksigning from Rizzoli in Beverly Hills for October 26th—

Please come!

Love,
Audrey

That night, I got all dressed up and drove to Rizzoli by myself. There was quite a gathering for such an iconic star, and I felt most comfortable hanging back for a while. I already had a signed book, so I could always wait in line a bit later to have a few minutes with Audrey.

Meandering into a corner of the bookstore, I discovered a woman who seemed to be intentionally avoiding the crowd too. When she saw me, her face lit up. "You're Stacey!" she said with enthusiasm in an adorable South American accent.

Feeling suddenly like a celebrity of sorts for the second time in relation to Audrey, I said, "Yes. How did you know?"

She pulled me into a warm embrace, then held me at arm's length. "I'm Norma, Ms. Meadows's housekeeper and friend. I've seen your pictures . . . and your letters."

"You have?"

"Yes. Ms. Meadows is always so tickled to hear from you."

My heart swelled. She and Audrey were obviously close, so I wondered if perhaps I could uncover a bit more of the mystery behind Audrey's and my uncommon friendship.

"That's so sweet. But Audrey must receive a *lot* of fan mail."

She didn't hesitate to confirm. "Oh, yes . . . she gets letters and requests all the time . . . people are always asking for signed photographs."

I was perplexed. I didn't think I was the *only* one who wrote to her at her home address, but still. "So if she gets so many letters, I'm surprised she took the time to write back to me so personally . . . and to keep writing to me."

At that she became serious. "Oh . . . you're not like everyone else. Ms. Meadows always knew that you were special."

I was sincerely in awe. It's true that I hadn't asked Audrey for anything in that first letter (or in subsequent ones, for that matter). I only wanted her to know how much I admired her and for her to see the cool photos I had of her on my wall. But I had been in one of the photos, so was it possible Audrey had connected with me on a soul level too?

When I shared my encounter with Norma with my mom, she too was blown away. "But I'm not surprised," she said. "I've always said you were a bit otherworldly."

I laughed.

"I still say, though, I don't know why she's never invited you to her house for tea or something. She knows by now you're not a crackpot. Plus, you know where she lives, and you've never just showed up on her doorstep."

I laughed again. "I know . . . but, I get it."

What I didn't get, though, was that Aletha had essentially done the same thing. My mom had never done anything to invade her privacy (well, since the big reveal), or to push the friendship more than Aletha was comfortable with. And yet, after two years of being in touch and sending cards to each other—wherein my mom could certainly have shown up on her doorstep if she'd wanted to—Aletha had always held back. She not only refused to allow my mom to come up to her home where she lived a quiet life with her kitties, or even to send a picture of herself to my mom so she could see what she looked like, she flat out refused to ever meet her in person at all.

Betrothed and Bewildered

I had been working for Nordstrom for five years, and right from the beginning, I had wanted to move up in the company as far as I could. I loved the family background, the strong values, and the commitment to top-notch customer service. Being a serial pleaser, and feeling so aligned with the company's moral code, I couldn't have been a better match to uphold their high reputation.

Nordstrom also valued experience and performance within the company, not a person's educational background or academic achievements. Since I had lost my once-fanatic school mojo, and since one didn't have to be a college graduate to hold any level of management position, I was able to put my failed college attempt behind me and set my sights on becoming a store manager. I knew it would take several more years and promotions to get to that place, but I saw Nordstrom as where I belonged, and I loved having so much responsibility, attending regional meetings every month (for which several of us managers deemed a perfect excuse to buy new outfits), and working in a beautiful store.

I had also started dating someone. His name was Kevin, and he was the first real boyfriend I'd had since my first love my senior year. Eight months into our relationship, on Christmas Eve, Kevin had proposed and I'd stupidly said yes. I say stupidly because while we were great friends, had fun together, and shared a wide range of interests, I felt absolutely no physical attraction to him.

Hmmm, you might be saying. *Where did those dots not connect??*
Well, I'll tell you.

In contrast to my mom, I had always been physically conservative, modest, and protective of myself sexually. In fact, I was committed to waiting until I was married to have sex, no matter how old I might be.

Whether that came about because I worried about my mom being such a sexual being and wanted to be the opposite, or because I was simply a completely different person from the time I popped out of the womb, I don't know. Either way, I had witnessed my mom swept into every relationship she had because of physical attraction and the whirlwind of the "in love" butterflies, and then I had watched those relationships crash and burn after that spark wore off. I saw myself more as an old-fashioned, "forever" kind of gal, and I was very choosy about who that one person was going to be. I also had the misguided notion that if I married more for friendship and shared interests, instead of for any feelings of lust I might have, the sexual appeal part would come.

Go ahead, say it with me.

What a crock of crap!!

So, here I was, engaged, and I didn't even like the way he kissed me, so I held fast to my "no sex before marriage" adage and focused on the fun we had at hockey and baseball games, going to plays, and watching old movies. Just *what* I thought I was going to do on that wedding night and beyond, I seriously don't know. I insisted on a two-year engagement, though, so I had plenty of time to prepare.

Whatever reservations my mom might have felt about this union, she didn't impose them on me. She could have easily told me I was making a mistake, or tried to talk me off the ledge of this ridiculous decision, but instead she took me wedding dress shopping and even put a nonrefundable down payment on the one I was giddy over, along with buying my veil. I suppose she knew that I had to make my own mistakes, that it wasn't her place to sway me away from something, even something this big. Or maybe she knew deep down that I'd get wise to myself and come to my senses on my own.

Or . . . maybe she actually thought it wasn't her place to tell me how to live my life.

Some months prior, I had come home from work to find my mom in her room. She was crying and said she had something to tell me. I sat down on her bed, concerned she might be ill.

"I'm pregnant," she said.

The words pierced me like a dart I hadn't seen coming and landed square in my chest. "What? But I thought you couldn't get pregnant."

"I didn't either. And I'm freaking out."

Knowing she hadn't been dating Dave all that long, the thought, *Why were you having sex with someone you barely know?* raced through my mind like an accusing parent. But I had no right to judge her that way. Sex was part of a relationship for my mom because for the wounded inner child in her, sex equaled love. I knew it. She knew it on some level too. Plus, after she nearly died from her last ectopic pregnancy and was told she'd never have more children, birth control had become a moot point; sex for her no longer carried the worry of an undesired pregnancy. But now, against all odds, here we were nonetheless.

The last time my mom was pregnant, I almost lost her. What would this one mean? *Certain death? A prayed-for miscarriage? Life-saving surgery? A sibling?* I couldn't imagine any of them except for the miscarriage, which I knew was a terrible thing to wish on her, but understandable under the circumstances.

Blessedly, that's precisely what occurred.

I wasn't even secretly relieved. I was outwardly relieved. She was too.

I also had my own internal dissonance I was contending with, and it was getting close to erupting.

Inner Stirrings

I'd been engaged for a year, and the wedding plans had already slowed to a halt. Kevin wanted to know why, and I wasn't sure what to tell him. My reluctance to let him touch me might have been a clue, but I think he was still holding out hope that he was getting a bona fide old-fashioned girl with old-fashioned values.

I don't have to tell you it was more than that. My mom had noticed the way I acted with him, and she asked me if something was wrong. I confessed that the physical thing was a problem for me, and not because I wanted to wait. I really didn't like the idea of being intimate with him at all.

"Then you shouldn't marry him," she said without hesitation. "I know you're nothing like me, and that's a perfectly wonderful thing. But honey, this isn't going to change once you're married the way you think."

I knew she was right. My first boyfriend and I had had love *and* chemistry. I *should* have both with someone I was going to marry, for gosh sake.

"I guess I just see how people who are best friends have the best marriages," I said. "And we *are* best friends in lots of ways."

"I know, Doob. But it's not enough. I'm not going to tell you what to do, but I see how this is weighing on you, and I just don't want you to stay in this relationship if it's not right for you. God knows I've done that enough for both of us."

I appreciated her frankness, and I knew she was right. But I decided that for good measure, I'd see a therapist to find out if there was something wrong with *me*, something that might be hindering any future relationships I might have if I broke off this one.

❦

Going to therapy this time was much different than the first. In high school, I hadn't known what was wrong and Bonnie had to help me uncover it. This time, I knew exactly what to focus on. Or so I thought.

After I explained my woes to this new therapist and saw her a few times, she walked me through a hypnosis kind of exercise, all the way down my body, asking me how I felt when we got to certain places. I wasn't truly under hypnosis, but when she "snapped" me out of it, she looked at me pointedly, having assessed the exercise and arrived at her question of all questions.

"Do you think you're gay?" she asked.

I thought for a moment. "I don't think so."

"Are you sure?"

"Um, well . . . I had a lot of chemistry with my first boyfriend. So, yeah, I think I'm sure."

She sat back in her chair with a thoughtful look on her face. "Would it be a problem if you were?"

"Not at all," I said easily. "I have a very open-minded family. I just don't think that's what it is."

"So, why do you think you're so unattracted to your fiancé?"

"I think he's just not the right one," I said, filling in my own blanks. "I'm really committed to only getting married once, and I want to be sure he's the right person. I think my body is just telling me *he's* not the right one. That's all."

She nodded. "That could very well be."

When I told my mom about my session, she found it interesting. "Have you ever wondered if you were gay?" she asked matter-of-factly.

I shook my head. "No, not until she asked me."

My mom was the most accepting person in the world, so even if I had told her right then that I was breaking off my engagement because I wanted to find a nice young woman to spend my life with, my mom probably would have said something akin to, "More power to you!"

But instead, I called Kevin and told him he should come over so that we could talk. He knew without being in person, though, what I was going to say. With tears on both sides, I confessed that I wasn't truly in love with him, and that we couldn't get married. He was grateful I finally admitted it, as much as it hurt. I offered to give him back my ring, and he said to keep it, that he didn't want it back.

And that was the end of it. As disparaging as it might sound, I felt immediately unchained. Embarrassed I'd let it go so long, but unchained.

I also felt horrible about the $600 nonrefundable deposit my mom had put on my dress.

"You being true to yourself is *way* more important than that money," my mom assured me. "Don't ever give it another thought."

I've carried those words with me ever since.

And I never had the heart, because my mom so generously bought it for me, to donate that beautiful veil.

A Fork in the Road

$\mathcal{I}$ had reached a point where I had to choose one of two paths—to marry or to break up—and once I decided, flowers bloomed, the trees applauded, and I skipped down that welcoming path with abandon. However, that wasn't the only fork I was about to encounter.

Not long before, Kevin had taken me on a short trip to meet his beloved uncle and aunt. He told me that his uncle was a brilliant man, but I had always been considered smart, so I wasn't too intimidated.

Until his uncle engaged me in conversation.

Within thirty minutes, I realized that the "smarts" that had landed me in the gifted program in elementary school, and in enriched courses in junior high, no longer amounted to a hill of beans. I was now an adult, and Kevin's uncle wasn't interested in the fact that I'd won the spelling bee all three years at Stanford (please know I didn't tell him that), or could calculate basic math in my head at lightning speed (that never came up), or got A+++s from my exuberant seventh-grade English teacher for always doing extra credit (I left that out too). This guy talked about current events, trade agreements, politics, the stock market—all things about which I was blissfully ignorant. If he'd wanted advice on how to dress, I was his gal. But a conversant partner on the assorted complex happenings of the world . . . fuhgettaboutit. I was toast.

I came home after that weekend feeling like I'd been skating on my childhood intellect a few years too long. I wasn't dumb by any means, but I had stopped engaging academically in high school, and the gap showed.

I had reclaimed my freedom as a single woman in February of 1994, one week before my twenty-fifth birthday, and the upcoming milestone brought that humiliating weekend of ignorance back to my mind.

Back in August of 1993, I had made a lateral management move at Nordstrom so that I would be on track to become a buyer, which was the required path toward being a store manager. The problem was, the buyers were always, and I mean *always*, running on stress. They were stressed about sales numbers, stressed about placement of vendors in the department, stressed about how quickly customers were approached, stressed about the easygoing way I managed my staff. Their stress put stress on me, and I refused to put that same stress on my team. At that point I realized that if I continued on my trajectory of becoming a buyer, that was likely going to be my life. And I did not want to be that person to become a store manager.

Thankfully, a few months after my breakup, I had a remarkable epiphany, one that resonated with me in the most surprising way: I felt ready to go to college. My lack of motivation the first time I tried was usurped by an insatiable desire to learn and excel scholastically, just the way I had when I was younger.

Right away, I started researching schools and buying books like *How to Get Straight As* and *How to Take Notes*. I bought a giant book of colleges and pored over all my options. Since I had never taken the SATs or college prep courses, and since I'd graduated high school seven years prior, what I needed to do was go first to community college to earn my stripes, then transfer to a college or university from there.

As enthusiastic as my mom was for my newfound spark for education, we had bought our townhome together, and my share of the mortgage was dependent on my manager's salary. Enrolling in three college courses each semester would mean stepping down into an hourly position at Nordstrom, probably part-time, which would mean making a lot less money. My mom was earning a good living by then, but still we had to crunch the numbers. Finally, she agreed to assume part of my share to support me in my academic endeavor, and in August, I officially started school at Cerritos Community College.

From the start, I was an eye-rollingly devoted student. I took every piece of advice from my *How to Get Straight As* book and followed it to a tee. As a result, I received As in all three of my first college classes and, sparked by a project in my English course, set a lofty goal of going to a prestigious women's college and re-engaging my sixth-grade career dream: becoming an obstetrician.

A Bend in the Fork

Early in my third semester of college, my mom came to my room like a cop who arrived to break up a perfectly respectable party.

"I want to talk to you about something," she said.

I looked up from my textbook. "Okay."

She took in a breath. "I'm seriously thinking of marrying Ben."

My mouth dropped open. "What? You haven't even been dating that long."

"I know. But we're good together. And I enjoy being with him."

"But are you even in love with him?"

She waffled. "I do love him."

I couldn't believe what I was hearing. And I didn't like the way she said "I do love him," as if she was trying to convince herself as much as me. "But what about us? What about our life together? Don't you love living together anymore?"

"I do," she assured me. "But I also want to be married again, to share my life with someone." I deflated before her eyes and a look of sadness crossed her face. "I don't mean to upset you. I just wanted to talk to you about it."

My shoulders slumped and I shook my head with an audible sigh. "I don't get it. We have a perfectly wonderful life, something it took us a lot of years to have again. I want you to be happy, but why would you want to upend everything to marry someone you can't even say you're in love with?"

She didn't have a good answer for me, but I knew she was serious. Something was pulling her toward yet another marriage, and while Ben was a nice guy and they were in the same industry, I knew in my heart she'd be making a mistake and told her so. I feel bad admitting it, but I didn't always go about these things with her the same way she did with me. From past experience, I wasn't so willing to let her run out into the street to see if she got hit by a car. I guess a part of me wanted to keep her firmly at the curb, safely next to me.

"Plus, what about our agreement?" I said, still completely blind-sided. "I can't afford to get a place of my own now that I'm in school."

She knew she'd knocked me down hard and apologized. "Okay," she conceded. "I'll tell him I'll think about it. Maybe you're right. Maybe it *is* too soon."

But it didn't take long before she'd thought about it long enough.

At the upcoming industry gathering in Hawaii, the wedding was on.

Making Amends

After I'd moved out of my dad's house, our relationship had been a bit distant. Hurt and resentment from the circumstances under which I'd felt I had to leave had muddied the waters between us, and though I'd forgiven him and we'd slowly found our footing with each other again, the phenomenal bond we had shared throughout my childhood seemed it had shifted irrevocably.

Once my mom made up her mind to marry, I had no choice but to make plans to move back in yet again with my ever-present supporters: my grandparents. I loved my mom's and my perfect place and the life we shared in it, but I could nowhere near afford it on my own. With my part-time gig at Nordstrom, three classes on my plate, and the cost of books and tuition, I couldn't afford much of anything on my own besides the basics.

Though my dad and I mostly communicated when I came to pick up one of my siblings for one of our regular "play dates," and I didn't want to tell him about the impending move, I didn't have a choice. Lindsay, in particular, came to our house on a regular basis, and my dad had to know my living arrangements were going to be changing.

I could tell he felt bad for me when I shared the news. No matter what had gone down between us, my dad cared deeply and I knew it.

"Where are you going to live?" he wanted to know.

Hesitantly, I told him I was moving back to my grandparents'.

"Maybe there's another option," he suggested.

Remember that primo bachelor pad my dad used to have behind my grandma Hill's house? Well, she currently had a renter living there, and my dad thought she'd surely be willing to give the guy notice to make a place for her granddaughter to live. Plus, she didn't really need the rent, which made the prospect of the arrangement seemingly ideal for both of us. She lived independently on her own with no problem, but it would be nice at her age to have me there to check in on her, and although my schedule was bulging at the seams, we could at least see other on a regular basis.

In short order, the renter agreed to move out (he'd been thinking about it anyway) and my dad offered to meet me there to check out the place. I hadn't been in that room out back for years, so I mostly had memories of it from my childhood.

Buoyed in my doldrums by what seemed like a gift from the heavens, I excitedly went over to see my new pad. When we opened the door, however, I was appalled.

The renter had had a huge aquarium, and it had leaked, soaking a huge patch of carpet, creating mold, and leaving a horrific dank stench. The carpet was filthy, and the walls were scuffed too. I wasn't a princess by any means, but the idea of living in that disgusting swamp instead of in my modest but lovely bedroom with the en-suite bathroom in our townhome was like a sucker punch to the gut.

"Oh my God," I moaned. "There's no way I can live here. This is awful."

"Well, wait a minute," my dad said in his usual positive manner. "We can fix it up. A coat of paint and new carpet will go a long way. And I'll take care of the mold."

"But I have to move soon. I'm sure it's going to take some time to do all that, especially with you working during the week."

He had a remedy for that too. "Well, you can stay with us until your place is done, in the spare room."

Now, this was supremely generous of my dad. But it also felt like I was sliding backward about a decade. My dad and Leah had added on to the house when I was in high school, and the whole upstairs was their room, so the kids and I would be downstairs with some degree of privacy, but still.

When I told my mom what had transpired, she looked relieved I'd found a perfect living space, that my dad was making it nice for me, and that I was slightly less upset with her now that I had a place to go. I could also see the cringe on my behalf that I would be staying temporarily with my dad like a revisited teenager until my digs were suitable for human occupation again.

"Well, it didn't make sense to move in with Grandma and Grandpa for a few weeks," I said.

"I guess not."

I looked away, trying to fight tears.

"I'm so sorry, honey," she said. "I know you probably hate me for this."

I turned to face her. "I could never hate you. But I really wish we could have stayed together. I'm sorry. But I do."

"I know. Part of me wishes that too."

Our townhouse hadn't gone on the market quite yet, but the newlyweds had already moved into their lovely new condo in LA.

My watery eyes met hers. "Do you think you're going to be happy with Ben?"

"I do. And it's great living in my territory. I don't have to do *as* much driving."

"That's good."

"And we're having a housewarming party soon. I hope you'll come."

"Of course I will."

She smiled slyly. "And you have to admit . . . there's something oddly sweet and full circle about you moving into the room where you were conceived."

Another New Start Apart

I'm not going to lie. I did not go gentle into that first night at my dad's.

In the shower that evening, I wept like there was no tomorrow. Then I got out, told my dad I had somewhere I had to go, and drove to our townhouse. Everything had been packed and moved, but I still had my key and my phone was still plugged in. I called my best friend for some solace, and after we hung up, I hugged my knees tight to my chest and felt my heart breaking in two as I sat against the wall and let the tears silently stream.

It wasn't that I expected to live with my mom forever, or that I would dissuade her from marrying again if she was truly in love. But in the space where the little girl in me resided, I felt like she had spontaneously decided to jump on a train and leave me on the platform, where the iron horse hissed and chugged and picked up speed with my mom inside, and all I could do was wave with a brave smile.

Both the child and the adult in me at once craved understanding and strove to see the providence in our latest breakup. But even with the prospect of having my little studio apartment, I still couldn't get over my mom's decision to marry Ben. I knew she wasn't in love with him, not really, and so I was left to wonder why she seemed set on leaving me again. We had the best relationship a mother and daughter could have: we never fought or really even disagreed, we had fun together, we watched our favorite movies—*When Harry Met Sally, How to Marry a Millionaire, The Big Chill, Enchanted April*—over and over, we laughed a lot, and we gave each other our space.

Did she want out from under my proverbial thumb? I wondered. I didn't monitor her every move or anything, and we definitely had our own lives. And I was incredibly busy with work and now school. But I still worried about some of the men she chose to date and the decisions she made. *Did that make her feel like she was living with the mother side of me—and she'd had enough of that, thank you?* She never gave me any indication that's how she felt, and when I hinted at that being the reason, she wholeheartedly told me that wasn't the case at all, that she appreciated how much I cared and looked out for her.

At the time, I couldn't figure out why my mom so seemingly easily left our lives together when everything seemed so wonderful for us. It wasn't until later, with maturity and reflection, that I came to understand that it was yet another time in our journey when she needed her space to grow wings, and I needed mine to plant roots of my own.

As promised, my dad went to work on transforming that sentimental space we once shared from when I was born until I was six—only instead of it taking a few weeks, it took two months. Part of the delay was that my dad wanted to do more than simply clean it up. He put in a new bathroom sink unit, shower door, and toilet; a secondary portable closet (since the built-in one wasn't big enough for my requisite Nordstrom wardrobe); and new linoleum in the kitchenette and bathroom. In fact, the next time I saw it, it looked like a completely new place. He'd been right: a coat of white paint and new carpet had changed its appearance (and smell!) entirely. I felt very grateful for all he had done, and I actually saw how cute it could be for me and started to feel a little excitement.

At the same time, while I was happy to live with the kids again—who were now eleven and eight—I was a college student now, and trying to study was admittedly challenging. I also felt uneasy [read: exceedingly awkward] returning to my teenage home, even if only for a short time. So, since the kids were busy with their own school and sports, I studied on campus as much as I could during that time, and went to my grandparents' house afterward whenever I could swing it.

Now that my mom lived in LA, it was a trek to go see her, just like it had been when she and Danny moved to Phillips Ranch. So we went back to the routine of seeing each sporadically, while I put laser focus on work and school and tried to soothe my heart's lament that my mom's and my wonderful living arrangement had ended much sooner than I imagined.

A New Devastation

$\mathcal{N}$ ot long after I squeezed all of my furniture into the perimeter of my 300-square-foot place and made it as homey as I could, our family received devastating news.

About ten years prior, my grandma had gotten hypnotized to quit smoking, and to everyone's happiness, she had never lit up a cigarette again. But the forty-plus years she *did* smoke had done their damage, and an x-ray revealed the one thing I'd always feared: that my grandma would end up with lung cancer.

Right away, she decided against chemo and radiation, which we all supported. But the doctor also said she probably only had a few months of quality life. At the time, I didn't know anything about healing cancer naturally; none of us in my family did. And I didn't know any better than to trust people in white coats as authorities when they gave people X number of months to live (that disillusionment is thankfully gone now too). So, just like that, I was facing losing the one person who had always, *always* been there for me without fail, and with whom I had shared a bond unlike any other, and the prospect of that loss was almost more than I could bear.

Just a month before, I had signed up for a summer study abroad program in Guadalajara, Mexico, where I would complete my second semester of Spanish in only five weeks. I'd never traveled out of the country, and my current Spanish professor, whom I adored, was going to be the coordinator and supplemental teacher for the American students. My grandma thought it was a wonderful opportunity and was excited for me to go. But after I found out I might only have a few months left with her, and that I'd be losing a third of that time abroad, I told her there was no way I was going.

"But I don't want you to miss out on this," she said. "This could be a once-in-a-lifetime opportunity for you. I'll be okay. I want you to go . . . and it's only for five weeks. I'll be here when you get back."

I fought her on it, but in the end she won out, and off I went at the end of May to Mexico.

It ended up being a wonderful decision to go, but I worried the whole time about my grandma, wondering how she was. Also, because she and my mom had never been particularly close, I feared my mom wouldn't drive to Lakewood often enough to check on her. Finally, I was able to get a phone card and call my grandma. When I heard her voice, I was elated. She sounded just like herself, and she also told me she'd decided to do the chemo after all, that she hoped it would give her more time.

When I got back a couple weeks later, she had already lost a lot of her hair, and she had decided to shave it and opt for wearing hats and headscarves. She was sick for a couple days after the treatments, but otherwise she was doing pretty well. She had also slimmed down even more, and she said she was glad about the decision she made, even though she felt terrible sometimes.

A check-up scan in the fall indeed gave all of us hope when it showed that her lung tumor had shrunk by half, and we actually entertained the possibility that she could beat it altogether.

But that didn't happen.

Far from healing for good, that Christmas of 1995 would be our last one together.

From Worse to Unthinkable

round midnight on the 19th of January, my grandma collapsed at home in the hallway. My grandpa had her rushed to the hospital, and we were hopeful it was merely an unfortunate effect from her treatment. But she had collapsed because she'd fallen into a diabetic coma, and her condition was delicate. Because of that, they wanted her to stay in the hospital for a few days at least.

At some point during her stay, a nurse peeled off my grandma's socks to discover that her left foot was turning black. She had obviously cut it at home days before without realizing it, but no one had removed her socks to notice it in the hospital. Now, having gone unchecked, it was becoming gangrene, and it was so perilous that the doctors said there was no option but to amputate her leg above the knee.

None of us could believe that my grandma was facing such a horrible decision: to go through with the amputation, or let the gangrene creep up her body and kill her. She had had such a tough time of it physically in her life—not to mention that we thought she was getting better from the cancer—that this felt like the cruelest joke.

By the time my grandma was a teen, she had varicose veins in her legs that made it challenging for her to be on her feet for long periods. She was a big-boned person and already struggled with excessive weight, and as I mentioned earlier, she had a hysterectomy (a likely unnecessary one) when she was only twenty-six. After that, she put on even more weight. Sometime in her thirties, she had to have all her teeth removed and get dentures, which the dentist made to look nothing like her original teeth, so it changed her entire facial structure and smile. When she was in her mid-fifties, she was diagnosed with diabetes (which she was thankfully able to manage with diet). When her dentures eventually needed replacing, they once again made them look completely different than her prior set, causing her to look like a different person to me, and of course yet again to herself too. Probably most challenging, though, was that her vision had significantly declined over the years due to macular degeneration. Then, only ten months prior, they had found the cancer in her lung. Now, she had to heavy-heartedly sign papers to let them remove her leg.

While our whole family was still reeling from the news, the surgery was scheduled for the following afternoon.

My mom went back to her condo that night, and I went back to my studio. Though terribly upset, I eventually fell asleep. But around 3:00 a.m., I woke up violently ill. I threw up, had diarrhea, and ended up lying on my bathroom floor, writhing in misery. As I lay there, a thought came strongly to me: *This must be how awful Grandma feels.* I broke down in tears, begging God to please not let my grandma have to go through with the barbaric surgery.

The following morning, at around 10:00, I received a phone call from my mom.

"Doob . . . I have something really hard to tell you."

Right away, I thought my grandma had died. "Oh God," I murmured.

"Last night, around 3:00, Grandma's organs all started shutting down. Honey, you need to come down. She's not going to be here much longer."

Tears immediately streamed down my face. There was no time to tell my mom how sick I had been myself. I hung up and threw myself together.

As I was driving to the hospital, the time my mom had mentioned hit me: both my grandma and I had gotten sick at 3:00 a.m. Right away, I took three things from that synchronicity. One, my grandma and I were so connected that when her organs started shutting down, *my* body felt it. Two, my prayer for her to be spared from that horrific surgery was answered. And three, physically feeling the misery I believed my grandma must have felt put me in a space of being more okay about letting her go, as okay as I could be about losing the person with whom I had always been inseparable.

When I arrived, my mom, grandpa, and uncle were there, along with my grandpa's brother Keith and his wife Joan. The two couples had been close friends for decades and did almost everything as a foursome, and they felt they were losing a sister too.

The doctor told us that my grandma was on morphine, still breathing on her own but very labored, and that she wasn't in any pain. They were going to give her a lethal dose of morphine, after which we would see her heart rate decline on the monitor, and she would probably leave us within thirty minutes.

Of all of us, I was the one who asked to have a little time with her alone.

My mom told me later that when my grandpa turned away from me, imagining what that goodbye was going to do to me, it was the first time she had ever seen him cry.

I was so overcome with emotion, I almost couldn't speak. But I took my grandma's hand and managed through tears to thank her for everything she had been to me and for everything she had done for me all my life. I wanted to say so much more, to list out all the ways she had made me feel like the most special person in the world to her, but that would have taken much more time than I had. Instead, I kissed her cheek, then her hand, and told her I loved her more than she would ever know.

After that, my family came back into the room and the nurse administered the morphine. All of us just sat staring at the heart monitor, and at her, and waited.

For thirty minutes, we were quiet. It felt irreverent to speak, and no one wanted to pierce the sacred space with words. But then another thirty minutes passed. My grandma was breathing in a labored cadence, but her heart rate was still steady. The nurse came to check on us—and on my grandma—and said that everyone passes when it's their time. Some people simply held on longer than others.

After a while, someone mentioned getting some food and bringing it back. Then we allowed ourselves some solemn conversation. Then the conversation became a little lighter, as if my grandma was only sleeping nearby, not dying. As the hours marched on, we started telling family stories and even laughing. It felt incredibly inappropriate, but this maudlin scene had actually become oddly humorous. At 6:00 that evening, though my grandma's heart rate had slowed some, she was still with us. I realized then that what my grandma must have wanted was to have her beloveds around her, not mired in sadness, but casually engaging with each other, and even finding reasons to laugh. It was her final wish, and we had unknowingly granted it.

Once she had spent all the time she could hanging on, my grandma's heart rate suddenly galloped downward. I rushed to her side and took her hand, squatting beside her bed so she wouldn't be alone when she took her last breath. And after she did, I stayed there, glued to her hand and sobbing for the longest time, until my mom was finally able to gently pull me away.

Mourning Alone

*A*fter my grandma passed away that evening, we all went our separate ways home. We were each at a loss for what to say, and it was clear that each of us was going to mourn differently.

When I arrived at my studio, I was in a trance of disbelief. It was January 24th, and my room felt like an icebox. Staying bundled in my coat, I pulled the floor heater toward me and curled up on the floor next to it. Even at that proximity, though, I almost couldn't feel the warmth. I was too in shock on the inside, too hollowed out by the still non-reality that the person I had the most unfailingly close and present relationship with all of my life was gone.

Twelve years prior, when I was fourteen, I had attended my first funeral, for my great aunt who died of cancer. She was a ray of light in our family, but I wasn't closer to her than I was to any of my other more distant relatives. My grandparents sat up front, and my mom and I were several rows back. During the entire funeral, I sobbed quietly but uncontrollably, more than anyone in that chapel, more than my aunt's own children or grandchildren. My mom had put her hand gently on my leg and whispered, "Don't think what you're thinking." She knew exactly what was going through my mind. I was imagining the devastation I'd be feeling had that funeral been for my grandma.

And I was certain she knew what that devastation was for me now.

One of the most remarkable things about my mom, and something I can't emphasize my appreciation and admiration for enough, was how despite the less-than-close bond she shared with my grandma, and the understandable hurt my mom carried from having a somewhat detached mother when she was a child, never—and I mean *never*—did she disparage the love my grandma showered on me, or me on her. She could have harbored deep resentment that my grandma was for me what she never quite was for her own children, but instead, she was profoundly happy that my grandma and I shared what we did. She saw me as my grandma's gift after she'd gone through so many heartbreaks as a young woman—not to mention likely suffering from undiagnosed depression, possibly for years—and she always expressed how grateful she was that when my mom needed her most after I was born, she never failed to be there.

The truth was, my grandma loved my mom deeply. But my mom could never overcome how she had been made to feel like a burden when she was young, and that had tainted any real closeness they might have fostered. She also felt like a perennial disappointment to my grandparents, even though they never said they felt that way. Some people's energies simply don't connect, and some wounds, if not healed, will fester for a lifetime. This was the dynamic between my mom and my grandma.

So now, both of us faced grieving this loss, but I understood that my mom wasn't going to grieve the same way I was. I had recently seen some show about foster kids being returned to their natural parents, when that parent was a stranger to them. They showed a toddler being ripped away from the only mother she had known, all because the birth mother had gotten her act together, and my heart split in two seeing the devastation that poor child experienced. On that night my grandma returned to stardust, and for a long time after, I felt she had been torn away from me in a similar way, without my having any say in it. But that was *my* experience. I knew my mom's grief was going to be more complex, and perhaps less intense, than mine, and I could never begrudge her for that, the same way she had never begrudged me for having a very different relationship with my grandma than she did.

As I lay there on the floor that night, feeling odd that my mom and I weren't together in this decidedly sorrowful moment, I also respected that we needed our space to mourn in our own ways. And indeed for both of us, that meant mourning alone.

Not one week later, I received a call from Norma that Audrey had been ill with cancer for months and had told no one, not even her sister Jayne. But she was now in the hospital and close to dying, and she didn't want me to hear about her death on the news.

Though Audrey and I had written to each other less over the prior years, we had shared a rare, undeniable bond that had been significant in my life. Norma assured me I would be invited to Audrey's private funeral, and that she would call me with those details when the time came.

Within days, Audrey passed away.

Still in shock over losing my grandma, I attended Audrey's funeral alone, where I sat in the back, too numb from both losses to even shed a tear.

Grass Under Feet

A s I had feared, my mom's marriage didn't last. Her debonair husband ended up being a serious alcoholic, something he had brilliantly hidden from her until they were married, and within two years, she had gone through her third divorce.

By then, I had completed four semesters of college with straight As, but I had abandoned my desire to go into medicine. I loved anatomy and physiology, but a lot of the other science courses weren't really suited to me. I still wanted to get into a small and prestigious women's college, though—in particular, Scripps College in Claremont, CA—and for that, I needed stellar grades.

One day, my mom suggested that we drive out to the campus, which was nearly forty miles from where I lived, and see if it indeed felt like the right school for me. I thought that was a brilliant idea and off we went.

As soon as we arrived, the campus was even more charming than the pictures had illustrated. Built in 1926, Scripps was like a secret garden of enchantment, with plentiful archways, multiple fountains, and ivy crawling up the historic buildings. The expansive lawns and thoughtful layout added to its allure (though the quaint library alone was enough to steal my heart). My mom and I spent a couple hours strolling through the buildings and gardens, taking in every detail.

"Oh, Doob," my mom gushed, "I *see* you here."

I faced her with my own joyful grin. "I do too."

"I don't think I could choose a more perfect place for you."

"And the fact that it's here in Southern California is amazing. Most of the women's colleges are back east, but we have this one *right here*. It would be a drive every day, but worth it."

My mom agreed.

Why, you may be wondering, would I sign up to drive seventy-five miles round trip to college every day? Well ...

It would take me two more years to finish all my transfer requirements at Cerritos, and I'd be a "beyond the traditional age college student" [read: ancient *twenty-nine*] by then. I'd mostly been an only child growing up. I'd never had to share a room or a bathroom with anyone, except when I'd studied abroad, and double dorm rooms and a passel of girls to one bathroom was definitely not for me. Even though Scripps was *not* a party school and had no sororities to worry about missing out on (you may be shocked to learn that my personality didn't jibe with either), I was still long past gathering in pajamas for late-night study groups or sneaking off at night to another campus in the five-college consortium to rendezvous with my boyfriend. Oh! And let's not forget I was graciously living rent-free in my little pad, thanks to the generosity of my grandma Hill. Moving closer to school, while convenient, just didn't make sense for me.

Beyond all that, this Scripps fantasy was not about having the full college experience. It was about my own personal dream of attending a beautiful school with a notable reputation. If I could earn the outstanding grades I needed, I might be able to get scholarships, loans, and financial aid to make it happen. *And,* if I got a second job, I could pay off my grown-up bills over the next couple of years and possibly have the luxury of working only one part-time job during my two years at Scripps.

And after the bumps in the road the two of us had been through, no one was more supportive of that dream coming true for me than my mom.

Becoming a Jew

One of the many things that was rare about my upbringing—and for which I was genuinely fortunate—was that I was raised with virtually no dogma. The only person you could call religious at all in my family was my grandma Hill, who was a quiet, faithful Christian who read her devotional every morning, said a brief grace before every meal, and went to church every Sunday, but she was in no way evangelical or religiously judgmental, and she never imposed her beliefs on anyone else. I had gone to church with her a few times growing up, but I was never too interested in making it a habit. I was perfectly satisfied being a nondenominational, non-practicing Christian for whom Christmas meant Santa, presents, and my grandma Hays making turkey dinners, turkey soup, and turkey sandwiches for a week afterward; and for whom Easter meant coloring eggs and hiding them, being greeted Sunday morning by baskets my grandparents filled, and relishing our traditional See's chocolate bunnies.

But in the summer of 1996, I'd done another month-long study abroad program, only this time I'd gone to Heidelberg, Germany. One of our field trips was to the former concentration camp in Dachau, which was now half old barracks, half museum. I hadn't known how I'd feel about going, but I was curious to learn and pay homage to the Jews who had perished there.

When I'd arrived in Heidelberg, they were having an uncharacteristic heat wave. But on the day we traveled to Dachau, it was dreary and bitter cold, which matched the haunting environment. Fairly quickly, I felt the emotional need to break away from the students I'd come with. Wandering on my own, I bent down and picked up a stone from the ground.

I wonder how much pain this stone has seen, I wondered.

I don't know why, but I placed that stone in my jacket pocket. For the rest of the afternoon, I kept warming my hands in my pockets and encountering that stone. When I clutched it, an overwhelming feeling came over me: I realized I knew nothing about Judaism, or the Jewish people, and I suddenly felt embarrassingly ignorant. I decided that when I got home, I was going to learn more, strictly out of respect. I'd had one close Jewish friend in high school, and one of the ladies I worked with in Century City was Jewish, but the latter wasn't particularly observant, and neither shared much about it with me.

Shortly after I returned home, I got a second job at the Barnes & Noble in the mall where I worked at Nordstrom, and I did just as I'd promised myself. During a break on one of my shifts, I combed the Judaism section and settled on a book called *What Do Jews Believe?*, which I figured should cover all the bases. What I didn't expect, however, was how much the beliefs would resonate with me. I'd gone to Wendi's Baptist church in high school and enjoyed being in the youth group with her, but I'd since grown to feel that the tenets of Christianity didn't fully align with me. I wasn't seeking religion in reading about Judaism, but something inside me connected too profoundly to it for me to ignore.

In short order, my Barnes & Noble discount began to fund an increasingly expanding Jewish library. I was fascinated by its history and drawn to its traditions, and I loved the way it spoke to me as a "quiet, peaceful religion." There was no proselytizing, no violent acts in the name of it, no "we're better than you" air (in fact, quite the often humorous, self-deprecating opposite), all of which had repelled me from other religions. I was even wowed by the fact that the number eighteen was significant in Judaism: the Hebrew letters, each of which had a number assigned to it, added up to eighteen in the word for "life," *chai*. Because of that, gifts and donations were often made in increments of eighteen, *my* number. I started celebrating my own Shabbat dinners in my studio by myself on Friday nights, and I asked my new and dear friend, Rita, who was herself a convert to Judaism many years before, if I could go to the synagogue with her sometime. In brief, as I did with everything I was ever passionate about, I immersed myself into Judaism as if I were Gregory Peck in the 1947 Best Picture Oscar Winner, *Gentleman's Agreement.*

One day, while my mom was over visiting me, she noticed the multiplying common-themed books on my shelf and commented on my ardent interest. She was also intrigued by my affinity for the Jewish people. Neither of us had thought about—or even knew about—the fact that a person could actually *choose* to be Jewish. But once I found out Rita had converted, I'd learned it was quite a long and complex process.

"*You're* not thinking of converting, are you?" my mom casually wanted to know.

"I don't know. It's a serious thing. But at the same time, in my heart, I *feel* like a Jew. I know that sounds weird, but I do."

My mom had always been fascinated by anything outside of what one would consider "the norm." She read books about psychic abilities, the riddles within the cosmos, the healing power of herbs, the list goes on. So my interest in possibly becoming Jewish didn't shock her world too much, but it admittedly surprised her more than a little.

"Isn't Judaism a patriarchal religion, though?"

She was right. Neither of us had ever been fans of anything—culture, religion, parental influence—that suppressed or manipulated people, particularly women. I despised extreme religion and wanted no part of that. But Rita's Conservative synagogue, which had quickly become my synagogue, was led by a self-proclaimed feminist rabbi who declared outright that any ritual or tradition that was oppressive to *any* segment of the population based on gender, race, sexual orientation, and the like within a religion needed to be changed, that if a religion didn't embrace its followers and serve to elevate them to be their highest, most authentic selves, it shouldn't be called a religion. He believed women belonged on the *bimah,* or altar, as equally as men, whether as a rabbi, a cantor, or a congregant during a service. He had even performed the same-sex wedding of his sister to her wife. He was quite traditional in many ways, but that was because he ascribed to the rituals of Judaism for the real reason they existed: to elevate the mundane to the sacred and strengthen our connection to the Divine—*not* to make people feel superior, or to carve a path to "salvation" through a list of deeds, or to foster favor with God.

For one example, keeping kosher was not about eating food "blessed by a rabbi"; it was about elevating what can easily become a mundane act (eating) by creating consciousness around what goes into our bodies: the ways food is raised or grown, the treatment of animals, the lifeforce energy, or lack of it, of what we ingest. Yes, some of those "laws," kosher or otherwise, are taken by some to an arguable extreme and can certainly become as rote as anything else, but the heart of those laws in particular is about being thoughtful in our food choices. It's pretty tough to argue the importance of that for the body *and* the soul.

It was within this context of liberal yet traditional Judaism that my heart found a home.

Once I made up my mind to take the requisite courses at the synagogue, follow that with the other requirements to make sure I was certain about making such a monumental decision, and teach myself Hebrew (nooo, I wasn't an overachiever)—along with maintaining my three-course-per-semester load at school (wasn't a handful of hours of sleep every night enough?)—my mom supported me 100 percent. In fact, after I officially converted in March of 1998, she delighted in calling herself a Jewish mother.

Almost right away, I decided I wanted to also have an adult bat mitzvah (nooo, not an overachiever at *all*). That would entail another eight months of studying with the cantor on a weekly basis, and a whole lot of studying on my own outside of that. And I wasn't content with only learning the minimum, which was *one* chanted Torah reading from the enormous scroll and another longer one called the *Haftorah*. I wanted to perform the reading of as many portions of the Torah as I could, along with a few other parts of the normal Shabbat service.

It was custom for parents to give a short speech during a bar or bat mitzvah ceremony, so I asked both my mom and my dad if they would be willing. To my delight, they both agreed. I knew that having a Jewish daughter was outside of what they had ever envisioned, but they both embraced it for me, and their heartfelt speeches were a beautiful and memorable part of the day.

After the reception Rita hosted for my close family, I walked my mom to her car.

She turned to me with genuine love and pride in her eyes. "This has been one of the best days of my life."

"Really?"

She nodded. "There are no words to tell you how proud of you I am."

"Thank you *so* much," I said, embracing her. "It means the world to me to have you understand and support me in something that I'm sure probably hasn't been easy for you."

She held me at arm's length. "Once I understood your affinity for the Jewish people and for their beliefs and traditions, it wasn't difficult at all for me to support you. Like I've said many times, you've always danced to your drummer. Seeing you happy and being true to yourself could never bring me anything but joy." She touched my cheek. "*You* have never brought me anything but joy."

Tears filled my eyes.

What more could a daughter ever be blessed to hear?

More Ch-Ch-Ch-Ch-Changes

On May 1, 1998—exactly thirty years to the date that I was conceived, in the very room I was standing in—I received the *big* envelope in the mail, which meant that Scripps had decided that despite my advanced age, I would make an excellent addition to the graduating class of 2000. In actuality, Scripps prided itself on its diverse student body, so lucky for me, my 4.0 GPA—which so many other hopefuls had busted their humps to earn too—wasn't my sole gold star on my application. My essay had detailed my enormous advantage growing up white and blond (and being lovingly compared to similar-looking Disney characters all my life), and that I had recently become Jewish, which now put me into a bracket of society that tended to be judged, stereotyped, and at times, even wrongfully vilified. (I think I was safe in saying no one else had leapt on that bandwagon for their application essay.) That, combined with my proximity to joining AARP, sealed the diversity deal.

My mom took me out to dinner to celebrate, contending she knew all along that I'd get in.

"I wanted to believe I had a pretty good chance too," I admitted, "but you never know who a school's going to choose. I couldn't really breathe until I got that envelope."

"I know. But I'll never forget the day we went to Scripps to check it out. I *saw* you there. After that, I never had any doubt that's where you'd go."

I smiled. "Seeing" me there was a nod to one of our top favorite movies, *Enchanted April*. We had seen it dozens of times and quoted it regularly. One of the main characters, Lottie Wilkins, could also "see" things before they happened, in a purely sweet and magical way.

As always, I appreciated my mom's confidence in me and her Lottie

Wilkins–like foresight. I also knew she would support another signifi-cant decision I'd made: I wanted to take a new surname. With no of-fense intended to my family (or to anyone reading this with that last name), I had never really embraced the name "Hill." It was so short and plain (and, once I fashioned a distinct signature for myself in eleventh grade, rather boring to write), and I had fantasized since I was a little girl about changing my name to something with more flair. Just like my mom had nearly twenty years before, I wanted to choose a name that suited *me*, and having converted and desiring a name that more reflected my identity, it was the perfect time to make that transition.

I pondered various names for weeks. I didn't have the Internet at home quite yet, so I used the phone book as my World Wide Web. I'd open it up randomly and search until I found a name I liked, sign my name dozens of times with it, and see if it fit. But after several tries, I wasn't yet settled.

My now Jewish mother with her Jewish sense of humor called regu-larly with suggestions and couldn't understand why in the world I'd re-ject such brilliant options.

"What's wrong with Finkelschmutz?" she might ask. Or "But Schlepsteinowitz sounds so perfect with Stacey."

"You're right," I'd say, "but they might be a little long to write on forms."

Then, one day, I decided to start at the beginning of the phone book (concept!), and BAM. There it was. *Aaronson.* It wasn't as tradi-tionally "Jewish" as say "Spielberg" or "Goldfein" or "Silverstein," but I wasn't necessarily going for that. With all respect to the origins of sur-names, what I really wanted was a name that felt like *me*. And Aaronson happened to be that name.

I penned my variety of signature options, pretended it was my name for a week, and was sold. When I called my mom and told her my choice, she loved it right away too.

By now, it can be no surprise to you that my mom thought it was the most normal and perfectly entitled act to choose one's own name.

Native American people do it at different stages of their lives to reflect who they've become, so why are we non-Natives so locked into a name a parent chose for us at birth, or obligated to take a spouse's name whether it resonates or not?

"Are you keeping Stacey?" she wanted to know. "Because if you're tired of it, I'll understand. I still love it, but I was only sixteen when I chose it. Maybe you want a different first name now."

I shook my head. "No. I want to keep Stacey. After all, you wrote it on the lid of a Yahtzee box. How could I mess with such providence?"

"Okay . . . but don't say I didn't give you the option."

"Oh no . . . not to worry," I said tongue in cheek. "But I do want to swap out my middle name."

My mom had been given the name Cynthia Ann, and so she'd given me the middle name Ann too. But she agreed with me that it didn't sound good with Aaronson. Plus, she had ditched her own "Ann" decades ago.

"I like Jane," I said. "You were named after your great-grandmother, Cynthia Jane. I like the way it sounds—you know, the rhythm of the syllables together, Sta-cey Jane Aar-on-son . . . and I like that it's from Grandma's side of the family. Plus, that would make my full name have eighteen letters, which makes it perfect too."

"Jane, it is," she said. "I love it." Then she added, "How do you think your dad will take it?"

To be honest, though I certainly didn't want to be hurtful to my dad, grandma, or siblings, I wasn't seeking permission to change my last name (I doubted anyone would give a whoop about my middle name). It was not at all a rejection of my family; it was *my* decision for *me*. I would explain it thoughtfully so they would all understand. And even if they thought I was a little cracked, my mom got it 100 percent, which was the only "stamp of approval" I craved at all from the outside.

Though I had been accepted into Scripps as Stacey Ann Hill, I would officially change it shortly after school started and graduate as Stacey Jane Aaronson.

∞

Shocks and Awe

Having a penchant for languages, I had decided to major in Spanish, which meant writing my thesis in Spanish (yes, for our bachelor's degree, we had to write a 40ish-page thesis to graduate). But that wasn't overachieving enough for me. Once I realized I could *double* major, I was elated to choose Jewish Studies for major number two. The only thing was, fulfilling those requirements meant studying abroad for a semester in Israel.

While I wasn't completely keen on leaving home for four months during my senior year of college, and frankly neither was my mom, it was the only way to earn the appropriate credits, and I admittedly thought studying in the Holy Land would be a remarkable experience. So, I filled out the paperwork and submitted it to the study abroad office for consideration for the fall semester of 1999.

During the summer, as I was gearing up for this grand adventure, I started experiencing something bizarre: an inordinate amount of static electricity began to surround me. At first, I thought it was my laundry, but I quickly realized that wasn't the culprit. One day, for example, I was sitting on my bed, nowhere near the remote, when the TV went on by itself. Another day, I was with my mom in her car when the radio station changed and neither of us had touched it.

I had told my mom how I was getting shocked whenever I touched something, and now weirder things like the channel changing by itself were happening.

"Wow, Doob . . . you really do have something electric going on with you," she mused. "What do you think it means?"

I had already told her that oddly, I wasn't scared. "I think it's

Grandma," I said. "I think she's trying to get a message to me, and this is how she's getting my attention."

My mom didn't think that was so odd, but she was curious as to what the reason would be.

"The only thing I can think of is that she doesn't want me to go to Israel. I think maybe I'd be in danger."

"Well, I *have* been worried about you going to such a volatile part of the world. But I know you have your heart set on that double major . . ."

I paused. "I do . . . and I don't. Seriously, I've been surrounded by this electricity for weeks. Nothing else makes sense to me except that it's Grandma trying to protect me in the only way she can get a message to me. My aspirations to do a double major aren't worth dying for, for God's sake."

"You've got my agreement on that one, sister. So, what do you think you're going to do?"

"The more I've thought about it, the more I believe I'm right. And what else could it be about besides this trip? Canceling my Israel semester seems like the only logical thing to do."

My next class day, I pulled my application for the program and changed my Jewish Studies major to a minor, which didn't require studying abroad.

Almost immediately, the electricity around me disappeared.

I believed in my heart I had heeded my grandma's guidance, but I had no idea just how significant that decision was going to be.

∽

$41.00 Plus Shipping

𝓑 y the time I entered Scripps, I had indeed paid off my grown-up bills by working three jobs my last two years at Cerritos, and I now had a promising career as the Foreign Language Lab Girl at Scripps. Translation: I'd left Nordstrom and Barnes & Noble, stopped tutoring students in Spanish at Cerritos, and was now making a whopping $6.50 an hour, two days a week, two hours per shift, at Scripps in something called a Work-Study Job. This scintillating, cash-machine of a career move involved sitting in a room (calling it a "lab" was a stretch and a half) with a table and a giant filing cabinet full of cassette tapes. Essentially, I would study between students coming in to check out a foreign language tape for their particular class. I had this coveted position for three whole semesters at Scripps, and I think I checked out a total of ten tapes, which meant that the majority of the time I was at "work," I got to study and get modestly paid for it.

I had gotten my first computer at the beginning of the year, and I had also fallen prey to procuring booty (which for me was mostly vintage sweaters) on a new auction site called eBay. Besides letting me live in my studio rent-free, my grandma Hill generously gave me a modest allowance to live on every month as her way of contributing to my education. After food, gas, and car insurance were paid for, I'd sometimes have enough for a sweater or two, as long as I kept myself reeled in.

But on October 26th, 1999, I went a little crazy.

The computer lab was right next door to my language lab, and my advisor had told me that if I ever needed to use a computer during my shift, to just put a note on the door to alert students that they could find me next door. I'd never taken her up on it, but on this day, an auction that I really wanted to win was serendipitously ending during my shift.

If you're familiar with eBay, you know you can place a proxy bid on an item you want, which allows the computer to outbid other bidders until they surpass whatever proxy amount you've chosen. On this particular day, I had my eye on a rare European Sarah Brightman compilation CD (I had become a huge fan) whose bid was around $20 to start. Truth be told, I had no business buying any more stuff on eBay. I was mostly living on pizza, tuna sandwiches, and a select assortment of fruit, and I should have been saving my extra money, or at least buying more vegetables with it. But I *really* wanted this CD, and my strategy was to thoughtfully win it [read: snake it at the last second].

I typed in my bid and was immediately outbid by the proxy feature someone else had set on the item. So I bid a little more. Still I was outbid. This continued until I had about two minutes left of the auction. Finally, with full adrenaline pumping, I typed in $41.00 just before the timer ran out.

The computer screen read: You are the highest bidder. Congratulations!

My elation was quickly usurped by the realization of what I'd just done. *Holy crap. I just spent $41.00 plus shipping for a flippin' CD. What was I thinking?*

When I got home that evening, an email was waiting for me.

Hey [username],
Congratulations on winning the CD. I was bummed to come home from work and find out I'd lost the auction, but at least it went to a fellow Sarah Brightman fan.
Enjoy!
Dana

These were the early days, when no one was freaked out yet about privacy and a person could actually email a winner of an auction directly. Not that anyone, *ever*, did that. Seriously. Who writes to someone after they've snaked their desired item to congratulate them? Again, no one in the history of auctions does that. Except, apparently, for this incredibly nice person named Dana.

Right away, I felt like the snake that I was. This poor person must have thought no one in their right mind would pay more than $40.00 for a CD, so she thought she had it in the bag. That is, until I came along. I wrote her back and thanked her for her kindness, promptly apologized for stealing her CD, and promised I'd keep an eye out to find her another one.

I did keep my eye out. And I did find one. I speedily wrote to this Dana person and told her.

She scored the CD for twenty bucks.

Declarations of Love

*Y*ou may be wondering why I told you the riveting story in the previous chapter and what it has to do with my relationship with my mom. Trust me. We're getting to that, but I had to set the stage to bring you on this leg of our journey with the full backstory.

Over the next couple months, Dana and I, both being major Sarah Brightman fans, started emailing each other regularly and fostered a friendship. We shared a few facts about ourselves with each other and felt fairly certain neither was a creepy, lying stalker guy posing as a friendly female. She was 37; I was 30. She lived in Indiana; I lived in Southern California. We were both born on the 18th (how cool!) of different months. That kind of stuff. Then Instant Messenger became a thing and we started doing that. Then a phone call here and there (it was long distance back then, so we had to be judicious). Then we thought it would be fun to send each other photos of ourselves so that we could put a face to all the messages we were exchanging.

In brief (because this story merits its own memoir, so I don't want to give too much away), Dana and I fell in love, purely through a soul connection neither of us could explain. Even for my supremely open-minded, supportive mom, I thought she might be a little concerned that I'd fallen for someone I'd never met in person, and a woman at that (hmm . . . I guess that therapist way back when was onto something after all). So, I kept this increasingly consuming relationship to myself while trying to do all the reading and research for and write my thesis, plus finish the courses for my last semester. The best word I can use to describe it is *madness*. But I had never felt this way in my life, and so I mostly operated on love butterflies (and pizza and tuna sandwiches) until graduation.

As you might imagine, Dana and I knew we needed to meet to see if this insanity was real or not. So, we planned for her to come out four days after my college graduation, on the auspicious date of May 18th.

My commencement ceremony was held on Mother's Day of the year 2000 on a gorgeous afternoon on the Elm Tree Lawn of our campus. It had taken me six years of devoted study and working my tail off, and I had accomplished my lofty goal of graduating magna cum laude. I had also been named in *Who's Who of American College Students* and been inducted into Phi Beta Kappa. The fact that my graduation was held on Mother's Day made the whole milestone event that much sweeter for my mom.

Despite it being a holiday, two of my dearest friends, Jay and Shirlie, who each had four grown children of their own, graciously came to my ceremony. When everyone gathered afterward, Shirlie said, "Oh Briana, you must be so proud of Stacey. You've done such an amazing job raising her."

"Oh," my mom said matter-of-factly. "I didn't raise Stacey. Stacey raised me."

My friends laughed. Then my mom said, "I'm serious. If it weren't for her, I don't know who I might have become."

The laughter faded into sentimental expressions. No one, including me, knew quite what to say. It was clear my mom was being genuine. And it was true that we'd both joked many times about how often I had been the mother within our twosome throughout all our years together. But to hear her say it like that, and to my dear friends, deeply touched me, and them.

"Well," Shirlie finally said, "I'm sure you've been more of a positive influence on her than you realize."

My mom tipped her head humbly.

I wrapped my arm around my mom's waist. "Believe me," I told my friends. "She has."

But Wait, There's More

*I*n the days leading up to my graduation, which were undeniably thrilling and included shopping for dresses with my mom (I loved that as much now as I did when I was a little girl), I was also in a glittery rainbow-swirl of anticipation about meeting Dana in person for the first time. As you might imagine, the excitement of so many huge events occurring in my life only days apart was almost more than my already full heart could take.

One of the things I wanted to do before Dana flew out was to doll up my studio a little more. By then, I had shared my friendship with Dana with my mom, but only that we had become close friends who wanted to finally meet. We had plans to go to Disneyland, watch movies, and do some typical SoCal things, like go to Hollywood and shop at the awesome malls (which was all true). My mom thought that was so cool, and she was a sweetheart about making curtains for my studio to make it look more like a home. At the time, she suspected nothing. Why would she? She was excited to meet Dana and offered to take us out to dinner one night while she was here.

Once Dana and I actually met in person and discovered that our soul connection was indeed not merely a cyber illusion, and having been suspended in a true-love orbit for days (part of which did include multiple trips to Disneyland, where we delighted in being a girl couple holding hands without so much as a sideways glance), we were approaching the date of the dinner with my mom. But I knew I couldn't sit across from her at a restaurant, with my new "friend" by my side, and pretend that's all Dana was—a friend—when I was in love, really in love, for the first time in my life. And unloading that news on my mom, with (a very nervous) Dana present, wouldn't be fair to either one of them, so I hatched a quick plan.

A couple years prior, after enjoying years of enormous success in her career as a sales rep for the fine paper company, my mom bought a beautiful brand-new home in a small, newly developed housing community in San Pedro, about thirty minutes from me in Long Beach. Dana and I were supposed to meet her there, then go out to dinner nearby. But the day before, I called and asked if it was possible to come by and see her now, at home. "Sure!" my mom said, looking forward to seeing us.

But when I arrived on her porch, my mom glanced around and asked, "Where's Dana?"

"Um . . . she's actually not with me. I wanted to have a little time with you alone."

"Oh," my mom said, a bit confused. "Okay."

I walked in and told her I wanted to talk to her about something. We sat down opposite each other, and I looked into my mom's beautiful, open, expectant face. Tenderly, I said, "I know this is going to come as a big surprise . . . but . . . Dana and I aren't just friends. It's crazy, I know, but . . . I'm in love with her. And she feels the same about me. We've actually been in love long distance for the last four and a half months, but I didn't want to tell you until we met and I knew for sure."

Her eyes grew wide, but a genuine smile spread across her face. "Wow. I *am* surprised. But this is wonderful news, honey! I'm so happy for you!"

I exhaled the breath I hadn't realized I was holding. "So you're not freaked out?"

"Not at all. Surprised, yes, but of course I'm not freaked out. I might just need a little time to digest it is all."

I threw my arms around her. "I'm so relieved you finally know. I've wanted to tell you for so long, but the whole thing was just so crazy. I didn't want you worrying about me if it didn't turn out to be what I thought it was. You would have had every right to be concerned about me thinking I was in love with someone I'd never met."

She nodded playfully. "I suppose . . . but then, magical things seem to always happen for you. And you're always so level-headed about everything that it's rare I would doubt you."

"Uh," I said sarcastically, "there was that engagement I wasn't so level-headed about."

"Well, yes," she joked. "But that was just a minor blip."

"But *this* is pretty out there. I would have been concerned if I were in your shoes."

"Well . . . I get why you waited to tell me until you were sure. But how in the world have you kept this to yourself all this time? And with writing your thesis and everything?"

"To be honest . . . and please don't feel hurt by this . . . I did tell one person. When Jay took me to Disneyland for my birthday. We had so much fun, and then we came back to my place. I was bursting to tell someone about Dana, and I felt like I could tell her."

Right away my mom understood. Jay, who had been a dear friend for several years and was close to my mom's age, was an extraordinary person and very young at heart like my mom.

"How did she react?"

"She was totally shocked. But she could tell I was in love when I told her and showed her Dana's picture. She just hugged me and told me that if I was happy, then she was happy for me."

Never one to be jealous, my mom said, "I'm so glad you had someone you could confide in. I get why you told Jay. I really do."

Again, I exhaled with relief. "Thank you for saying that. I didn't want you feeling hurt that you weren't the first to know."

"Not at all." Then, my mom grew suddenly excited. "So when do I get to meet her?"

"Tomorrow night. If dinner's still on."

"Of course it is! I can't wait to meet your love."

Butterflies upon Butterflies

$\mathcal{T}$he next night, I was eager for Dana to meet my mom. But Dana's butterflies were almost too much to bear. She had grown up in highly conservative northwest Indiana, in a Born Again Christian family, who believed that being gay was a sin punishable by hellfire. And so while she'd had a few serious, long-term relationships in her life, she had always had to keep them hidden, or pretend that her beloved was only a good friend. The engrained belief that there was something wrong with her for loving a woman, and her fear of what that meant for her soul, was so intense that she had deliberately stayed single for the past decade, even praying for God to bring her a man if that's what was meant for her.

Now here she was, in ultra-liberal Southern California, in love with a recent convert to Judaism who had never believed there was anything wrong with same-sex couples (and neither did her rabbi), and whose ultra-liberal mother embraced the idea of us immediately and was ready to meet her "other daughter" only minutes after the big reveal. The possibility of complete acceptance was such a foreign concept to Dana that she almost couldn't believe people like my mom and me existed.

True to her nature, my mom embraced Dana from the moment she met her. It didn't matter how starkly different Dana and I were in a multitude of ways—our upbringings, our religious persuasions, our educational levels, our family dynamics, our exposure to other cultures and languages, our social escapades. If *I* loved Dana and felt a profound soul connection with her, then my mom loved Dana too. But she didn't only love her because I did, she willingly—and genuinely—took her into her heart as a fully accepting mother to an overwhelmingly kind, caring, and wonderful person. Yes, Dana had come into my life carrying a lot of emotional and spiritual baggage from all the conditioning she'd been raised with, and yes, she had been a bit sheltered never having left her insular, dogma-heavy community. But she also knew what it was like to escape into the gay-bar scene near Chicago, the only place she could be her authentic self with her partners and friends, and partake of the party life that came with it, which was something completely foreign to *me*.

But that night, over dinner, my mom looked across the table at us in our sparkly love-butterfly world and emanated nothing but joy to see us so happy together.

"You know," she said. "I told Stacey yesterday that I needed a little time to get used to the idea of you two. But I really didn't need much time at all."

"I'm glad," Dana said nervously. "I know this is big. It's big for *me*. I can't imagine what it's like for you."

"Well, I'll tell you . . . this morning I was sitting out in my courtyard with my cup of coffee. And I felt like a fairy landed on my shoulder. In that moment, I knew everything was exactly as it should be. And any worry I might have initially felt just melted away."

I squeezed Dana's hand under the table. "I told you she was special," I said, referring to my mom. "You don't have to hide anymore. Not here with me."

Though it would take many years to chip away at all the cement Dana had been encased in, she moved to California only three months later to be with me, and she became my mom's other daughter from that day forward.

We all also realized why my grandma had worked overtime from beyond to keep me from studying abroad during that fateful semester. Had I been in Israel, I wouldn't have been at school that day during my work-study job to snag that CD—from the person who was destined to be my soul mate—for $41 plus shipping.

Gilmore Girls

*A*bout a year into Dana's and my cramped but genuine bliss, my mom called one evening while visiting some friends.

"Hey, have you two heard of a show called *Gilmore Girls*?"

"I've heard of it but we haven't seen it."

"Well, it's on right now and a couple of my friends said I *had* to see it because it's about a mother who had her daughter when she was sixteen, and they have a kind of role-reversal relationship like us, where the mom is like me and the daughter is like you. And the mom doesn't get along that great with her mom, but her daughter does. It's so like us, you wouldn't believe it!"

"Really? What channel? We're on it!"

At this point in the chapter, if you've never seen an episode of *Gilmore Girls*, one of the sharpest, cleverest, funniest, most creative, heart-centered shows ever produced, I urge you to put this book down, spark up your Netflix account (where they're available free), and take in an episode. Even if it's only one. In fact, if you're a Gilmore virgin, and you're actually going to try it out just for me, I suggest watching season one, episode six. The cast is gelling by then, and this one will give you a good glimpse into how daughter Rory is much like bookish me, how mom Lorelai is free-spirited and the queen of sarcastic and witty repartee like my mom, and how the two of them together have their own signature "thing." Do note, however, that my grandparents were almost nothing like rich and snobby Richard and Emily. Yes, Richard and my grandpa both worked in the insurance field (!); and yes, Emily and my grandma were both stay-at-home wives. And yes, they were all generous when it came to Rory. But otherwise, the main resemblance to them is the strained and distant relationship between Lorelai and Emily, and even that is more a bit more strained and distant on the show than it was for my mom and grandma. But nonetheless, in scary-similar ways —even though I didn't live with my mom as a teen—this show is uncannily *us*. Lorelai even makes dresses for Rory!

Up until *GG* aired, neither my mom nor I had ever encountered anyone with our dynamic. It was so unlike what other mothers and daughters had that people sometimes had a hard time grasping it. It was clear she was no June Cleaver or Carol Brady, but how did my decidedly unconstrained mother end up with a square, conservative, perfectionist like me? Now, thanks to the brilliant mind of writer Amy Sherman-Palladino, the world now had a glimpse of the uncommon magic my mom and I shared. In fact, the question "What's your relationship with your mom/your daughter like?" was now quick to be answered with, "Have you ever seen *Gilmore Girls*?"

∽

Shocking Diagnosis

*D*uring the year of our delight at being portrayed on TV in a hit show, when my mom was forty-nine, she went to see a chiropractor to once again address a persistent problem: she'd been experiencing numbness in her hands and feet for over a decade. She'd gotten used to it to a point, and she'd seen chiropractors before who believed it was pinched nerves that were causing it, but it had never gone away permanently with adjustments. Now, it had become so pronounced that she could barely feel her feet, and walking and driving were becoming more of a challenge. Having a job that required loads of both, she was determined to fix it once and for all.

This new chiropractor, however, didn't believe it was merely pinched nerves. He refused to work on her without an x-ray first, and after he slid the film onto the screen, he refused to work on her at all.

"I want you to see a neurologist," he told her. "I don't want to scare you, but you're showing some lesions on the brain stem that could be what's causing your problem."

"Lesions? What does that mean?"

"Well, I'm not in a position to diagnose you, and like I said, I don't want to scare you, but I've seen this in patients who have multiple sclerosis."

"MS? I can't have MS. I'm a perfectly healthy person."

"I know. This is why I want you to see this neurologist." He handed her a business card. "This is his specialty. He'll be able to assess it more clinically than I'm trained to do."

During the consult with the neurologist, he confirmed what the chiropractor had suspected: he believed my mom had MS. In fact, he believed she'd probably had it for nearly fifteen years without realizing it, which in hindsight was a blessing. Had she known in her mid-thirties that such a frightening fate had befallen her, she might have progressed much faster than she had, precisely because what the mind focuses on typically manifests—good or bad. She knew that people could unknowingly walk around with a disease for months and feel fine—until they were told they had it. Then they would often decline, especially if a doctor gave them a grave prognosis, because their mind now struggled to focus on anything other than the disease.

As you know, my mom was no stranger to the idea of what people call "alternative medicine," which in reality refers to what's been used for millennia to heal and foster health in the human body. Pharmaceutical medicine superseded herbal remedies and igniting the body's natural healing power back in the 1930s, which unfortunately has virtually no focus on prevention of disease. My mom and I weren't completely clued in to that at the time, but we still knew that the mind-body connection was powerful. And my mom decided that she wasn't going to let MS take over her life. She did sign on for an experimental "cocktail" injection that she had to administer to herself once a week, which was promising for keeping the telltale brain-stem lesions from multiplying, but she continued to work, take health-boosting supplements, and eat fairly well. The numbness in her feet caused her gait to become a little tentative, and she'd had to give up her beloved hikes in the Palos Verdes hills, but other than that, she was as glowing and ebullient as she'd always been.

But even with her commitment to keeping a positive outlook, she couldn't help but fear that she would eventually be robbed of her mobility and end up in a wheelchair.

I'm not going to lie. The idea that my young, vibrant mom could possibly be saddled with a physically debilitating disease weighed on me too.

∞

Giving It the Ol' Fourth Try

Over the last several years, my mom had been immersed in a long-time, on-again off-again love affair with a younger man that she finally realized had to come to an end. After that painful breakup, she had been swept into a whirlwind romance and briefly engaged to a man I knew in my heart wasn't right for her, and eventually she had to concede the same. Although my mom loved her independence, she also loved being in a relationship and longed to be in one again, so she decided to create a profile on eHarmony.

As you might imagine, she received lots of hits. One of the men who was interested in her seemed like a good match, so they met for drinks. After the date, she told Dana and me that the guy, whose name was Rick, was handsome and interesting, but intense.

"That's the best word I can use to describe him," she said. "Everything he talked about had an intensity to it."

"Well, is that good or bad?" I wanted to know.

"I'm not sure. But I think I'd like to see him again."

I won't prolong this for you. In a nutshell, they started dating, she gave full disclosure about the MS diagnosis and what that might mean for the future, and he said he didn't care about that, that he loved her and wanted to be with her no matter what.

And so, on May 7, 2005, in an intimate celebration in her home, with a lovely female ecumenical minister who performed a touching ceremony, and holding the elegant bouquet I made with love for her as her gift, my mom got married for the fourth time.

As with marriage number three, I was concerned about the short engagement and questioned the "in love" part of the equation. But my mom had made up her mind, and so all that was left was to support her, as she had supported me.

I just didn't realize that Rick, almost immediately after the wedding, was going to literally whisk my mom away from me.

Big Moves for the
Little Ladies

For their honeymoon, my mom and Rick went to Santa Fe, NM, where Rick's sister was getting married. They attended the wedding then spent a week or so there and fell in love with the landscape, the peacefulness, and the expansive views. My mom had already been forced to go on long-term disability because she couldn't manage all the walking and traveling her job required. So, when my mom returned, she told Dana and me that she and Rick had not only decided they wanted to move to Santa Fe, but they had already looked at houses in an upscale area and found a brand-new one they loved.

As I mentioned, my mom had bought her beautiful house in San Pedro all on her own, and she adored that house. I had figured Rick would move in there after they were married, since she was the one with the nice digs. I never imagined she'd want to move away from it—and out of state at that. But here she was, already moving on to her next chapter. Only she didn't want to sell her house, not yet anyway.

Dana and I had moved to San Pedro (after proving that we must be made for each other if we could live in my 300-square-foot pad for nineteen months without driving each other nuts) only two miles from my mom, where we rented a homey duplex. But besides adopting our first kitty, who we found as a stray in the complex, we'd encountered a few unsavory things living there over time that made us consider a move.

"What about moving into my house?" my mom suggested eagerly. "You can pay your same rent to me that you're paying now, and that would buy me a year to think about selling, and buy you girls a year to find your ideal place."

Being a person who hated to move, I wasn't that keen on the prospect of moving into her house, then moving again in only a year. But my mom's house had three bedrooms, which included a spacious master suite, and it was in an endearing gated neighborhood that would only extend our commutes to work by five minutes. Dana and I had started a greeting card business on the side, so living there would give us an office *and* a guest bedroom. Plus, we would be helping my mom while having a beautiful home to live in. So, within the next few months, she and Rick moved to their new adobe home in the high desert, and Dana and I moved to Nantucket Lane, into my mom's hard-earned storybook house only minutes from the ocean.

Another Piece of the
Biological Puzzle

After a year had passed—the time span we'd agreed upon to live in my mom's house—she still didn't want to sell, and we most definitely did not want to move, so we stayed in her lovely home and continued to make it ours.

Over the next few years, though my mom and I talked almost every day on the phone, it was yet another adjustment not to see her on a regular basis. Even when we'd lived so close to each other, and Dana and I had been too busy with our own lives to visit all the time, it was still nice to know my mom was only five minutes away.

This was particularly true when my mom called one day to tell me she'd received some sad news: Aletha had passed away. For the past eighteen years, they had spoken periodically by phone, where Aletha had "thawed" with my mom and they had actually discovered ways they were alike and gotten a kick out of each other at times. "She's a kook like me," my mom had told me. But their relationship had never gone further than those phone calls and the exchange of cards. Aletha maintained that my mom looked nothing like her, that she hadn't thought about her after giving her up, and that my mom's birth father was practically a one-night stand who went off to the Korean War and never knew about the pregnancy. She was also adamant that she didn't want to meet, flippantly saying, "Oh, you don't want to see me in person. I'm an old lady now anyway." Of course, my mom didn't care if she looked like a bag lady; she simply wanted to hug the woman who carried her for nine months and brought her into the world. But Aletha would never cave on it, and my mom stopped holding out hope she would change her mind.

Eventually, despite seeming manic about keeping the whole sordid affair a secret all these decades later, Aletha told one person—a treasured niece—about my mom's existence and their reunion. It was this niece who delivered the news about Aletha's death.

"And Briana," she said, "there's something else you need to know. I know Aletha told you she didn't want to meet you, but that wasn't true. She *did* want to meet you, but she was afraid."

"Afraid of what? I told her I didn't want anything from her."

"I know. She wasn't afraid of that. She was afraid that *she* would want more from *you* if she saw you. She loved her independence, but she also loved her friendship with you. At the same time . . . she thought you'd be disappointed if you met her in person, and if you made that connection and then pulled away . . . well, that was part of her fear. Acting like she didn't want to meet was just a defense mechanism, not her true feelings."

For my mom, this disclosure was the source of several emotions: shock, sadness, disappointment; compassion, solace, happiness. The first three for the lie and for what they missed that they could have had; the latter three for Aletha's inner struggle and for knowing she cared more than she had ever let on.

"I can email you some pictures," the niece told her. "Some younger ones and a few recent ones."

"Really? Oh . . . I would love that."

As soon as my mom received the photos, she called and sent them to me for my real-time reaction.

"Oh my gosh," I said, "I can't believe she said you looked nothing like her. You *do* resemble her . . . a lot."

"I do, don't I?"

"This must be so surreal for you . . . finally seeing your birth mother . . . and seeing yourself in her."

"It *is* surreal. And look . . . we finally know whose hairline you got."

It was true. Both my mom and dad had high foreheads and baby-fine hair, and I had Aletha's hairline and, as an adult, more the texture of her thick hair. Up to then, I hadn't felt much connection myself to Aletha, because the relationship had always been only between her and my mom. Plus, I'd never felt that my grandparents weren't my "real" grandparents; blood meant nothing to me when it came to that side of the family. But now, seeing Aletha for the first time, and traits I'd gotten from her, did extend our little branch on the family tree a bit further for me.

Then my mom shared what the niece had told her about Aletha wanting to meet but being afraid to.

"That really breaks my heart for you. I know how much you wanted that," I said.

"I did . . . and it makes me sad too. But just knowing she wanted to, and that she seemed to love me . . . that's something."

Once again in our relationship, I felt anguish for my mom. I was glad that Aletha had more feeling for her only child than we knew, but I hated that my wonderful mom was having to settle for these bread-crumbs. I wanted to hold her in that moment, to comfort that little girl whose mothers—both of them—were only capable of giving her so much, both of them coming up short. But she was nine hundred miles away, so I had to settle for reminding her how remarkable she was, that her mothers' shortcomings were theirs and had nothing to do with her.

"Thanks, Doob," she said.

I could tell her words were genuine, and that she had relished shar-ing all of this with me by phone, but I still wished I could have been there with her in person for such a monumental moment in her life.

As an interesting side note, adding to the odd parallels between Aletha and Audrey Meadows, they both left this Earth, fourteen years apart, on the exact same date: February 3rd.

Downs and Ups

*N*ow that my mom and I saw each other only once or twice a year, and one of us had to travel a distance to make those visits happen, it made the progress of the MS even more apparent.

While I had already witnessed my mom's stride become a bit unsteady, on one of her trips out to see us, she lost her balance and fell at the airport. She wasn't seriously injured, but her confidence was shattered. She was so embarrassed that she couldn't stand up on her own and needed help, and so afraid of it happening again, that she decided to start using a rolling walker to help her feel secure. Not so long ago, she had gone on regular power hikes and walked thousands of steps a day in her job as a sales rep. Now she was feeling more and more dependent on an unwelcome crutch just to get around, not to mention terrified of what the next phase of her life would look like if she became completely reliant on a walker.

Committed to doing whatever she could to reverse or halt the damage that the disease had seemingly already done, and no longer feeling aligned with the intra-muscular injections she'd done for a few years, she stopped that and turned to various supplements. Being in Santa Fe now, where a strong community of healers of all types existed, my mom took it a step further and embarked on an ancient treatment that was promising for MS: apitherapy—the use of products derived from bees as medicine. In her case, this involved not only taking royal jelly every day, but two sessions per week of being intentionally stung by bees in specific places on the body, releasing the healing venom. This may sound barbaric, but my mom's opinion was that despite the obvious pain it entailed, there was something profound about connecting with the bees, and for each one to lose its life to help her. The sessions became deeply ceremonial, and she gave thanks to each bee for its gift as it traded its lifeforce for the betterment of hers.

Whether the bee venom itself was therapeutic, or my mom's belief in its healing power helped to halt the progression of the MS, no one can know. I imagine it was some of both. Either way, even though she continued to use the walker for stability, her level of mobility remained fairly stable.

Unfortunately, she couldn't say the same about her marriage. Though it had now lasted longer than any of her previous ones, she and Rick had already grown apart. As Dana and I had both feared, she had once again wed a man she hadn't known long enough to discover the ways in which they weren't compatible, only now she felt less inclined to leave the way she had in the past. They had a home and a life in Santa Fe, her mobility was compromised, and she could no longer work and afford to buy another house on her own.

During one of her visits with us, my mom remarked, "I feel so much better here than I do at home. It must be being with you girls."

Of course we all loved the idea of that. But we also realized her heightened energy could be from being back at sea level again. The elevation in Santa Fe is 7,000 feet, which some say has significant health benefits, but for my mom, she said she felt "heavier" being at home than she did when she was in San Pedro.

"Maybe it's time for us to move so that you can leave Rick and move back here, into your house," I suggested.

But despite the fact that Rick wasn't the best match for my mom and they had drifted in opposite directions, she had no interest in returning to crowded LA county once she'd tasted the serenity of Santa Fe and made a treasured group of girlfriends.

So, believing she had no choice but to enjoy the good parts of her life and make the best of the not-so-good ones, she decided to remain in the largely loveless marriage with Rick, continue with the apitherapy, and pray for a health miracle.

⚘

My Darkest Hour

*M*y fancy education, which my mom and I were both extremely proud of, didn't quite project me where I thought it would career-wise. I'd entertained the idea of going into academia and perhaps becoming a college professor, but I changed my mind when I got a repelling whiff of the politics. I'd gotten what I thought was a wonderful job selling textbooks to colleges, but within a short period, I'd soured of the ridiculous expectation that I be "on call" 24/7 (umm . . . as a textbook rep?) and return all emails within two hours of receiving them (really?). So when the owners of one of my mom's accounts, a small boutique retail company, were looking to hire someone to run their three stores, my mom had asked me if I might be interested.

I owed thousands of dollars in student loans, and frankly, I thought I should, at the very least, work in a field that reflected *why* I owed all that money. I'd already done retail for ten years, and I really wasn't considering going back to it. But after the interview, where the three of us clicked beautifully and I presented all kinds of ideas on how I could better the company, I was actually hopeful they would offer me the job. They did. And so, returning to where I'd excelled in the past, I became their director of personnel and customer relations on May 14, 2001, one year to the day I had graduated from college.

I adored my job and blossomed in it in multiple ways, but by 2010, I had stayed in it about two years too long. The recession had hit in 2008, and my once fulfilling job had been diminished to running a single store. I'd had aspirations at Nordstrom to be a store manager, but in this case, it was a major demotion, which included two detrimental pay cuts.

While I was grateful I still had a job, it was clear I needed to move on. Despite having to kick my own booty out of my comfort zone, I embraced the idea of a fresh employment chapter in my life and set out to discover what that might look like. The owners of my company even offered to let me stay while I found another position, and I honestly believed that with all my experience and education behind me, I'd be packing my retail bag within a few months.

Boy, did I shoot that arrow way off the bullseye.

Not only was I not being scooped up and into a new and exciting career opportunity, but the entire world of job hunting had changed dramatically since 2001. I quickly learned that for every position listed online, it wasn't uncommon for the company to receive five to eight hundred applicants. *Five to eight hundred.* It wasn't just that I hadn't landed a new job yet; I struggled to even score acknowledgment of my application and resume, let alone an interview.

In no time, the generous timer my bosses had set swiftly buzzed at zero, and I had no choice but to leave and go on unemployment. Yes, I'd paid into it; and no, there was nothing shameful about needing it. But Dana had lost her job too due to downsizing, and our unemployment benefits didn't begin to pay our monthly expenses, one of which was a hefty amount every month to my mom for the rent.

Akin to jumping on a speeding train, I immersed myself in newfangled methods to make myself stand out. I took an online branding course. I spent hours researching the companies that offered the positions I coveted and wrote thoughtful cover letters to the appropriate people, by name. I refashioned my resume for each position, so that the skills of mine they were seeking were up front and center, not buried in a formulaic CCV. I used a splash of color. I took a night course for weeks at a local college to get certified as a PHR, Professional in Human Resources, and designed a professional logo for myself. I became a veritable dog in a circus jumping through hoops, but the crowd wasn't going wild. In fact, the stadium remained filled with crickets, and I couldn't understand why.

As the months clipped by, I grew increasingly depressed. Our savings depleted fast, and so my mom stepped up in the most generous way, making up the difference on our rent when we couldn't afford the total, and even a couple of bleak months covering all of it when we couldn't swing it. After all those years of not being able to afford to have me with her, she was making up for it and then some. But my dependence on her weighed on me heavily. At forty-one, with an expensive education under my belt and twelve years of being in leadership roles with massive amounts of responsibility, I couldn't believe I was in this position. Dana wasn't faring any better in her job hunt, and our once-successful card business had slowed to a halt. I cobbled together income by working part-time for a dermatologist's office, doing design projects for an entrepreneur, anything I could use my skills for that paid, all while working a "full-time job" applying for jobs. Dana had always been a saint as the one who orchestrated the total care and feeding of us, and that had intensified as we moved toward a more healthy eating regimen and stopped eating out. Taking amazing care of us became *her* full-time job, and the truth was, without her making all our meals, juices, and smoothies, and managing our supplements and wellness routine, I could have never put so much effort into finding a new career path—or stayed healthy while I was doing it.

Still, one day, I finally broke down on the phone with my mom.

"I can't bear having you pick up the slack like this. I hate that you're helping us so much. I can only imagine the stress this is putting on you and I feel horrible about it."

My mom knew I was leaving no stone unturned and that I was doing everything in my power to unearth another career path, but still I felt like a massive burden.

"I know you hate this," she said tenderly. "You've always been so independent. But think about how wonderful it feels for me to be in a position to help you like this. There were so many years when I couldn't afford to have you with me . . . or that I wasn't in a place to do something like this for you. But now, I can . . . and being able to provide you girls with a home . . . think of how serendipitous *that* is, that you're still living on Nantucket during this difficult time. I know you'll find your way. And I know you're working *so* hard. Something's going to happen for you soon . . . I just know it."

Buoyed by her seeming gratitude and delight in getting us through my darkest hour, and with immense appreciation for her support and belief in me, I vowed not to let this demeaning stage of my life break me completely. But after finally scoring first and second interviews for two jobs I sincerely wanted, and not getting either, I hit rock bottom. So many people in the nation were unemployed that benefits were extended for a second year, which helped, but I increasingly questioned why the Universe had me hitting so many brick walls.

Soon, though, I was finally going to find out.

Reinvention

Every one of us comes to this Earth school with gifts to offer. Sadly, many people's gifts are suppressed; others are believed to be impossible to use to earn a living; and others are beautifully hatched and nurtured, which can happen at any stage of life. Still others know they have certain gifts but aren't sure what offering them to the world might look like. For me, that epiphany happened in 2011.

Though I had achieved some level of success in my career as a leader, my dream was always to be a writer. Books had been cherished companions all of my life, and writing was the one area where I felt I possessed some degree of talent. Then, around 2004, I had become a self-taught graphic designer when Dana and I launched our hand-embellished greeting card business, and I loved that creative expression too. But writing and design were consistently side pursuits; while both lit me up inside, parlaying either or both into a career just never crossed my mind.

But it *had* crossed the Universe's mind. In fact, a beautiful plan had been hatched for me and was already in place—only I didn't know it. This was why every time I applied for a position that focused on my "old" skills of leadership—the only skills I thought made sense to highlight to score another job—the Universe pressed a giant rejection buzzer. After a year of having my self-confidence repeatedly crushed into gravel with a steel-toed boot, I finally concluded that I had no choice but to try to reinvent myself completely. It's not that I hadn't wanted to do that before, but it was a huge chance to take with my mom chipping in for our bills nearly every month. I simply didn't think it was feasible or that the timing was right.

But then an opportunity showed up, one that pushed the Big Black Button in my mind and clicked on a bright light.

An author I knew was looking for someone to design an ebook cover for him. I jumped at the opportunity, designed a cover he loved, adored doing it, and immediately heard a chorus of angels as a new pathway seemed to radiate through parted clouds of the heavens: as a cover designer for independently published authors. I immediately threw myself into learning all the strategies and trends of cover design for different genres, and I believed I'd finally arrived on the stage the Universe had pointed the spotlight on for me.

"I love this for you!" my mom had gushed. "Working in books . . . being a designer . . . how perfect for you."

To grow this newfound pursuit, I needed to build a portfolio and a website. But before I had the chance to do that, my vision got kicked up a notch.

The author whose cover I designed met another author at a conference who was looking for a cover designer for *her* new book. He referred her to me, and I scored my second gig. Only after I did the cover, she wanted to know if I could do the interior too.

"I've talked to layout people," she told me. "But none of them do the complex book I'm doing. You get my vision, so if you're up for it, I think you'd do a great job with your design sense."

Design a book interior?! I squealed inside. *You want me to do* your *book as my first one ever?* I had never thought about designing a book interior, and this prospect ignited a whole new spark in me. In short, I ended up creating this client's cover and interior, and she loved it. And then another client—one of New York's leading executive coaches—came from that client. This woman had the resources to hire any professional she wanted, and to my surprise and delight, she picked *me*. I flipped! The Universe was definitely working its magic, and it wasn't long before more swirled around me.

"Do you do editorial work too?" this new client asked.

Can this really be happening? I wondered. *Can this be my next chap-*

ter? Being a book designer AND editor? I was honest and told her that I'd never done it professionally, but that I'd been born to be an editor with my love of the written word, nerdy obsession with grammatical rules, reading language-related books for fun, and possessing a sort of "musical ear" for how sentences best danced with each other. Plus, I'd done writing projects and edited people's work multiple times, just never for money. I told her that if she was willing to hire me to prove myself for that part of her project and wasn't happy, she wouldn't have to pay me.

She agreed—and in executing every part of that book project, I had never felt so aligned with my gifts. She not only happily paid me, but she wrote me a glowing endorsement.

I set my sights on becoming a top-notch editor and book designer by embarking on further self-study to hone my skills. In the process, I discovered that the majority of editors were like me: not formally educated in the craft of editing, but rather they boasted a particular penchant and talent when it came to the written word. They were predominately self-taught in the mechanics, and often took courses or workshops, but were otherwise simply blessed with a gift. Thrilled to finally align with this calling, I fell completely in love with this "work" and couldn't believe how fulfilling it was.

It seemed a brilliant, providential light had indeed been shone on me, obliterating my darkest hour at long last. The Universe hadn't been trying to break me with all the rejections; it had been pushing me to reinvent myself so I could finally utilize these gifts lying in wait, which I never would have had the motivation to do if I had gotten any of the jobs I'd been considered for. I now saw the whole serendipitous path clearly and was awash with gratitude for the fresh direction my life had taken.

Unfortunately, the ominous cloud that had hovered over Dana and me for so long, the one I thought had only been affecting us, had —for different reasons—stationed itself without my knowledge above my mom in Santa Fe.

Her Darkest Hour

Besides Dana and me, no one was more ecstatic about my new-found career than my mom. Seeing me use gifts that had been dormant to a degree and that I was developing with such excitement brought her immense joy. Every book I edited and designed, I also facilitated the publishing for, and I became committed to producing self-published books with the same level of excellence as books from traditional houses. As I continued to hone my skills, I quickly became a rare "one-stop-shop" partner for authors of all types.

But as I was bursting forth in my new passions, my mom was falling inward, hiding an ever-growing depression. For months, she hadn't wanted to add to my deflation, so she had kept her own dispiritedness tightly locked inside. But I could tell something wasn't right with her and finally dragged it out of her on the phone one day.

"I feel trapped," she confessed. "I'm not comfortable going out anymore, so Rick is doing all the shopping and errands. I order certain things online, but I basically don't go anywhere. I can't even get up our driveway to get the mail because I can't use the walker in the gravel. I look at my life and wonder what happened to me. I feel like a prisoner in my own body."

My heart cracked in two. "Oh my gosh . . . I'm *so* sorry. How long have you felt this way?"

"A while."

The lilt in her voice told me that "a while" meant a pretty long time, and because I'd been mired in my own muck for well over a year, she'd kept it to herself so she wouldn't upset me.

"You're not going out at all?"

"Not really. I hate being stared at, and I hate being dependent on people to help me. And I really can't shop by myself. I just never imagined I would be this person."

Though the source of my defeat and deflation hadn't been exactly the same, I related to those feelings on a deep level. I had never imagined my young, vibrant mom being reduced to this state either.

"How's Rick been with you?" I asked her.

"He's picked up the slack and does what he can, but there's just no real connection between us. We live such separate lives mostly. We go to Mike and Deb's for dinner sometimes, but that's about it. He says he loves me, but you know I don't feel the same."

"I know." Then I ventured, "Well, it's not too late for you guys to split up, you know. You shouldn't stay in the marriage if you're miserable."

"With my situation what it is? There's no way. I don't see how I'll ever be able to be independent again. I'm stuck. And neither of us would want to leave our house. So this is my life now. I have to get used to it."

After everything my mom had done to support me over the past year and a half, both financially and morally, I couldn't believe that *I* was getting this remarkable opportunity to reinvent myself while my mom was shrinking into herself as if she'd stepped in quicksand with no one around to pull her out.

Eager to do whatever I could to shift her mindset, I had the idea of buying her a journal for Mother's Day that year—one that I would write encouraging messages in at the bottom of the pages so that she'd have my words to lift her as she used the journal herself. Dana and I had become immersed in the Law of Attraction and positive affirmations, along with our much more health-focused eating regimen, over the past couple years, and even though my mom was on that journey with us, it was clear she wasn't using these techniques to pull herself out of her funk—or to hasten her healing. At least it seemed like she wasn't.

I found the perfect journal for this project, with a beautiful cover that said "Everything you can imagine is real." Then I wrote her the following letter on the first page:

Bree ~

This is a place for you to write down your daily list of goals so that you can feel a sense of accomplishment for tending well to yourself . . .

But I wanted this journal to be more than that for you . . .

I wanted you to also receive words of inspiration and encouragement, knowing how important it is for you to hear those things regularly.

So I hope you'll find my periodic reminders strengthening and smile-inducing . . .

I believe in your power to heal yourself . . . and that everything you can imagine is real.

I love you,

Doob xo

The journal had 160 pages, and I wrote a message at the bottom of every fourth page, which meant she received forty energizing messages, such as:

"Every day, you are writing the story of your healing."

"Everyone – and I mean everyone – is on your side."

"Of all you possess to heal yourself, your mind is the most powerful (and the right foods are a close second!).

"Create a statement of intention and repeat it daily until it becomes something you can't NOT say."

You get the idea. Maybe her mobility wasn't getting *too* much worse, but the depression was definitely getting the better of her, and I hoped this journal would help. She had also gained about twenty pounds, which she was bemoaning loudly. She'd always been fairly thin, and being overweight was adding to her desolation. So, I found a picture of a highly fit celebrity putting on running shoes, and I photoshopped my mom's head onto her body so that she could easily visualize herself well, trim, and completely mobile again.

When she received her gifts, she gushed over them as always and deeply appreciated the time and thought that went into creating them. But I couldn't help but wonder how much she was taking all my advice to heart. Before we hung up, she said, "This is all wonderful and so helpful. *Thank you.*" She paused. "But just knowing *you're* doing well does a lot for my heart. As long as I have you to boost my spirits and make me laugh, I'll be okay. I'll just live vicariously through you."

And into my court the ball returned—until something beyond my control woke my mom up.

⚮

A Loss and a Gain

*I*n November of 2014, after several mini-strokes he'd managed to recover from, my grandpa landed in the hospital again. Only this time, it became apparent that his body was finally tired of bouncing back. My mom flew out, we brought my grandpa home with hospice, and within a week he passed away on December 1, at the age of ninety-two, with me holding his hand and all of us surrounding him.

My wonderful grandpa had been a truly magnanimous patriarch: he was the rock who had always been there for his kids and me, and after my grandma died, he had sweetly taken over the family traditions my grandma had always been in charge of: buying us birthday and Valentine's cards, dyeing eggs and making us Easter baskets, and stuffing the stockings and buying us Christmas gifts, even as adults. (Yes, I still celebrated these holidays as a Jew because I believed it was more important to partake in these cherished traditions with my family, none of which were religious for us, than to stand on ceremony over them.) He generously offered to pay for the fixings to cook—or order—the holiday dinners Bree or Dana made for the family, and he was consistently at the ready with one of his goofy jokes or stories of mischief from his boyhood.

We all felt his absence and the heartbreaking close of a long chapter in our lives, but my mom felt a particular sense of abandonment.

"I'm an orphan now," she lamented. "It's the weirdest feeling. It doesn't matter how old you are when you lose your last parent, you feel like an orphan."

My mom and grandpa had always been close. He was a genial, loving father who had swiftly gotten past the pregnancy bomb and been easy-going and supportive ever since. He had sent her flowers every Mother's Day, and he had sympathized with her when she confided, after my grandma passed away, that she had found her birth mother and that the connection hadn't been exactly what she'd hoped. And now that parental touchstone for my mom was no longer physically with us.

During this time of loss, my mom of course stayed with us. It had been a while since she'd come out, and she found using the walker in our house to be a nuisance. We had narrower walkways than she did in Santa Fe, and so she parked the walker in the garage and decided to try using our furniture to steady her from room to room. Amazingly this worked, and the walker remained in the garage for the entire trip. She even managed the stairs, though with a slow climb, which she didn't have in her Santa Fe house.

After my mom ditched her walker during that trip to see us, she decided she was going to ditch it altogether. If she could use furniture and walls to steady herself at our house, she could do the same at hers. And she had grown tired of letting her limited mobility keep her at home—and dependent on Rick—much more than she liked. The fear that was instilled in her after the fall at the airport had resided there far too long, and she simply decided to kick that fear to the curb. She boldly donated her walker, got a walking stick in case she needed it, and tenaciously taught herself to take steps as steadily as she could. When she wanted to go grocery shopping by herself, she parked near the carts or asked if someone could bring her one, using that as her stability device; when she wanted to go on outings with her girlfriends, they happily offered their arm.

But she didn't attribute this revisited semi-independence solely to her own tenacity.

Though she hadn't been inclined to ask my departed grandma for anything, she did appeal to both her parents once my grandpa was gone. She told me that after returning home, she had asked them out loud to please help her get her life back. After that plea, she sincerely believed they had come together to give her the strength and resolve she needed to regain her mobility. She still struggled to some degree, and she didn't have extended stamina, but for someone diagnosed with MS to go from a walker to an occasional cane or no steadying crutch at all—*not* from a walker to a wheelchair—was remarkable indeed.

That kind of magic had happened before for us—you'll recall my grandma and the great electricity episode of 1999—and now it seemed my mom was finally getting some magic of her own.

Delayed Revelations

*T*he next time my mom came to visit, she was still sans walker. She wasn't the steadiest person on her feet, but by gum, she was one determined sister to no longer need a crutch (unless it was a person, which we were all happy to provide when needed).

You'll recall that when I was a child, whenever my mom came to school, my friends always commented on how pretty and cool she was —and I reveled in having a mom who attracted such positive attention. In fact, we tended to attract attention pretty much everywhere we went together during the years I was growing up, and even beyond. Although we looked nothing alike in our facial features (I mostly favored my dad from eyes to chin), we both had long, light blond hair and lean figures. Those two qualities, plus our hard-to-pinpoint age difference, seemed to always spark people to ask how we were related. A common conversation would go like this:

Outsider: "Are you two sisters?"

Me: "No, she's my mom."

Outsider: "Your *mom*? *NO*. She's your daughter?"

Bree: "She is." (Big smile)

Outsider: "But you don't look old enough to be her mother."

Bree: "I'm almost not."

Outsider: (Head tilt)

Me: "We're only sixteen years apart."

Outsider: (Eyes wide) "You don't even look that far apart."

Bree *and* Me: (Big smiles) "Thank you."

We had sustained ourselves on this diet of compliments for a few decades, and I'll be truthful, it never got old. My mom always looked young for her age, and I loved seeing her glow from the surprise on people's faces. But now, her affected mobility made her feel old. Her face still looked young, and we still got asked sometimes if we were sisters, but my mom felt she had "fallen" a bit in my eyes. This, of course, was ridiculous; that thought never crossed my mind.

Just after my grandpa's funeral, the three of us were craving a distraction from our grief and decided to watch a movie. Part of the storyline was that one of the kids was bullied. When the movie was over, my mom said, "That poor little girl. I was bullied like that. It was so awful."

"What?" I said, as if she'd just told me she was a natural redhead.

"Oh yeah. Not so much in elementary school, but in junior high. I dreaded going to school because of the bullying. Kids were relentless. They stole my lunch, made fun of me, chased me home . . . it was horrible. I had no self-esteem at all."

I sat dumbfounded. After all these years of our open relationship, she had never told me anything about being bullied like that.

"That's terrible. Didn't you tell anyone you were being terrorized?"

"No, I guess I didn't think anyone would do anything about it. I didn't want Grandma to think I was more of a burden than I already was. And I didn't want to bother Grandpa with it. He always worked so hard and had that long commute to LA every day. So I just suffered through it."

My mouth dropped open. "That breaks my heart for you. I had no idea." She shrugged. "But I don't understand. When I was growing up, I never saw you as anything but a glowing, confident person. How did you go from having no self-esteem to being the mom I wanted to flaunt everywhere we went?"

She smiled and said softy, "Because I had *you*. People were always drawn to your white-blond hair . . . and you were always so smart. And *I* was the mother of that extraordinary child, which made *me* feel extraordinary."

I couldn't believe what I was hearing. "I never realized it felt like that for you."

She nodded. "It did. Within a year after having you, everything changed. What felt like the worst thing happening to me as a teenager turned out to be the best thing that ever happened to me."

After all the things we'd shared with each other—even after she told people regularly that *I* had raised *her*, that I had just "popped out" the way I was and she didn't have much to do with it, or that I'd always "danced to my own drummer" despite how she "tried to corrupt me"— this declaration was particularly touching to me.

"I'm serious," she said. "I believe I was headed for a really bad path. But you stopped me from going there."

"What do you mean 'a bad path'?"

"Well, after being bullied so badly, and not being very happy at home during that time . . . with Grandma's and my relationship the way it was . . . and her smoking I hated . . . I think I would have dropped out of school, or maybe finished high school, and then become a stripper."

"A *stripper*? Why?"

"Because the only thing I had going for me was my nice figure. That was the one thing I thought I could capitalize on. But then I got pregnant, and my body got ruined . . ."

She shot me a sarcastic smirk and I mirrored it back.

"But seriously," she continued, "if I hadn't gotten pregnant with you, I really think I would have become some kind of exotic dancer, and who knows what might have happened to me."

I thought about that for a moment, hating the idea that she would have felt that was her best option, and how demeaning it would have ultimately been.

"So you really think I saved you?"

"I don't *think* you saved me," she said with complete honesty. "I *know* you saved me."

Secrets and Lies and Genes, Oh My

℘ropelled by persistent questions my mom couldn't shake, in early 2016 she bought herself the gift that can open a can of worms: a heredity kit.

Aletha had told my mom that she was one-eighth Cherokee Indian, which my mom thought was immensely cool, even if that meant she only got one-sixteenth of it. So besides wanting to see evidence of that tidbit on paper, my mom was curious what she got from her elusive birth daddy. To remind you what Aletha had written on the paperwork my mom received from the Department of Social Services: her birth father was of Anglo-Saxon ethnic descent, of the Protestant faith, with blue eyes and dark hair. But Aletha had also said she was twenty-six at the time of my mom's birth when she was really twenty-eight (why fib about two years?) and that she'd had only one brother, when later she told my mom she had several brothers and sisters. Again, why?

These fabrications had piqued my mom's interest in what else Aletha might not be honest about. She hadn't been terribly forthcoming about her past during their conversations, and her insistence that she knew very little about my mom's birth father had always seemed a bit suspect. But my mom was decidedly not prepared for the report she got back six weeks later.

On March 31, I received this text from my mom:

"I'm a Jew!"

Me: ???

Her: Check your email for details. No Native American showed up. Strange.

Me: OY (apparently your word now as well). Did you do a DNA analysis through ancestry.com?

Her: Yes. So obviously you've been a Jew all along!

Me: Wow! Very interesting! I just looked at your ethnic results . . . so fascinating!!! I wonder why no Cherokee? But it's something that your ancestry is mostly European Jewish. No wonder I was drawn back to my people!

Her: Maybe that's why I've struggled with faith all along. I was looking in the wrong place, never imagining I was Jewish! Please do this DNA thing too . . . I'm so curious what yours will show. 😂

Wow, I'm a Jew! Interesting too that Aletha married a Jew and never told me. What in the world is going on here?!!!

Me: It's getting more curious by the minute. Those papers she filled out said your dad was a Protestant. ??

Her: I know. But I have to wonder if Meyer is my bio dad.

Me: What? I thought he came later.

Her: They married about a year after I was born. There are so many possible scenarios here. Maybe he was in the Korean War and when he came home they got back together. Who knows!

Me: Whoa . . . the fact that she kept you such a secret could explain Meyer being your father and her never telling him. This is curiouser and curiouser . . .

Her: I have a little info about him somewhere. I'm going to investigate. Wowsa, what a morning! It's hard to know what the truth is here. Maybe she did tell him after all was said and done. Maybe he found out about me after I had been adopted. The plot thickens . . .

Me: The plot definitely thickens!

Her: I wish you were here. I'm finding all kinds of stuff!

Me: Wish I were there too!

Her: I'm something now and that makes me happy. We're little blonde Jewish girls from Europe and that's that!

Me: Who knew?

Her: I think I'll change my name to Briana Jane Aaronson. Do you agree?

Me: That would be a lot of name changes for you, but I like it a lot. 😊

A little while later . . .

Her: How about this! I'm looking around in ancestry.com and found the military enlistment for Meyer. He was blonde! BLONDE!

Me: What??!! And Aletha said your birth father had dark hair. Another weird fib! Are you sure Meyer is your bio dad?

Her: Yep. He has to be. The dots are all finally connecting. Aletha sure went to a lot of trouble to keep secrets. And I don't think I'll ever know why.

Me: Grandma died with a lot of secrets too. I think in both cases, we're probably better off not knowing what they were.

Her: Amen to that, sister. 😊

❦

Another Chapter Closes

*D*ana and I had lived in my mom's wonderful Nantucket house for nine years now, and while we were beyond grateful, we had also been craving a change. Having lived in Southern California all my life (except for my third-grade year up north), I never thought I would leave. I loved the weather and our proximity to Disneyland, Hollywood, Scripps (where we loved to go visit), and everything else that made So-Cal a wonderful place to live. But Dana missed the season changes of the midwest (not all the harsh weather, mind you, just the seasons), and I had to admit that I was growing tired of it taking forever to get anywhere because all the cities were so heavily populated. So, we had started investigating other places we might live in the US, and we fell in love with the idea of moving to Washington—the Evergreen State.

As always, my mom completely supported our desire to experience a different landscape, and being a tree lover herself, she delighted in the idea of Washington. We'd loved living in her darling neighborhood, but the houses were also right on top of each other. We lived high up on a hill, but from that vantage point, the view was of the sprawling port of Los Angeles. Yes, the ocean was only a few minutes away in the opposite direction, but we never went to the beach, and both Dana and I realized what we really wanted in our next chapter together was trees, wildlife, serenity, and a slower-paced life.

I had no intention, though, of moving while my grandpa was still alive. With my mom in New Mexico, I didn't want to leave him. But he'd been gone now for over a year, and my mom was finally ready to sell her house and send us north with her enthusiastic blessing.

After making a trip to Whidbey Island and deciding it was definitely where we wanted to live, we waited fourteen months for that "just right" rental home to pop up—a small but lovely west-facing A-frame with enormous windows that looked out to Puget Sound and the Olympic mountains, with a sizable basement for storage, a large, beautiful loft for an office, and plentiful deer that roamed the land of our quiet cul-de-sac. In the meantime, we orchestrated—at her request and expense—the remodeling of my mom's kitchen, along with some other home improvements to get the house ready to sell, which felt like the least we could do after all she'd done for us. Dana also packed a lot of our things to signal to the Universe that we were indeed ready for this significant change.

While my mom was completely on board, and had said multiple times that she had no desire to move back to LA, selling her house proved to be a highly emotional transaction. A lovely woman and her two grown daughters ended up buying it, which warmed my mom's heart, but it also brought the end of this era to a tearful close. That house had symbolized my mom's professional success, which reflected her personal success too. Far from the exotic dancer she feared she might become, or the many jobs she'd held in her early-adult years to make ends meet, she had been named salesperson of the year more than once in her fifteen-year career with the fine paper company, which was no small accomplishment. The long-term relationships she had cultivated with her accounts had afforded her the kind of life she had dreamed of, and the house was an enormous part of that dream. She had used her design talents to make it a warm and welcoming space inside, and used her flair for landscaping to create an outdoor sanctum. She had raised, and lost, several beloved kitties there; embraced Dana into her heart there; shared laughter with cherished friends there. It had replaced my grandparents' house as the family gathering space for holidays, and it had been our saving grace during my dark night of the soul.

Now, after serving its deeply appreciated role in our lives, the house stood poised to welcome a new family under its eaves, to be their protector, their stability, their sanctuary.

On August 14, 2016, with my dad at the wheel of our U-Haul, and us with our two kitties in our SUV, Dana and I drove down Nantucket Lane for the last time. As we did, I felt my heartstrings tugged hard, not so much for our lives in California because I was ready for our new adventure, but because of how much the house had meant to my mom, and to us. Even though I knew she didn't want to return to LA, I liked that it was there for her, like a lighthouse in a storm—because I could sense that's what was brewing for her in Santa Fe, and I wished so much she could come back to her safe haven, if only as a stop where she could begin a new chapter.

∞

A Trip Through the Wormhole

Once the escrow closed on the Nantucket house, my mom officially had no plan B for leaving her marriage. Though moving back, as you know, was never *her* plan B, I still believed it was a viable option, even if it was only temporary. For a brief time, she entertained the idea of buying a small condo—since that was all she would be able to afford—if she and Rick went their separate ways and sold their house. I knew it would feel like a step backward in certain ways, but I also knew that regaining her independence could certainly outweigh that, and I gave her my genuine encouragement toward that end. She also entertained the fantasy, after visiting us for the first time over her birthday in 2017, of moving to Washington to be near us. She loved the landscape of Santa Fe, but she loved the trees and the weather of Whidbey, and she delighted in the deer that frolicked daily on our property. She went so far as to check real estate listings on the island for a while. But, after exploring all of these options, she ultimately decided to remain under the same roof with Rick and try to make the best of it.

Feeling her resignation on the phone one day, I suggested having a reading with my dear friend, Susan, a gifted intuitive and medium.

"Maybe she can tap into some things for you," I offered, "to help you see the bigger picture. Maybe it would make you feel better about your situation since you've decided to stay."

"I'm totally up for that . . . but I don't even know what I'd ask her."

"Well, maybe you could talk about what Rick's purpose is in your life . . . your mother wounds . . . or about us . . . whatever comes to you in the moment."

My mom liked the idea and made an upcoming appointment.

"You have to call me right afterward," I said. "I want to hear everything!"

"You know it, girl . . . I'll call you the minute I hang up with her."

That day, their session was supposed to last for one hour, so when that passed, and then *another* hour passed, I started to wonder what was up. But I didn't want to interrupt if they were still immersed, so I didn't call. Finally, three hours later, my phone rang.

"I *just* got off the call," she said. "Susan had so many things shown to her during our session that the time just flew."

"Wow. I can't wait to hear!"

"Well, for starters, you and I have been together before, just like we've always believed."

"Well, there's a big surprise."

"I know. But get this . . . we were *twins*."

"Really?"

"Yes. It was during medieval times. She said we were identical, and that having two girls during that time was seen as a curse or something, so we were kept in a tower together, alone. Only one of us got let out, so we would switch places to relieve each other's burdens."

"Whoa. Kind of like how we switch between our mother and daughter roles in this life."

"I guess so. Isn't that a trip? She said we were crafty, resourceful, and older than our age."

"That sounds like us! But it's so deep too . . . the whole idea of relieving each other's burdens. I wonder if we've done that in other lives together too."

"I wouldn't doubt it. Look how we are together. I wouldn't be surprised if you've been my mother before."

"Oh, I wouldn't doubt that either. But Susan didn't pick up on that, huh?"

"No . . . but that doesn't mean we haven't been. And that's not even the most profound part. She said we made a pact to always find each other 'from here to eternity.'"

My heart swelled. "Oh my gosh . . . I *love* that. We've always felt that kind of connection . . . and now to hear that we actually made that pact centuries ago? That's amazing."

"I know. I'm not surprised, but to hear it just brought us so full circle to me."

"Like the last time we were souls together, we said, 'Okay, see you soon!'"

She laughed. "And you just swooped in the first chance you got, didn't you? I didn't even have a chance to grow up. First time I had sex, you were like, 'I'm comin' down!'"

I cracked up, then said cheekily, "I guess I didn't want to wait because I thought you needed me."

I could hear the smile in her voice when she said, "How right you were."

I took in the serendipity for a moment. "So what else did she reveal to you?"

"She asked me who Lucy was. I told her it was Lucille, my mom. She said, 'I'm getting that Lucille is the self-appointed CEO of the first level of heaven, which is closest to the human level, so that she can look after her baby birds.'"

"Her baby birds? That's us! How sweet!"

"I know. She also said that she was burdened in her childhood and left with a lot of secrets."

"Well, we've always known that."

"And she said, 'Things were different with Stacey. Do you know what that means?' And I said, 'Oh yes . . . I know exactly what that means.'"

"This is so fascinating! I love that she saw Grandma, and that she's looking out for us. That must warm your heart too."

"It does. And I *have* believed that she *and* Grandpa have helped me regain my mobility."

"And your intuition was right." I paused. "I know you've always kind of questioned it because of your childhood, but I know Grandma loved you deeply. I really believe she had her own burdens that had nothing to do with you."

"I think I'm starting to see that too."

"I hope so." Then I jumped to the other topic I was curious about. "What about Rick? What did she have to say about your marriage?"

"Ha! We never even talked about him. Between talking about us being twins, and Grandma, and Aletha, and other interesting things that came up, I forgot to even ask. And anyway, I got what I wanted most."

"What was that?"

"Knowing that you and I made a pact to find each other from here to eternity."

∞

Milestone

T he dawning of 2019 meant only one thing worth talking about. On January 7th, I sent my mom the following text:

Holy merde . . . six weeks from today, I'm going to turn 50!

Which my mom followed with:

Not so, my beloved, I'm claiming 50! That leaves you at 34, Dayni at 36, and me feeling much better about the whole thing!

I countered:

LOL! Ok then . . . I'll take 34, which actually makes Dayni 41, and you 50. It's all mindset anyway, right?

She volleyed:

No no no! It freaks me out to have a daughter in her 40s. Dayn goes back to 36 . . . right away!

All kidding aside, I was taking my milestone birthday very seriously, not in terms of age, but in terms of celebration. A week later, I texted her:

I've decided to have a Five-Day 50th Birthday Extravaganza . . . a day of fun for each decade! I'm masterminding it now 😁

A few hours later, my masterminding had birthed more ideas for experiencing new places than a mere five days could hold.

Me: I think I might need a week off now for my bday extravaganza . . . and why not? I almost NEVER take vacations.

Her: Well rock on, birthday girl! I'm going to want to see your itinerary!

The next day, I typed out all of our thrilling plans for each day of my birthday week—including the new organic restaurants I'd found to eat at near every venue—beginning on February 14th, building up to the crescendo on the 18th, and keeping the celebratory momentum strong until the 20th.

Her: My goodness, how fun! Excellent birthday week plans. You're really doing it up right to turn 34. 😜

When the make-merry week arrived, Dana and I indeed reveled in one pleasureful day after another: exploring the LeMay Car Museum, roaming the antique haven of Snohomish and the shopping mecca of Bellevue, taking in Rock of Ages at a theater in Seattle, and more. Then, on the morning of the milestone, I received this text from my mom at 7:22 a.m.:

Well, 50 years ago right now I was screaming my head off . . .

Until 8:47 . . .

You're out! OMG, you're a girl! A real babydoll for me. Now what??? 👶🤍

I hated thinking of her screaming her head off, but her words *did* crack me up. *Now what???* I knew that was exactly how she'd felt.

And it *did* seem incredible to think we had spent half a century on the Earth together in this lifetime—five decades of her messing with my head, me trying to keep her on the straight and narrow; her trudging through countless valleys, me offering my hand to pull her out; me groping through the dark year of my soul, her being an indisputable reason I made it to the light; me experiencing great joys, her being by my side for the biggest ones; us being apart, us being together; her gifting me with total acceptance and freedom, me reveling in it; the list went on and on.

But as much as this particular week had been about celebrating this milestone age I had reached, and as much fun as Dana and I had every place we had chosen to visit, the best part was the trip home every day, headed back to our little island, when we called my mom and shared every detail of our latest adventure. Reliving the moments with her, from the seemingly mundane to the magical, and knowing how much it meant to her to be as much a part of it all as she possibly could, made the whole sublime week that much sweeter.

On February 25th, I received this text:

> So, if it's not too much trouble, I would greatly appreciate if you and The Dayn took another week to explore more places and dine some more. You see, I miss my dailies!

I knew she had loved those calls from us, but I had no idea just how meaningful they truly were until August of that year.

A Crushing Blow,
a Hopeful Plan

*B*y the summer of 2019, I'd heard my mom bemoan being bloated more times than I could count. As far back as May 30th, I have text messages saying "My tummy is pretty sore and distended." We'd gone back and forth about what it could be—what she was eating, the need for a digestive enzyme, a reaction to gluten or lactose, etc. But while it would go away for a bit, it would flair up again. I'd had bloating issues at times in the past, and we chalked it up to certain food choices. But after trying to uncover her culprit, we kept coming up short.

By this time, Dana and I had long ago transitioned away from a Western medicine mentality and were firmly ensconced in food as medicine, which included eating almost 100% organic and very few processed foods, taking a handful of top-quality supplements and tonic herbs, drinking lots of healthy water, and regular detoxification. My mom had jumped on this train with us too, but she wasn't *quite* as devout about the food and detoxing. I didn't want to harp on it, but I couldn't help but be concerned that her body needed a serious detox, simply from living for so many years without doing one. She'd done colonics in the past, but it had been years. So this persistent bloating was beginning to worry me.

During the second week of August, my mom told me that the bloating had gotten so bad that she was having horrible pain.

"I look like I'm six months pregnant," she said.

"Well, we know *that's* not it," I joked.

She laughed, but said, "I wish I *could* give birth to whatever this is and stop feeling so miserable."

The next logical thing I had to ask was, "Are you constipated?"

"Constipated? Oh, honey," she joked, "I'm beyond constipated."

"Why? How long has it been?"

"Oh . . . a week . . . maybe ten days."

"What?! That's so unhealthy for you! No wonder you feel awful. Have you tried that poopy tea of yours to loosen things up?"

"I've tried it all. Even laxatives, which I know you don't approve of."

"I don't. But even that didn't help?"

"Not really. And the pain's just getting so intense."

She was actually moaning between some of her sentences and catching her breath, and I realized this was progressing way beyond a gluten intolerance or being dehydrated. "Maybe you need to go to emergency," I said. "Or an urgent care clinic."

"I think maybe you're right. But Rick's not home, and neither is Deb. Maybe I'll go tomorrow."

"Do you think you'll be okay until tomorrow? You sound like you're in so much pain. I'm really worried about you."

"I know. I'm worried too. I just don't want to have to go to the hospital."

The next day, Saturday, August 17th, my mom was still in pain and I begged her to go to the urgent care, at least. Deb was able to drive her, and Dana and I sent her heartfelt healing energy as I waited for a report.

Later that morning, my mom called to tell me that she had an obstruction in her bowel, and that she'd had a horrible accident while waiting for the doctor. A massive rush of diarrhea had flowed out of her, as if a dam had burst from her insides.

"They're taking me to the hospital for surgery," she told me.

At the time, I didn't understand how she could have released what seemed to be the obstruction, yet still required surgery. But we didn't have time to discuss it. They were already whisking her off.

"Rick or Deb will call you," she said before hanging up.

A few hours passed before I received a text from Rick, telling me that my mom had gone into surgery to remove the obstruction from her colon and release the pressure, and that the operation should only last about an hour. I asked what hospital she was in and told him I was going to fly out on Monday. He gave me the name but also said my mom thought it might be best if I waited to come out until she came home. I wanted to be there to support her and didn't like the idea of waiting, but I agreed to hold off booking a flight until I was able to talk to her.

A few hours later, my mom called me. She didn't sound good, and I didn't think it was only because she was groggy from the anesthetic.

"The doctor was just here," she said. She took an audible breath. "He said I was really close to dying. If I'd waited another day, I'd probably be dead."

"Oh my God. I *knew* you were in trouble." I swallowed hard. "That's the second time that's happened to you . . . being saved in the nick of time."

"I know."

The line fell silent, then I heard her breathe like she was crying.

"Doob," she said, her voice breaking. "He told me I have cancer." Her fear reached out and gripped me, as if seeking a steady place to land.

"Okay," I said calmly. "Where?"

"In my colon . . . and my liver."

You would think that in that moment, I'd be awash with fear myself. But to my immense good fortune, Dana and I had watched the powerful and eye-opening *The Truth About Cancer* docu-series when it premiered in 2015, and we had continued to get educated on the cancer "industry" ever since. I knew how patients were manipulated into toxic treatments, and there was evidence that those treatments were frequently the ones to ultimately cause metastases and end patients' lives. I had learned that statistics were skewed and that Big Pharma was giving huge incentives to doctors to prescribe chemo. But most importantly, I knew that cancer was not the death sentence that society had been duped for decades to believe. In most cases, it came down to the body being toxically overburdened from one source or another, cells mutating into cancer as a result, and that the cancer was merely the body's "voice" speaking to it in symptoms saying, "something's wrong here . . . I need help getting back into balance." Further, these mutations had virtually nothing to do with genetics, again as society had been duped to believe. Yet, oncologists, by and large, weren't focusing on this reality. Instead, they routinely told patients that poisoning the body with chemicals, or cutting off the affected body parts, was the way to "kill" the cancer cells. I, however, knew this couldn't be further from the truth.

With complete calm and confidence, I told my mom, "Okay. I know you're scared. But remember we know that cancer is *not* a death sentence. Your body is brilliant and was designed to heal itself. This is just your body telling you it needs help. We'll figure it out. Just don't worry about anything, okay?"

To be honest, my biggest concern was how the doctors were going to swoop in any minute to fill her with fear and lay out the toxic protocol they believed she had to start immediately, and I told my mom this.

"They've already done that," my mom confirmed. "Some asshole doctor came in and started pushing his chemo and radiation speech on me. I said, 'I'm not doing that.' And he basically made me feel like I was an idiot. He had no compassion whatsoever. You know me, I don't like to cry in front of people, but the way he talked to me . . . he made me so upset. I actually said to him, 'I want you to leave.'"

"I'm so glad you stood up for yourself. But what a jerk! Did he leave?"

"Yes, but he was shaking his head, saying, 'Fine, it's your life' with his hands thrown up."

"Screw him. Just stay strong in your convictions about refusing chemo. This is *your* decision, not the doctor's."

She tearfully said, "Okay," then added, "And I have a colostomy bag."

"I know . . . Deb told me. But it's only temporary, right?"

"I don't know. I hope so. I can't imagine having this for the rest of my life. But right now, I'm just so overwhelmed."

"I know you are. I'm coming out Monday. Is that okay?"

"Yes," she said, "good." Then she added, "Doob . . . I don't want to die. I *can't* leave my girls without a mommy."

"Well, then it's good that you're not dying. Because I can't imagine my life without you in it."

"You know I love you very much."

"I do. And I love *you* very much."

I heard a nurse in the background and my mom told me she had to go.

After we hung up, I immediately jumped into rescue mode. During *The Truth About Cancer* docuseries, Dr. Tony Jimenez and his cutting-edge non-toxic treatment center in Mexico called Hope4Cancer was featured. Seeing the multitude of ways they bolstered, not suppressed, the immune system with holistic therapies had stayed with me. And they didn't only focus on the physical—they understood that emotional and spiritual health had just as much to do with a person's healing, so they focused on those elements at the clinic too. Sadly, these remarkable, strengthening therapies, none of which had any negative side effects, weren't "approved" in the States. I knew there were some quack clinics in Mexico too, but this one was the real deal, and I had mentally filed it in the back of my mind should anyone I loved ever need it.

Now, that time had come.

I found the clinic's website, read more about the protocols, and watched some videos. Feeling completely aligned with this being right for my mom, I sent in a patient inquiry form so that I could be ready with all the details when I saw her. I even had a phone consult on my mom's behalf. I explained that when the surgeon opened my mom up, he found two tumors blocking the lower colon, but his priority was saving her life, which meant diverting the colon above the blockage with a colostomy, not attempting to remove the cancerous ones below. He had also discovered a large mass in her liver, along with what appeared to be several cysts. While he believed the liver cysts were likely benign, and he didn't biopsy any of the tumors during surgery, he felt certain that they were cancerous. The rep from Hope4Cancer told me that in my mom's situation, biopsies were often detrimental because cells can be disrupted and released throughout the body during the procedure. I was relieved, as I didn't know if my mom would need biopsies to be admitted to the program, and now I knew it was good she didn't have any. The rep went over all the immune-boosting treatments my mom would be able to receive, and while it was going to be a significant investment for the three-week intensive, I knew my mom had the money in her nest egg—and I had every confidence the expense would be worth it.

On the morning I was supposed to leave for Santa Fe (Dana was staying home with Shaia Luna, our senior kitty who was in delicate health), Dana woke up with horrible pain in her jaw from a problematic molar we were hoping to save. I couldn't believe the timing, but there was no way I could leave her to face a surgery alone. So, I postponed my trip a day and rushed Dana to our biological dentist in Seattle, where she ended up needing an emergency extraction. With her back home safely, and with her own healing protocol she assured me she could handle, I left the following morning to go see my mom.

When I arrived at the hospital, I poked my head around the door jamb and said, "Did someone order a daughter?"

"Yes! I did!" my mom said all bubbly. "Hi, honey." She reached out her arms and I gently fell into them. "I'm so glad you're here."

"Me too."

I pulled away and sat next to her.

"How's our Dayni?" she wanted to know.

"She's actually doing really well. She felt so bad about delaying my trip, but I'm so glad I was there to take her."

"I'm so glad too." She spread her arms and gave the room a cursory glance. "And it's not like I was going anywhere. I'm just glad she's okay, poor girl."

"I know." I smiled. "You look so good!"

"Why, thank you."

"And you're in such good spirits."

She shrugged playfully. "You know me . . . wacky as ever."

"I'm so glad. I wasn't sure how you'd be feeling."

"Well, you told me not to worry and that you had a plan. So . . ."

I'd sent her the information about Hope4Cancer and encouraged her to watch some of the videos in hopes that the prospect of their natural healing therapies would obliterate some of her fear.

"Were you able to go to any of the links I sent?"

"I saw one video. The nurses come in and out of here constantly, so I'm always being interrupted. But the one I saw sure looked hopeful."

"Good, but I want you to see the rest too. I've already had a consult with them and they sent me a written protocol proposal so you can see all the amazing therapies they offer."

She shook her head with an impish grin. "When you said you'd figure it out, you went straight to it, didn't you? Just like always."

I smiled and she clasped my hand.

"Thank you, honey. I could never be facing this without you."

"Well," I said, squeezing her hand tenderly, "luckily, you don't have to."

Stark Realization

*D*eb had dropped me off at the hospital the evening before, and Rick had picked me up after my visit and driven me back to their house. He was used to being in bed by 8:00 every night, and it was already past 9:00, so he went straight to his room, and I went straight to the office that doubled as a guest room on the other side of the house, next to my mom's room. I used the guest bathroom, then changed and crashed on the pull-out bed. Dana and I talked for a while—I got the scoop on how she was feeling from her surgery, and I shared how good my mom looked and how "herself" she was. Finally, we hung up and I fell asleep.

In the morning, Rick left early for work so I had the house to myself. My mom was supposed to come home that day, but probably not until late afternoon. So I planned to stay at the house, catch up on some emails, and tidy up her room and bathroom for her. I hadn't really looked around the night before—and I hadn't been to her house in several years because she preferred to come visit us—so it wasn't until the light of day that the reality of my mom's life hit me.

My mom had been feeling physically crappy for a good two weeks, so I didn't expect her normally clean and orderly house to be immaculate. Plus, Rick wasn't a housekeeping kind of guy, so it wasn't surprising to encounter some disarray on the surface—the living room coffee table piled with random items, loads of dirty dishes in the kitchen sink and on the counters, my mom's room and bathroom in a state of unusual clutter, that kind of thing. But it was what I encountered behind closed doors that set off my internal alarm.

When I opened the refrigerator, it was packed—only not solely with fresh food. Rick's mostly dried-up leftovers from take-out cluttered one shelf, while dozens of expired sauces, dressings, and the like surrounded them. There was some fresh produce and other healthy, unspoiled items, don't get me wrong. But it was as if my mom hadn't really inspected what was in her fridge for months, only added to it. The freezer and pantry reflected the same. This distressed me, no doubt, but that wasn't all. When I went to put clothes, towels, and toiletries away, most every closet and cabinet I opened were full to overflowing. I was immediately consumed by an abrupt and disquieting overwhelm that my beautiful mom, who had always taken such pride in her home and in herself, had, over time, become physically, emotionally, and spiritually buried in her own house.

As I changed her sheets, hung up her clothes, and cleaned her bathroom, I couldn't get the perplexity and despair I felt for my mom out of my head. Growing up, she had loathed that my grandma didn't keep house well, and that every corner was a cluttered disaster—so much so that she was too embarrassed to ever invite any friends over. In the apartments and houses she'd lived in as an adult, however, she was the exact opposite of my grandma. All of her homes had been neat, thoughtfully and creatively appointed, and filled with plants; her Santa Fe adobe was likewise decorated beautifully, and she had a wonderful housekeeper come twice a month to do the big stuff. But all of her lovely furniture, and her specially chosen art, and her treasured collected keepsakes belied that my mom had been injuriously depressed for much longer than I realized.

I ended up spending the entire day not only brightening up my mom's bedroom and bathroom, but her newly remodeled kitchen too, and I had just enough time to make the living room welcoming again before I had to go pick her up.

When we arrived home, she noticed right away how much cleaning up I'd done.

"I'm so embarrassed that you saw the house in such a mess," she said. "I haven't had Silvia here for a month . . . thank you for making everything look so nice, honey."

"I was glad to do it. And don't feel embarrassed. I know you weren't feeling well."

"I just hope you didn't clean my bathroom . . . then I'll *really* be embarrassed."

I scrunched my face, which said it all. "I did . . . but please don't worry about it. I couldn't let you come home without a fresh start."

"Ohhh," she said in her signature funny way, signifying that she was mildly mortified, moderately undeserving, and supremely grateful.

I decided that her first night home, after having barely survived this latest episode—and saddled with a colostomy she now had to be trained by a nurse to care for—was not the time to probe what had really been going on these last months that she wasn't telling me.

∞

Coming Clean

y mom was pretty spent that first night she was home and was craving uninterrupted sleep for the first time in days. But the next night, after Rick went to bed, my mom and I sat up talking. I could tell she still needed some time to digest what she'd been through, and the option of going to Mexico for holistic treatment, but I also knew it was the time to delicately broach the subject of the chaos I'd encountered behind the scenes of her life at home.

"I don't want you to think I was digging through your stuff," I said, "or disrespecting your privacy . . . but when I was cleaning up the house, I was really shocked to find how much stuff you have everywhere . . . your closets . . . the pantry . . . and it startled me because this isn't *you* . . . all this clutter." I put my hand on hers. "It really feels to me like you're *buried* here."

She nodded gently. "I *am*."

I exhaled solemnly. "When did this happen? You've never been the hoarder type."

"I know." Her eyes clouded with shame. "I've just been so depressed for such a long time. I guess I stopped seeing it."

My heart cracked in two. "Oh, Bree . . . I know you've been unhappy in the marriage, and that you've been depressed, but I didn't realize how bad it was."

She nodded again and looked away.

"I'm not proud to admit this," she began, "but for a long time, I've pretty much spent my days sitting right here on this couch, watching HGTV or shopping on my iPad, having a little vape in the afternoons and dreading hearing the garage door go up. I know it's not all Rick's fault, but I'm just so unhappy in this marriage." She turned to me. "The only highlight of my day is when you call."

I looked at her sitting there, imagining that being her daily routine, and felt a mixture of sorrow and disappointment flood me. *Why hadn't she left years ago?* I screamed inside. *Why had she stayed in a marriage that made her so miserable? She'd never done that in past relationships. Why this one? Was staying in her house really worth all this?*

"I had no idea," I said. "I could tell you seemed a little more 'carefree' when we talked sometimes, but I didn't know you were vaping every day."

"Not *every* day . . . but, you know . . . it's my little bit of time out of mind."

Truthfully, my mom, Dana, and I had become so much more educated about cannabis and some of its benefits that thinking of it as a hard-core drug anymore was ridiculous. We chalked that up to years of more collective deceit and found humor in the fact that I'd stopped being such a goody two shoes about it. But it was the image of my mom wanting so badly most days to escape her life that hit me on such a visceral level, and I hated her vaping regularly as a way to bypass emotional wounds she needed to heal.

"What about your time with your girlfriends? I thought that was part of why you decided to stay here."

"Oh, yeah . . . that's always wonderful. We have our Friday dinners out, and Deb and I do the grocery shopping together sometimes, or go out to lunch, or have a girls' day at the consignment stores. But the rest of the time, I just have my calls from you to pep me up. That's when I get to live vicariously through you."

"Wow," I muttered.

"I just can't believe that I got cancer. *Me.* I've pretty much reversed MS, and then I get *cancer?*"

"*I'm* not surprised."

Her eyes grew wide. "You're not?"

"No. After what you've told me, I see this as your giant wake-up call.

Seriously. How long would you have continued in this routine if something drastic didn't happen to you?"

My mom looked shaken by my response, but I could tell it made sense to her too. "I don't know."

"Exactly," I said tenderly but honestly. "If you had nothing to look forward to except outings with your friends and calls from me, and those things weren't enough, what would have made you snap out of your funk?" I didn't wait for an answer. "The Universe has been whispering to you for years to get out of this marriage, but you didn't. Then it got louder, and you still didn't leave. The only way left to get your attention was for all this melancholy and negative energy . . . and all the stuff from your childhood you've been carrying around to manifest itself in an illness so that you'd have no choice but to do something to change your life." I put my hand on hers and said genuinely, "I don't see this cancer diagnosis as a negative at all. I see it as your second chance at getting your life back."

She thought about my words for a few moments, then nodded in resignation. "I guess you're right. Who knows how long I would have continued this way."

"I know it sounds weird, but I'm grateful for this cancer. This is going to be a new beginning for you. And I'm going to help that be your reality."

Hope Springs

𝐼 had bought a one-way ticket to Santa Fe, having no idea how long I'd need to stay, or how much help my mom would need having a colostomy bag. But trooper that she was, she took her instruction on how to tend to it like a mother caring for a child, and it gave her reason to treat herself tenderly. So, instead of the new appendage being a burden, which I fully expected, she embraced the routine wholeheartedly. She even named her new little friend (the stoma part that stuck out of her body) "Pinkie," since it being pink meant that it was healthy.

"It's weird never going poop, though," she remarked.

"I bet. Do you feel like you have to go?"

"No, not really . . . because there's nothing there. Anything that was came whooshing out at the urgent care."

I made a face. "Oh, that's right. But it's temporary, isn't it?"

"I hope so. I have an appointment with the surgeon next week. So I guess I'll find out then."

"I'd like to go with you. Is that okay?"

My mom perked up. "Of course. I'd love to have you there with me. But I didn't expect you to be able to stay that long. You need to get back to Dayni . . . and to work."

"I know. But I can do some work from here. And Dayn is doing great. Plus, she's taking care of Shaia . . . and she knows my priority right now is taking care of you."

She tipped her head with a smile. "Well, if you're sure. You know I'd be thrilled if you never left."

With plans now to stay for a full eight days, our next focus was on the prospect of going to Hope4Cancer. My mom took the time to read through the protocols and watch some more videos, and in short order, she fell into my camp and believed it was the right path to healing for her.

Once my mom decided to go to Hope4Cancer, we had two hurdles to jump. One, she was somewhat reluctant to take the money for H4C from what she was determined to leave me one day as an inheritance, which was profoundly meaningful to her. Thankfully, I was able to convince her that having her here with me was much more important to me than having her money. Two, her sisterhood of girlfriends, who were a mix of Western- and alternative-minded gals, were a little skeptical of the clinic, but after we presented it to them with all the facts, they became the supportive tribe she needed.

After all the arrangements were made, we agreed that I would fly down and meet my mom in San Diego, which was only miles from the border of Mexico, and spend the first week at H4C with her. One of their perks was offering double rooms as part of the cost—along with the three organic meals they provided each day—for a companion to accompany a patient for some or all of their stay. While my mom was more than capable of taking care of herself, we both knew how much it would mean if I could spend part of her sojourn with her. I sincerely wanted to support her through every step of her healing journey, and I also wanted to see firsthand how the clinic operated and the therapies my mom would be partaking in every day.

So, after securing her dates at the clinic from October 2nd to 23rd, my other priority became lightening the negative energy load in my mom's house. While I couldn't do anything about the marriage, I could do something about the areas that fell into my expertise.

"Is it okay with you if I clean out your refrigerator and freezer?" I asked.

"Oh gosh," she said. "I'm so embarrassed you feel you need to do that for me . . ."

"Oh come on, it's just me."

She smiled. That line was from *Terms of Endearment,* another one of our favorite movies. Debra Winger's character, Emma, says it to her mother, Shirley MacLaine's character, Aurora, when Aurora is trying to keep something personal to herself. "Hey, if you're up for it, more power to you!"

"Good! Do you mind if I start right now?"

My mom laughed. "You've always been so motivated when you want to do something. I can't believe cleaning out my fridge is exciting you this much, but I sure do appreciate that you're willing."

"Willing? I can't wait!"

I proceeded to spend four hours pulling everything out onto the counters and organizing items into sections of expired, keep, and dump. Then I scrubbed the fridge and freezer inside and out, replaced everything by themes in the doors and on the shelves, and gave my mom a tour so she could maintain the new layout and categorization features I believed would vastly improve the refrigerated and frozen aspects of her life.

"This is amazing, honey. It really does feel like a fresh start. Now I know what I need and what I don't for my new, healthy eating plan."

We had had an appointment with her naturopath the day before, and she had given us her heartfelt approval on Hope4Cancer and their pioneering therapies, along with a list of foods she wanted my mom to eat—and avoid—to obliterate the cancer.

"I'm glad. Now can I clean out and reorganize the pantry? I already have ideas for making it so much more functional for you."

Again, my mom laughed. "Sure. Be my guest. I don't *expect* you to do all this . . ."

"I know. But this is Operation Heal Bree, Phase I. I *want* to do it. Plus, you know I'm in my element."

She shook her head and said with a playful lilt, "I know you are."

Once the pantry looked like a mercantile my mom could shop from and was unburdened of anything no longer viable for consumption, I said, "I know I don't have much more time here, but I can't leave without redoing your hall closet. Can I? You can just relax and weigh in from time to time on if you want to keep certain things or not."

My mom held out her hand like a game show host toward the hallway. "I'm sure you already have a brilliant plan for that too."

"You know I do."

So off I skipped to spend another half day in my organizer's paradise.

By this time in her life, my mom had lost thirty of the pesky pounds she'd put on a few years ago, and I suggested some donations.

"Just do the pants for now," she said, "the rest we can do another time."

You may be thinking, *Why only the pants? What was the big whoop about donating other items?* Well, here's what the whoop was. My mom had about *sixty* or so pairs of pants. These lived folded in the lengthy hall closet, alongside her pajamas and scads of layering shirts. Then there was her *bedroom* closet, which housed a volume of beautiful blouses, jackets, and tops—and when I say "volume," I mean she could have opened a shop of her own. *And then* there was her extensive collection of shoes, sweaters, and sweatshirts that were relegated to their own bins and cubbies. In other words, expanding her adorable signature style by contributing generously to the stock value of Anthropologie, Zulily, Sundance, Keens, and Zappos, not to mention wearable gems on Ebay, had been a huge source of light in the darkness for my mom these past months and years. So, I'm not exaggerating when I say it would have been too big an undertaking to thoughtfully sort through more than pants for donations in the time I had left that week.

"You know I'd love to do your bedroom closet and everything else too," I said. "But that will have to wait."

"That's fine, honey," she said. "When I'm feeling better and can move around without pain from the surgery, I'll work on it. I know I have a ton of things I need to donate now that will never fit me again, sad *and* glad to say."

So, I went to work on transforming the hall closet into a mini clothing, linen, and apothecary shop that said "aaahhh" when my mom slid open the door, and made a stack of about forty pairs of pants she could schlep to the thrift or consignment store.

"Oh, Doob," she marveled when it was finished and I'd hauled away all the trashable items she'd approved, "you've really given me space to breathe in again. This truly is a wonderful fresh start for me."

"I just wish I could do more before I had to leave."

"Believe me, this is more than I could have imagined. You're really helping to put me on the right track."

"And this is only phase one. Just think how amazing phase two is going to be in a month when we go to Mexico."

The next day, we had the appointment with the surgeon for a follow-up and to have my mom's staples removed. Pointing to the scans of her liver and intestines, the doctor explained where the presumed cancer resided.

"Before the lower intestine tumors can be removed," he said, "they need to be shrunk. I recommend a couple rounds of chemo and radiation."

My mom stood firm. "I'm not doing that. I don't believe in chemo and radiation. I've already made plans to go to a cutting-edge clinic in Mexico where I'll be receiving all kinds of immune-boosting therapies, as well as therapies designed to shrink or kill cancer cells without toxic side effects."

I silently cheered. I loved witnessing my mom standing up for herself, and the conviction with which she spoke.

"Well," the surgeon said, "I'll admit I don't know anything about these alternative therapies. I'm a Western-trained doctor through and through. But I also believe this is your body, and you need to do what you feel is best for you. My recommendation is chemo and radiation, but if that's not what you want to do, then I give you my blessing to try this other path."

I admit, the fact that he wasn't demeaning or pushy was a welcome surprise. I appreciated his frankness and also his support, even if we could tell he wasn't really on board with the idea of Hope4Cancer.

"So," I chimed in with my confident air, "once my mom's tumors shrink from her treatment down in Mexico, can you remove the rest of them and reverse the colostomy?"

My mom wanted to know the same.

"I don't know," he said tentatively. "It depends. I may not be able to do that if you haven't gone through chemo first."

And there it was. The maddening state of our current medical establishment that so often no longer supported the body healing itself without toxic chemicals. I was grateful beyond measure—and told him so—that this surgeon had saved my mom's life, but this infuriated me.

"You're saying that you won't be able to put my mom back together, after her tumors have been shrunk naturally?"

He shook his head. "When cancer is involved, that's usually the protocol. I'd have to see once you got back what the situation was."

As much as I liked this surgeon, and I admired that he truly seemed to care, I also couldn't help but see the heavy influence of Big Pharma on him. Truthfully, I felt bad for him. He had given so many years of his life to study medicine and to help people as a surgeon, but in this situation, he was bound by these ridiculous rules, even if he wanted to remove what was left of my mom's tumors when she returned from H4C.

"I guess we'll just have to see what happens then," my mom said, projecting a sense of disappointed resolve.

The doctor nodded. "No matter what, I hope you'll let me see you through this when you get back."

My mom agreed hopefully while I silently said, *If that means pumping my mom with chemicals in order to satisfy some nonsensical requirement, after receiving three weeks of the most fortifying protocols to restore her health, you can forget it.*

⟊

That night, I made my mom a master list to reference for the next five weeks. It included all the recommended foods and supplements from her naturopath, mindful breathing techniques, the best activities for helping the body heal (laughter being at the top), and a few resources I thought she'd find helpful.

"Thank you so much, honey," she said. "This is a *huge* help."

The next morning, it was hard to pull away and leave for the airport, but my mom assured me she would take good care of herself.

"You and Pinkie will be okay without me?" I said.

"Not *as* okay," she teased, "but yes."

We hugged tightly and kissed each other.

"You're going to be okay," I said. "Just remember that. This is your wake-up call, that's all."

"I know. I believe that too."

The morning after I got home, on August 29th, I received this text:

Her: Good morning, girls! Mommy is up and ready to go get my passport! I'm enjoying my oatmeal right now. All is well. I haven't felt this good in a long time. Toxins be gone!

Me: What a wonderful message to greet us! We are over the moon (and moved to tears) to hear that you haven't felt this good in a long time. Yes, toxins be gone!! We are SO proud of you . . . And we'll be bantering in person again in no time . . . and in a magical healing place! 🌱

Later, on September 4th:

Her: Every time I open my hall closet, I smile with wonder and gratitude. It's so awesome! And don't get me started on the kitchen! 😄

Me: Aww . . . I love that your closet and kitchen make you smile. I felt so gratified being able to do that for you. 🙏

Her: I'm nominating you for daughter of the year. You'll win in every category! Don't worry, no swimsuit competition. You are precious, little girl! 😘 💜 😘 💜 😘

Me: Wow! What a huge honor! I'm very touched (and relieved about the swimsuit competition). 😘 💜 😘 💜 😘

September 30th, the day before departure:

Her: I'm feeling very anxious right now. My damn stoma has herniated and it's sticking out really far! Great 😩

Me: Oh no! What the??? Don't worry . . . I'll stick it back in at the airport. 😆

Her: 😳

Between our wackiness together and the first-class healing therapies my mom was about to receive for the next three weeks, I truly believed she was headed for a no-fail reboot that would ensure we'd be making each other laugh for decades to come—and she believed it as ardently as I did.

∞

Over the Border We Go

As planned, on October 1st, I flew from Seattle to the San Diego airport, and my mom flew in from Albuquerque just a couple hours after me. I killed time chatting with Dana, and then I went to meet my mom in the baggage claim area.

Though it had only been a month since we'd seen each other, her improvement was staggering when I saw her. She was walking more steadily than I'd seen in years, and she was down to 118 pounds, which she hadn't been since pre-, well, *me*. She was wearing one of her usual adorable babydoll tops that hid Pinkie perfectly as she ambled toward me.

"You look amazing!" I gushed. "You told me how tiny you were, but geez . . . I don't think I've ever seen you this small."

In her cute little-girl voice, she said, "I know, huh?"

I immediately nicknamed her "Slim," like Humphrey Bogart called Lauren Bacall in *To Have and Have Not*, which she (not surprisingly) embraced.

Since I'd left at the end of August, she had been diligent about eating the right foods, and she looked like the picture of health except for one thing: she had (weirdly) slipped two weeks prior and fractured her right elbow when she landed on her tile floor. She couldn't believe the timing and hoped it wouldn't impede any of her therapies. There wasn't much to do for it, though, other than refraining from using it too much. So, trooper that she was, she oozed eagerness for our journey in Mexico and we both fully expected glowing results.

That first night, we stayed in a hotel in San Diego, and then we were picked up in the morning by the clinic's driver. He was a darling man who regularly shuttled patients over the border and assisted them with all the paperwork to make it easy. So, once passports were verified and our temporary visas were issued, he delivered us to the clinic just fifteen minutes away.

The facility itself was very modest—more than we expected—but when we met the intake doctor, he explained that the clinic was essentially a hospital, but one that was designed to feel more like home. No, it wasn't a spa-like environment, but it also wasn't a sterile and unfeeling environment. Unless a patient was close to end of life and required it, there were no machines to be hooked up to, and no nurses waking patients throughout the night.

"Sleep is an incredibly important part of the healing process," Dr. Salenas said. "Here, no one will bother you in the night. If you need something, there's a nurse stationed outside, but they won't come into your room and disturb you."

I loved hearing that. My mom and I both knew how vital sleep was to health, and how little of it people got in hospitals back home.

"As you know, besides sleep, we'll be focusing on nutrition, and on emotional and spiritual health, along with all of your therapies. You'll meet with our nutritionist in just a bit."

Again, we were thrilled, because again, nutrition—which is so crucial to health—is all but left out of American medical school curriculum. It's absolute lunacy. But here, we would be eating three organic meals a day, prepared according to each patient's particular needs.

"We can actually get you started today with a B-17 infusion, and then you'll have your baseline tests. Then tomorrow morning, you'll meet your assigned doctor and begin your full daily protocol, okay?"

"Okay!" my mom said. "Let's do it!"

It's true that the facility wasn't a glamorous place: the furniture and art were simple, and the decor was sparse in the rooms. But we had a nice big bathroom, a TV, plenty of closet space, and a balcony that faced the street and the ocean just beyond. There were four private patient rooms in our "suite," with a nurses station in the middle, and the dining room just across the hall. My mom had a hospital bed so she could adjust it for certain therapies she would take in our room, and I had a twin bed that suited me just fine.

"Just think," I said to my mom after the doctor left, "so many people don't even know this is an option for them. Or if they do, they can't afford it. But here you are." I glanced around our room. "It may be on the humble side in terms of how it looks, but how fortunate are you that you get to be here, where every therapy will make you feel great, not like you want to die after being pumped with chemicals."

"Amen to that, sister. I'm very grateful indeed. And I'm especially grateful that you're here with me."

"I'm so happy I'm here too."

⚮

Let the Healing Begin

While this part of my mom's and my story is decidedly not meant to be a running advertisement for Hope4Cancer, laying out the therapies my mom had to look forward to each day will give you a sense of the routine we quickly settled into:

Indiba (a procedure that raises the temperature locally in the area around the tumors to make the cancer cells unstable)

hyperbaric oxygen chamber (which she was worried she couldn't get into with her cracked elbow, but they found a way to make it work)

vitamin C infusions

B-17, or laetrile, infusions ⟶ (these two occurred on alternating days)

near infra-red lamp

Sono-Photo Dynamic Therapy (for inhibiting cancer cell growth)

Pulsed Electro-Magnetic Field Therapy (PEMF) (delivery of non-invasive, painless biofeedback to detect and repair areas of cellular imbalance and inflammation)

Unfortunately, because of the colostomy, my mom had to forego two of the recommended therapies—coffee enemas and rectal ozone therapy—and because she had adverse reactions to extreme heat, she had to skip on the infra-red sauna sessions too. I didn't want her missing out on *any* of the treatments available to her in the program, but there was nothing to be done about the rectal ones, and she was adamant that she'd be a noodle for hours if she did the sauna, so she focused on getting the maximum benefits from all the others.

One of the perks about the H4C therapies was the flexibility of scheduling for the patients and the relative autonomy involved. This put my mom's healing journey mostly in her own hands, which was highly empowering. She'd go down to the treatment rooms for two of her therapies, but the rest took place in our room, either assisted by a nurse or on her own. While I could be with her anytime I wanted, and we had all our meals together, I was able to spend some time during the day working downstairs in the open atrium, and then we'd mostly have the evenings to hang out in our room, watch TV, and talk.

Because all of the patients came and went in their own three-week cycles, certain people were more on our cycle and we saw them often, while others left soon after we got to know them. My mom made one particularly close friend named Jacqueline, along with a couple others. Each person had a unique story, but in almost every case, they'd been through conventional cancer treatment, had gotten sicker from it or had experienced a relapse, then came to Hope4Cancer with the hope of finally getting their body back into balance. My mom and I were not only the sole mother/daughter duo in our group, but we were the only ones who had come straight to H4C after diagnosis. Everyone was curious to know how that had happened, when there was so much pressure from American doctors to do surgery, chemo, and/or radiation.

"Stacey's the one who knew about this place," my mom told them. "She did the consult and got all the information for me before I even left the hospital."

"How nice that you would do that for your mom," someone said. "My daughter wouldn't have a clue about a place like this."

I shrugged. "I was just fortunate to have seen the docu-series where Hope4Cancer was featured . . . and that something told me to file it away in my mind."

That led to spirited discussions about natural healing, people's discontent with a lot of doctors, particularly oncologists, in the States, the grueling procedures they had been through, and so on. But perhaps the saddest story was Jacqueline's. She had already been to H4C before and had been doing well until a doctor at home went against her wishes and performed a biopsy of her tumor during another procedure. That biopsy was akin to breaking down a retaining wall that was keeping the cancer in a holding tank—releasing a flood of cancer cells into her abdomen. This was why she'd returned to Mexico, and why she was so aggrieved at the current medical system in America.

"For emergency medicine and putting people back together after accidents, there's no doubt that we're top notch," I said. "But what's sad is that there's virtually no preventative care in our country. It's all pharmaceutical, which so many of us know has nothing to do with keeping people healthy or well. It only masks symptoms so that the body has to speak louder and louder for the help it needs."

"And make money for Big Pharma," someone chimed in.

Everyone grumbled and nodded in agreement.

But *my* mom hadn't fallen into the trap or been manipulated. The surgeons had tried, but she had kicked one out of her hospital room and told the other flat out that she wasn't doing chemo. Armed with information, she was able to make her own decision—and that decision was coming *here*, where every therapy was boosting her immunity and diminishing the cancer cells naturally. As much as I felt for these people who had been through so much pain, trauma, and heartbreak, I was immensely grateful that that wasn't going to be my mom's story. At least I *hoped* it wouldn't be.

Only I knew that the physical part of my mom's healing wasn't nearly the most crucial.

As I mentioned, H4C recognized the importance of emotional and spiritual health. In fact, it's becoming more widely known that emotional wounds cause disease more than the physical assaults of chemicals, poor food choices, heavy metals, the environment, EMFs, and the like. To that end, my mom had two appointments with an H4C counselor to help explore what hidden traumas could have served as triggers for her cancer, as well as what her current life situation could have contributed. Two sessions could never address all of a person's wounding, but it was meant to be a catalyst to uncover the sources of a patient's dis-ease so that he or she could further pursue their emotional healing at home.

But my mom and I hadn't needed to wait to get to H4C to have this conversation. Yes, there were the emotional wounds from both of her mothers that I wanted my mom to heal—and those were indeed critical to address—but what I saw as more urgent was what was going to happen after her three weeks in Mexico.

Our second night at the clinic, I sat on my bed, notebook open with my pencil poised, and said, "Okay, Little Bree . . . we need to make a plan for you."

"A plan?"

"Yes. There's no way you can come here, invest all this money in your healing journey, and then go home to your unhappy marriage. You can't continue to heal in that environment. It just won't happen . . . and you know it."

She nodded. "I hear you. But what can I do?"

I asked her what her ideal life would look like, what it would take to achieve it, and how much it would cost. I wrote all the options down and explored them with her to show her what was feasible.

"I just really don't want to leave my house," she said.

"I know. It always comes back to that for you."

"That's because I *do* want to stay there with the kitties, but I also want to be able to leave half of it to you. You know I always planned to leave you Nantucket, but that plan changed."

My shoulders slumped. "Bree, I love you for wanting to leave me an inheritance, and I know how much that's always meant to you. But don't you know by now that I don't care about that? I want *you* here, *with* me, for decades more. That's *all* that matters to me. If you spent all the money or equity you've been saving for me, I'd support you 100 percent if that's what it took to get your health back."

My mom smiled. "I know you would. And it's not like it's *only* the house I'll have to leave you. But I really want that for you."

"And I *really* want you out of there."

She tipped her head. "So what do I do?"

"I say you go back to proposing a divorce, selling the house, splitting the difference with Rick, and using that money to buy a cute little condo you can redecorate to your heart's desire."

"That does sound appealing. But I just don't know if Rick will go for it."

"Too damn bad! Why should it be his decision that you stay trapped in this marriage? You've always bailed in the past when things weren't right. Why not now?"

My mom sat across from me on her bed, holding the little bunny Dana and I had gotten her for her birthday that year, her feet dangling just above the floor, looking so much like a sweet little girl but with an adult's anguish punctuating her face.

"I guess it all seems so much more complicated now," she said.

"Then let's uncomplicate it so you can know what you're going to do when you get home. Because there's no way you can go back to that life. I *know* it's a big part of why you got cancer. It's your wake-up call, remember? Your wake-up call to take care of *you* and to finally get out of that environment that's not feeding your soul."

"I know you're right."

"So it's a non-negotiable. Part of your healing will happen here, and a huge part of it will happen when you get out of the marriage. It might take some time, but think how relieved you'll be when it's done and you have your independence back. And you'll still live near all your friends. It feels like a win-win to me."

"It does to me too."

"Before I leave, we're going to map out a serious plan for you, okay?"

She nodded. "Okay."

A Change of Plan(e)

I had planned to stay at the clinic for six days and fly home on Monday, October 7th, but my intuition was nagging at me that it was too soon. Plus, once my mom's doctor reviewed the scans they took when she arrived, he told us in one of our meetings with him that he believed she was a good candidate for an additional treatment called IPT, or Insulin Potentiation Therapy—which, in effect, was a safe and innovative low-dose chemo.

"Chemo?" I protested. "Why would you even suggest that? I thought chemo was off the table here."

"Conventional chemo, yes," he said. "But this is very different. IPT usually has virtually no detrimental side effects, and because cancer cells have highly active insulin receptors, IPT takes advantage of that and can be very effective at killing cancer cells."

I still wasn't convinced, and neither was my mom.

He went on to explain the careful way it would be administered, with my mom's blood sugar monitored closely the whole time, and how they would have a large meal ready for her as soon as the treatment was finished to re-stabilize her.

"And I won't lose my hair?" my mom wanted to know.

"There is a chance, but it's very rare," he assured her.

"And what's the real advantage of doing it?" I asked.

"Liver cancer can be particularly hard to treat," he said. "That large mass in the liver is a concern. I know we don't have proof that it's cancer, but it definitely looks like it is, and a biopsy would be dangerous. So this would work in conjunction with all your other therapies to give the cancer in both the liver and the colon a stronger punch, if you will."

He outlined the recommendation of a six-week protocol, one treatment a week. "It's completely up to you, Briana. I just think that in your situation, this is a really good option for you. I've seen it work well for a lot of patients. But mindset is very important. If you're against it and don't believe in it, it probably won't help you. But if you think it can truly help you, it probably will."

We both loved how much he understood the power of the mind. What he was saying was so true. But it was still a big decision.

"Think about it," he said. "If you want to do it, you could start while you're here, this Wednesday, and then you'd just have to arrange to stay another four weeks near the clinic, maybe in an Airbnb."

After the meeting, our heads were spinning. Just the word *chemo* was an assault on our sensibilities. So I went online and read about it, and it did seem like something that could help my mom. But she wasn't so sure she wanted to stay another month in Mexico, making her time away from home seven weeks total.

"Think of it this way," I said. "It could be the Universe giving you more time away from Rick . . . more time to feel what it would be like to regain your independence so that it will be easier for you when you get home to stand strong in your decision that you want to go your separate ways."

She thought about that for a moment. "It could be."

"We have to look at everything the Universe is doing for you right now. You're here, and you have the chance to get this additional therapy, which I know sounds totally wrong but actually seems like it could be a good thing. And, like Dr. Rivera said, you shouldn't have any side effects except for some fatigue on the day. Plus, you'd be able to pay for a plan to have your meals here, so you'd still be eating healthy food. Or you could walk down to the organic restaurant sometimes and eat there too."

I really wasn't trying to force my mom into doing this treatment, but I did want her to consider all the angles.

At lunch that day, she found out that Jacqueline and Kate were both going to do IPT too, so she wouldn't be alone. They had found lodging in an inexpensive hotel across the street, and they told my mom she should check it out to see if there were any more rooms.

"I do think I should do it," she concluded, "as much as I hate throwing more money out for the treatment *and* whatever it will cost to stay longer. But figuring out where to stay . . . right now, I just feel so overwhelmed."

"I know . . . and I've been thinking about it. I don't feel right about leaving on Monday."

My mom perked up like a little girl getting extra tickets for rides at a carnival. "Really?"

"I know it's not a lot more time, but if I stay until Thursday, then I'd be here for your first IPT on Wednesday, and I can look into the hotel option, or find you an apartment."

I don't have to tell you that there wasn't a shred of protest from my mom's side about this plan.

I promptly changed my flight, got to work on securing accommodations for the month after my mom's clinic stay would be over, and made sure she'd have transportation to and from the clinic on Wednesdays. Just in the nick of time, we were able to reserve a nice Airbnb apartment only a few residential blocks away, with a lovely mother and son who promised to look out for my mom during the four weeks she'd be staying there.

As planned, I was there for her first IPT session, and other than being tired, she did really well. She even took (stuffed) Bunny with her as a support animal, which her friends and doctor thought was awfully cute.

"Just keep envisioning everything you're doing here obliterating the cancer cells and leaving healthy pink organs in their place," I said. "Don't underestimate the power of that."

"I won't. I know it's important."

Then she made a face, and I knew why.

"I know . . . I wish I didn't have to leave tomorrow. It's really hard to pull away from being here with you."

She nodded, but was a big girl about it. "I'll be fine," she assured me. "You don't have to worry. You've already done *so* much for me. I can't thank you enough for everything."

I knew that if I could stay for the next six weeks, she'd be over the moon. But that wasn't feasible for me, and she never would have asked it of me. Plus, what I really wanted for her was to have her little apartment all to herself for a month, to have that taste of independence I knew she craved and hadn't had for so many years. I was certain that after seven weeks away from home, she'd never want to go back to living in that beautiful but suffocating house, as much as she loved it.

Plus, we'd mapped out a plan.

All my mom had to do was stick to it.

∞

Leaving My Girl on Her Own

That next morning, as I rolled my suitcase toward the door of our room to leave, I had to take deep breaths to keep the tears in check. My mom seemed so little and vulnerable, yet brave too, sitting on her bed trying valiantly to appear strong. I knew if I hugged her one more time, I'd completely lose it, so I told her once again how proud of her I was and how much I loved her, how happy I was that I'd been able to be there the last week and a half, and how excited I was for her to continue on her healing journey.

She nodded, trying to keep her tears in check too. With her signature smile and twinkle in her eyes, she assured me with complete conviction, "I'm going to be fine."

Before I walked out the door, I said, "I'll see you soon" and she echoed it, which felt much better than saying goodbye.

During my flight, I reflected on the last ten days we'd shared and realized that we had never, not once, been away together for that long. We had been on a cruise one time—my mom and a dear friend, Dana and me—but even then we had separate state rooms, and that was only for six days. This had been a singular experience, sharing a room and a bathroom, eating all our meals together, me being there for every doctor visit, every decision. It had been so seamless for us to be together all the time. Sure, it had taken a couple days to figure out the maze of the clinic, but once we did, it grew quickly to feel like home, and within that home, we had our routine.

One of the best parts of the clinic was the daily structure, which was exactly what my mom needed. But because the therapies were largely self-guided, I also noted she could have a tendency to want to skip one (or two) if she didn't feel like doing it, and so I'd had to be the motivator at times to keep her on track. I couldn't understand why she would invest so much time and money in this wonderful opportunity and then squander even a sliver of it, and it was that tendency that made me a bit uneasy about leaving her. Overall, I felt I'd left her in good hands with her doctor and the nurses in our suite, but I did hope she wouldn't slack once I wasn't there to encourage her from time to time.

The other thing was, I could imagine my mom lamenting after I left that she no longer had anyone to play with (you'll recall the occasional petitions from her side in my early years to *please* stay home from that pesky, demanding institution called school). Don't get me wrong: I did not labor under the delusion that my mom couldn't get along without me, but I *did* know how important it was for her to laugh—both for her soul and for her immune system. She had her friends, in particular Jacqueline, but there weren't witty antics going on there. So I hatched an idea I thought would brighten her spirits.

One of the things we'd been looking forward to during the nights in our room at the clinic was watching our favorite movies together. I'd brought a nice array, and after she'd gotten all propped up and cozy in her bed that first night, I popped in *When Harry Met Sally*. Nothing happened. I took it out and put it back in. Nothing. "Oh man," I whined, "do we have a DVD player but it doesn't work?"

I promptly called the front desk and told the sweet man we needed a new DVD player because ours seemed to be broken. It took a bit, but someone brought us a new one and hooked it up. Again, my mom got cozy, and again, I slid the disc in. Nothing. No enchilada, no burrito, no chimichanga. *Nada*. Finally, it dawned on me: we were in *Mexico* with a *Mexican* DVD player, meaning it only read discs that were region four, not the region-one DVDs we played in the US.

I let out a long pirate-y sound of frustration. "I can't believe it! The one thing we were so looking forward to for fun we can't do!"

My mom let out an equally whiny sound.

After that, we'd had to resort to watching the couple of stations we got in English: History and some other serious channel. Translation: *No teníamos nada que ver para hacernos reír.* Translation: We had nothing to watch to make us laugh. (The best I was able to swing was a Spanish version of *Bridget Jones' Baby* with English subtitles that I scored on a field trip to the nearby Walmart.)

So, after I got home, I went online and found my mom a nice-sized portable DVD player and ordered her a dozen of her best-loved humorous DVDs, a few of which had four movies in the set, to be shipped to the clinic. It was going to take a few shipments and ten days for them all to trickle in, but I figured that would give her plenty to make her laugh during the extra weeks she'd be living in Mexico, and she would love receiving all the packages. I also reminded her that *Gilmore Girls* was on Netflix, which she had on her laptop, and that she could stream those too.

Yes, I was concerned that she'd get bored, not right away, but eventually. I also wanted her immune system to get all the healing qualities that laughter provides. In short, I didn't want to wake up one day and wonder if I'd done everything I could to help my mom reclaim her health, and realize I could have done more.

By October 15th, five days after I got home, my mom sent a text saying she was hitting her wall, but that everyone talked about that happening about two weeks in, *and* that she wasn't getting any laughs. So, to cheer her up, I caved and told her she had a surprise coming.

Her: Ooh! How exciting!

Me: Just hang in there, Slim! I think your surprises will make you smile (and some laughs are even guaranteed!) 😊 You should get them early this week or next. Stay the course, baby, stay the course. You can do this!!! 🙌

Her: Sweet, sweet message . . . thanks, darlin'!

I kept the pep-talk messages coming, just in case she was truly feeling inclined to hurl her IV infusion pole out the window and into the sand across the street, particularly after she expressed her discontent with the repetitive protein portion of the dinner meals and how much she missed Taco Tuesdays.

> **Me**: I know you're getting tired of salmon, but just think of everything you're eating there as nourishing your body to beat the invader. EVERYTHING. That makes it all so much more powerful. 😘
>
> **Her**: [bitmoji that says "True Dat"]
> But I sure could use and enjoy a 🌮 or 🌮🌮

When I knew it was time for another IPT day, I hauled out my Song-leader verve from high school:

> **Me**: Happy healing to you today! Yay for healthy breakfast! Yay for IVs! Yay for IPT! Yay for Indiba! Yay for everything you get today that's healing your body, mind, and spirit! And don't forget your new app . . . slip in your earbuds and enjoy a short meditation. 🧘 😘 🧘 Most of all delight in this amazing opportunity you have at H4C . . . I miss being there with you!
>
> **Her**: Miss you too! I made it through another round of IPT. This one was rough on me, though. But I've had breakfast, lots of it, and I'm perking back to normal. Jacqueline, Kate, and I made it through together! I'm going to lie down now. Thanks for the big cheer this morning. It made me smile!
>
> BTW, I forgot Bunny and was already hooked up so I couldn't go get her. And guess who got her for me? Yup, Dr. Cutie Pie. Precious! He's even the one who noticed I didn't have her!
>
> **Me**: Come ON!!! That is the sweetest story! What a doll he was to go back to your room and get Bunny for you. That seriously made my day. 😻

And when she sent a deflated moji that told me without words that she was feeling weary, I again hauled out my cheerleader poms:

Me: I know it's a lot, but just try to keep the perspective of why you're there . . . to beat the invader from every possible angle. 🗡 Be excited for IPT even, if you can, because it's stopping it, messing with it, shrinking it, killing it, so it can't do any damage, along with all your other amazing therapies that are costing you my inheritance 😏 (hee hee) But seriously, you can't leave me, remember? 😢🙏 AND you have a new chapter of life just waiting for you! Yee hoo!! 🥂 You got this!! I believe in you 🧚

Her: I do got this! All is well. 🖤🖤🖤🖤🖤🖤🖤

As the date neared for what I expected to be the delivery of my mom's first package, which was supposed to be the DVD player, I was getting excited. I had told her that the boxes were coming separately, and that she might have to wait for what "went with" the first one, meaning the DVDs themselves. Only that's not quite how it went down.

Her: Oh my goodness! I just got a package from you. My favorite movies! Only you would know my faves. Thank you sooo much! 😄 5 of these beauties arrived!

Me: What??? Oh man . . . okay. Well, that's cool, but like I told you, stuff is supposed to go together. 😳 You'll have to hang tight . . . maybe till Friday 😉 But yay!! So happy you got surprised!!

Her: ["So excited" bitmoji]
Thrilled! Off to Walmart I'll go for a DVD player! Yippee!

Me: Umm . . . don't do that yet.

Her: [bitmoji that says "Oh no you di'nt"]

Realizing the jig was up, I nonetheless thought a little humor might create a diversion from the wrong-sequential-order delivery.

Me: I heard you can get a DVD player on the street for cheap in TJ. When you're feeling better, I figured you could flash some slim leg and those pearly whites 😁

Her: Do those players off the street come with a cord or connectors? I guess I should have brought my short shorts!

Me: Yes, you should have. That's how you get cords. And with a bare midriff, you can snag installation too. 👍

Her: 🌑

Now, my mom and I bantered like this in texts and on the phone all the time, so it never dawned on me that she wasn't completely onto the fact that she actually had a portable DVD player coming too. But then she told me she tried to put one of her new DVDs into the player in her room and it didn't work. *Duh*, I'm thinking. *I didn't buy you region-one DVDs that we already know don't work in that player.* Back and forth we went about it, with her thinking she somehow got the wrong DVDs. I'm cracking up on my end as she's sending these hilarious bitmojis of disappointment. Finally, I lied and said I'd check on the order and get back to her.

The next day, I received this message:

I'm getting another delivery! . . . Well, this answers the conundrum!

I called her right away. "Did you really think we'd send you a bunch of movies with no player to watch them on? You had me laughing so hard yesterday thinking your DVDs were broken!"

She played it all cool, like she knew all along, but I could tell she didn't.

"Please tell me you didn't actually go buy one at Walmart."

"Well, no, not after you told me I could score one on the street if I flashed some leg."

"And how did that go?"

"I think having the portable IV pole took away from my sexiness."

"And here I thought you'd know to leave that in your room."

Yes, my mom and I could play silly till the cows came home.

Which was how she troopered through those next five weeks. Well, that, along with a bazillion texts, calls, and bitmoji exchanges between us, devouring every one of the movies we sent, and binge-watching all seven seasons of *Gilmore Girls*.

≈

Awaiting Operation Heal Bree,
Phase Three

*W*hile my mom was still in Mexico with access to her doctor, she explained her concerns about the forced chemo in the US before another surgery could be done, and asked him about the possibility of having whatever was left of her tumors removed and the colostomy reversed by a surgeon down there. He told her it was definitely possible, though it wouldn't be covered by her insurance, and gave her the name and number of a top surgeon (we'll call him Dr. Z) he had worked with for ten years.

Although Dr. Rivera didn't want to do any scans until my mom had finished IPT and was close to going home—which meant it was impossible to know what, if any, shrinkage had occurred of her tumors so far—she had a phone consult with the recommended surgeon, and in short order decided he was probably going to be the person to ultimately put her back together.

Having her surgery in Mexico would mean her returning sometime after the first of the year, and of course my mom didn't want to face that alone. I didn't want that for her either. So, we had a tentative plan that I would fly down when she was about ready to be discharged after surgery, stay with her in a hotel for several days while she continued to recover, and then when she'd had her staples removed and was well enough to fly home, I would accompany her to Santa Fe and stay for a week or so to take care of her before coming back home to Washington. This was all predicated on receiving those final scans and knowing if the surgery was indeed going to be viable after all the therapies she'd received.

As Thanksgiving neared and my mom was gearing up to go home after seven weeks in Mexico, she had her long-awaited scans done.

"Are you ready for some good news?" she asked when she called.

"Yes! I want some good news!"

"Well, my scans show that the colon tumors have shrunk, one by about half, and the other one about a third. The liver tumor seems a bit smaller too, but that's still a little iffy."

"Oh my gosh," I gushed. "I'll take it! This is great! So this means you can have them removed like you planned, with Dr. Z?"

"Yes, but I'm still going to have a consult with Dr. Williams first, just to see what he says. If I can have the surgery done at home and have insurance cover part of it, it would be so much easier."

I understood her desire to keep things simpler and less of a financial ding, so I supported her wishes and believed that whatever was best for her would come to fruition.

After packing up her little apartment and saying goodbye to her friends and therapists at the clinic, my mom returned home to the waiting arms of three of her best girlfriends at the airport. She had lost a bit more weight, but overall, her friends marveled at how healthy she looked.

I, of course, was eager for her to put her plan in motion for moving on with her life, but she'd been through a lot, and she felt she needed to get through the next major surgery before she made any big moves. I was impatient but understood.

"I just don't want anything toxic at home to unravel all you've done to get better in Mexico," I told her.

"Believe me," she said, "neither do I."

A couple weeks later, on December 18th, my mom told me that Rick had just announced he was going out of state for Christmas.

Me: Well, won't you be kind of glad to have the break and the house to yourself?

Her: It's just so sad to be alone at Christmas. 😢

I empathized and gave her some ideas of what she might find fun to do, as I planned to be home with Dana in Washington for the holidays since I'd be returning shortly to Santa Fe.

> **Her:** I know, I'll make the best of it, and your ideas are wonderful. I'm scared, that's all. It occurred to me that this could be my last Christmas. That's a horrible thought, but it's possible. I'm not in a very good place right now. 😿
>
> **Me:** Oh man! You need a rescue! This is definitely NOT your last Christmas!!
>
> I listened to an amazing podcast episode this morning and it helped me SO much today. Please listen to it . . . I think it will help you too. Will you do that for me?
>
> **Her:** Yes, for you I'd do anything! I'll do it right now.

I really did believe the marriage would be over soon, and that this solitary Christmas week for my mom would give her the space to chill with her kitties, have a movie marathon (our prescription of choice, as I'm sure you've surmised), pamper herself, and be goofy with us on the phone without interruption. I also thought, as I did when she had her apartment in Mexico, she could revel in having her house to herself, which would show her just how wonderful it was going to be when she reclaimed her life of independence.

On New Year's Day, my mom sent me a bitmoji that said, "THIS IS MY YEAR" with sparklies and her smiling face. I wrote back and said, "Yes!! This IS your year!!"

I couldn't have received a better welcome into 2020 than my mom's exuberant pronouncement that all was going to be well with her.

Within a week, my mom had her appointment with Dr. Williams, and considering the progress she'd made in Mexico, he told her he was willing to reverse her colostomy and see if he could remove the remaining colon tumors. He told her it was outside what he normally felt comfortable doing, as she hadn't undergone traditional Western therapies, but he would do it nonetheless.

When my mom called to tell me, she was relieved. A big chunk would be covered by insurance, and she wouldn't have to travel. "But will you still come out and help me while I recover?" she wanted to know.

"Of course," I assured her. "I'll do my best to make it work with my publishing schedule . . . and I can work from your house too."

"It doesn't have to be for too long. Just until my body gets to working properly again."

"You got it, sister!"

But when my mom received the call to plan the date of her surgery, Dr. Williams confessed that his decision had been weighing on him, and that he couldn't in good conscience do the surgery after all. My mom thanked him for being true to his personal ethics, but hung up dispirited by yet another assault from our current medical system.

And so, after a lot of back and forth, my mom obtained approval and a date from Dr. Z to do her surgery in Mexico on January 29, 2020. We went back to our original plan, bought the plane tickets, and counted the days until Humpty Breesky could get put back together again.

∞

Bye-Bye, Pinkie,
Hello, Whoosh

When my mom woke up in the surgical center in Mexico, Pinkie had been snugly tucked back in and reattached where she belonged, and it was only a matter of days before my mom could begin eating mild, soft foods to warm things up and her miraculous body would start processing nourishment through her intestines like normal again. Dr. Z had also removed those pesky remaining colon tumors and extracted what he could from the liver, though some cancer still resided there that he simply couldn't remove. Brilliantly, he concocted an infusion from the antibodies of my mom's tumor that was intended to get the invader to retreat permanently, and my mom would take that antidote orally for the three months following her surgery, along with the immune-boosting therapy she had brought home from the clinic as part of her protocol.

The days that followed were rocky, as my mom didn't have any English-speaking nurses like she did at the clinic, and she was experiencing a lot of pain. I was able to help a bit by speaking to one in Spanish over the phone, but cell service was sketchy to nonexistent there, so I could only do so much.

"You know I'd pull an Aurora Greenway if I could," I told her.

"Oh, I know you would."

(You may recall this reference to Shirley MacLaine's iconic scene in *Terms of Endearment* when she goes berserk in the hospital when her daughter's in pain. "GIVE MY DAUGHTER THE SHOT!!!" she bellows, prompting the staff, who had said she wasn't due for pain meds yet, to hustle to it.)

Overall, my mom couldn't wait until I arrived and we could go to the hotel—which was used often for patients who fled to Mexico for surgery, and whose cost was included in the surgical fees—where she was sure she'd be more comfortable and we could resume our typical verbal antics.

Once my mom was discharged and we were shuttled to the room we'd call home for the next several days, I was relieved I could help her in a more comfortable environment. What I couldn't help with, though, was how quickly her body was going to begin functioning normally again, which the doctor warned would be a messy, bloody affair that might "kick in," shall we say, more quickly than she could move.

Here, I'll just say that we only had to wait a couple days, and that he was right.

"I'm *so* sorry, honey," she kept saying. "I had no idea what I'd be putting you through. This is so embarrassing."

Once again, I quoted one of our standard *Terms of Endearment* lines, "Oh, come on, it's just me." But it didn't assuage her mortification in the least. Honestly, I was glad it was me taking care of her and not some stranger. To keep the topic light, I joked, "Hey, if I decide to change careers and become a crime scene investigator, this is great preparation." She laughed, but she still hated that I was the clean-up crew to her newly-operational colon.

Even though our relationship could certainly handle such awkwardness, and she had come prepared with plenty of feminine hygiene products for the occasion, still I felt for her. She had been through so much more than I ever had. And after going through the worst pain of her life to bring me into this world, and now all of this, I figured some hazmat duty was the least I could do.

"I know," I said, "I'd be feeling kind of weirded out if I were in your shoes. But at least this means your body is working again the way it's supposed to! How cool is that?!"

My mom conceded with a grimace, "That *is* pretty cool."

Dr. Z had told us that this frequent "whoosh" would probably last a good couple of days, and now that my mom knew what that whoosh looked like, she was growing increasingly stressed about the trip home. Not only did we have to cross the border by car, but we had to be at the airport two hours early, then have a two-hour flight to Albuquerque. Then it was another hour-plus drive to get to her house. When we added it all up, my mom couldn't imagine how she could get anywhere without having a horrible accident. Frankly, I wasn't sure either.

"Maybe an adult diaper?" I suggested.

"Well . . . yes . . . I guess so. But there's nowhere for you to get that for me around here."

Then I remembered that the hotel was regularly used for post-surgical patients and set out to find someone who might have access to supplies. Even with my semi-rusty Spanish and their broken English, though, I was out of luck. So, on the morning of our trip, we improvised the best we could, my mom passed on her freshly made glass of juice we'd ordered from room service in favor of an empty stomach, and fortuitously, one big whoosh happened before we left, which we believed was a good sign.

Off we went to the border and then on to the airport.

"You okay?" I kept asking her, as I whisked her through the terminal in a wheelchair.

"So far, so good."

After we checked our suitcases, we carefully and strategically placed her backpack and a carry-on in her lap, then hung another bag off one of the wheelchair handles so that I could use both hands to push. Luckily, we found a seat at the gate where I could park my mom next to me and unload all the bags she was holding into another seat. We sat chatting for a bit, and then I started feeling like I needed the bathroom.

"You sure you don't need to go?" I asked. "Because I do."

"Well, okay . . . maybe I should. But you'll have to help me."

So, we packed her and the wheelchair all up again and found the nearest restroom.

The stalls were fairly deep, and the handicap one was full, so I rolled her in facing the back wall, unloaded her lap, and then awkwardly helped her maneuver onto the toilet. We were both relieved there were no accidents to deal with, and I got her back into her chair and loaded her up.

By then, my stomach was doing flip-flops. "Oh crap," I said, "I think I might be sick."

I swiftly left her in the stall, closed her door, and dashed across the aisle, barely making it before I experienced a whoosh of my own. And then another. And then *another*. Every time I got up to dress myself, there was more. *What is going on?* I wondered. *This is so freakin' weird! Bree is fine, but I have diarrhea??*

Fifteen minutes passed of this intestinal episode while my poor mom was parked like Aunt Edna in *National Lampoon's Vacation* in the stall across from me. Finally, my nightmare ceased and I was able to return to her.

"Oh my gosh," I whispered, "I'm so sorry! But I just had the worst outbreak of diarrhea."

"Oh no," she said. "I wondered what happened to you. You were gone for so long . . . I thought maybe you decided you were done with all this crap, no pun intended."

In that moment, with her sitting there packed full of baggage, facing the toilet wall right where I'd left her with nowhere she could go, and me squeezed in there describing my own whoosh woes, the hilarity of the whole situation hit us. We both started laughing—not just a ha-ha, that's-so-funny kind of laugh, but the kind where sound barely squeaks out because you're laughing so hard, and every time you look at each other, you laugh even harder. And being in a bathroom stall, where people don't typically break out into hysterics, made it that much funnier.

When we finally regained some level of composure, I wheeled my mom out and avoided making eye contact with others as we washed our hands. If any of them had caught the sounds of our wheezing guffaws, I figured averting my eyes was the best way out the door.

Once we were settled again at our gate, my mom said, "I wonder what happened to you."

"I don't know. All I had this morning was my big juice . . . and *your* big juice."

"You drank mine too?"

"Well, it was such a wonderful organic juice, and you barely had any of yours . . . and I hated the thought of it going to waste."

"Well, no wonder!" she said. "Here I'm worried about *me* having diarrhea, and you give it to yourself by drinking all that juice within an hour."

A look of sheepishness covered my face. "It never crossed my mind I'd set such a surge in motion. I had no idea that could happen!"

"Well, at least it happened before our flight."

Relief washed over me. "Oh my gosh . . . you're right."

Whether it was my grandma sprinkling fairy dust once again, or simply the Universe giving us both a break, we got all the way to my mom's house in Santa Fe without either of us needing a pitstop.

And it definitely didn't escape us that we'd always have the airport bathroom incident to conjure in case we needed a dose of comic relief.

Slow Leak

After spending another week at my mom's to nourish her post-surgery, I realized she wasn't going anywhere anytime soon, meaning moving out and on her own again. For one, though the body is phenomenal at healing itself, having a colostomy reversed is a substantial surgery and can take months to fully recover from. Two, she had lost more weight and desperately needed high doses of healthy food, but she didn't have a very big appetite, so she tended to run on the low-energy side. Three, the intention for moving on with her life newly single was there, but the motivation to actually make it happen wasn't, at least not right after she got home.

In truth, those next six months for me with my mom were often like pumping up a tire with a pinhole leak: it would stay inflated for a bit, but the air would slowly drain out. When I noticed the deflation, I'd pump it up again, searching everywhere for the leak and patching various spots, hoping I'd found the right one. The patches came in the form of inspiring infographics and videos; protocols to look into; inner child healing programs; the work of pioneering people in the wellness world; podcast episode recommendations; uplifting bitmojis, texts, and phone calls; easy, yummy recipes for meals and smoothies; the list goes on. But despite the irrefutable resilience my mom had demonstrated all her life, the leak remained in the form of old emotional wounds, fatigue, and overwhelm, so ending her marriage felt for her like just too heavy a door to pry open and walk through.

There had been reasons of one kind or another for so many years for why she didn't leave Rick: she was too dependent physically to be on her own. She didn't want to leave her house. He was resistant to splitting up. She didn't want to break up the four kitties between them.

She wasn't feeling well. She was facing another major surgery or recovering from one. The amount of effort it would take legally and physically to get a divorce, prep and sell the house, and buy and move into a new one felt, despite its obvious perks, more daunting than staying.

From a spiritual perspective, I couldn't understand why she would ever remain in such a joyless situation and expect to continue healing from cancer; from a reality perspective, though, I got why it all seemed like just too much for her. I also had to accept that there was only so much I could do. I couldn't force her to leave her unhappy marriage, or unburden herself of excess belongings, or get excited about decorating a new little condo in her signature style—or even to make herself a healthy smoothie in the mornings or a balanced meal for dinner. She was a sovereign being who had the right to make her own decisions and navigate her life on her own terms.

But my mom had always expressed so much sincere appreciation for all the pep talks, and helpful information, and caring guidance I had given her. On the day I returned home from this last trip, I received this sweet text from her:

> You've literally saved my life with your intuition, love, and support and set me on my next journey with all the tools I need. I couldn't be more grateful, honey. 🩶

How could I possibly let her down by ceasing to be that consistent source of encouragement? And how could I be that in every way when I knew that on most days, remaining in that marriage was sucking the very life out of her? This was my mom's health we were playing with, and I have to admit that the narrow space between being loving and supportive of her decisions and refusing to let her lose sight of the future she deserved felt worrisome at best and crushing at worst. To lovingly push and prod her self-care was one thing. To stand back and let her slip away was unthinkable.

∞

Up and Down
and Back and Forth

On June 30th, my mom infused me with a tremendous rush of hope:

Her: My new motto!

"I haven't come all this way to fall apart now."

Diggin in! 😊

Me: I LOVE IT!

But within only weeks, by the end of July, when I would check in to see how my mom was feeling in the mornings, she began to repeatedly tell me that her tummy was uncomfortable and that she was experiencing dull pain, nausea, or shooting pain, or sometimes a combination of all three. She scheduled an ultrasound for August 6th, very concerned about her liver being the culprit.

"Well, the liver can be cleansed," I told her, "and it regenerates too. So I'm sure if that's what it is, there's a way to make it happy again. I know it might sound corny, but talk to your liver and tell it how much you appreciate everything it does, and that if it needs help, you'll find a way."

"I like that idea," she said. "I'll do that. It's just that this year has changed me . . . I see my mortality a little too clearly." Her friend Jacqueline from the clinic, the one whose doctor unleashed her cancer cells with an unauthorized biopsy, had recently succumbed to her illness, to the profound shock and sadness of all of us. "Losing Jacqueline was a bit of a wake-up call. But I also know several girls from H4C who are living with cancer and thriving in their own way. It's just this feeling of debilitation is so new and that's what's scary."

"I know."

"And I have so many responsibilities here at home . . . I'm falling behind. As you know, I have virtually no help and I'm overwhelmed."

There was no use lamenting that her home life remained what it was because she was in no condition to change it, so I fell back on empathy and positivity, and hoped it would help.

"Oh, Little Bree . . . I totally understand. I really do. But I also believe there's no reason you won't be okay . . . we may just need to crack another nut to figure out this slump, but you *can* get past it and come out stronger on the other side. You've been in resilience training all your life for this, and you have all the tools you need . . . and if there's still one missing, we'll figure it out, okay?"

I could tell by her response that she wanted to believe me but that she was at a loss too.

"Do you want me to come back?" I offered.

"Oh, honey . . . of course I would love that. But no . . . I need to take care of myself. You can't be putting your life aside. You've already done that for me when I needed you most. I know I need to dig deep here. I'm just trying to find my way."

But in the days that followed, my mom gave me increasingly alarming reports about her physical and mental state. She told me she had zero energy, zero stamina, and that she couldn't eat or she'd throw up. "I'm nauseous, sad, and scared," she said. "Other than that . . ."

My heart cracked in two. "This is terrible," I told her. "I don't want to be a source of worry energy, but I *am* very worried about you."

"I am too. I don't know what's wrong with me. I was doing so well for a while, and now I feel like I'm going downhill fast."

I kept my emotions in check, trying to stay positive. "At least tomorrow is your ultrasound. Maybe that will turn up something."

"I hope so. I'm just devastated that my life has come to this."

Again, I tried to keep her spirits up. "I know . . . and I hate that you're feeling that way. But I also know this is your body telling you in every way it can that it needs help. It's figuring out *why* that's so challenging. But you *will* figure it out. You *will*. Just hang in there. Maybe try asking your Spirit guides what's going on."

"I do ask for help and understanding every day," she assured me. "I'll see how the next couple days pan out and go from there."

A bit later that day, I felt compelled to resort to loving imperiousness:

Me: I'm not losing you, and that's final. 😊

You're sticking around no matter what it takes. Got it?

Her: Got it! I love your optimism 🖤

Me: Well, I think that's the best way to go through life, if we can. And I also think that when we made a pact to come into this life together, we planned to grow older together, not you taking off on me in my early 50s. That is NOT in the plan. So that's it. You hit another bump in the road is all. You're a warrior princess, remember? 👸 🖤

Her: Copy that, sister! 👸

The next day, when I asked her how she was feeling, she said:

Warrior Princess is doing well. I'm actually basking in a wonderful calm. 🖤

Me: That's great to hear!

But that calm was partially induced by her cancelling her ultrasound. She admitted she was dragging her feet because she didn't want to hear a definitive diagnosis. And I couldn't help but feel that my mom was wasting precious time to get herself on a new protocol.

At this point, I honestly wasn't sure what my role was. My mom had been firm on not expecting me to come out and take care of her, whatever that might have looked like, and that she knew she needed to "dig deep" and find her path toward healing. But day after day, with her frequently throwing up whatever she ate, bemoaning the pain she was in, having bouts of prolonged constipation, and not doing anything proactive about it, I felt compelled to get pushy (which, thankfully, she said she appreciated).

To that end, I sent her a long list of things to explore, possibilities we had discussed before but that she hadn't pursued for whatever reason.

> **Me**: I get that you're scared, but you need to check out all your options and really take charge of getting well. I'm worried that you're just sitting on it and giving up when there's so much you could be doing right away to support your body. I'll do whatever I can, but I want you to get serious . . . this is your life we're talking about! 😘😘
>
> **Her**: You're right, you're right, I know you're right. [one of our oft-spoken lines from *When Harry Met Sally*] I am starting a program called Matrix on Friday that two of my friends are doing. I'll get info on it for you. 💜
>
> **Me**: 😄 Okay, yes, I want to hear! But if I can just say this: I think you need to adopt the mindset of being radically proactive. And screw a "diagnosis." I say, don't even scare yourself. Just go forward as if you just need to radically heal yourself, because you DO need to do that. Matrix might be one component, but there have to be more. Definitely schedule the vitamin C infusions. Make your wellness your priority or even a game of hunting down other healing modalities.

I reminded her that that's what our dear friend who had been living for over a decade with stage IV cancer did, and continued to do. I also reminded her that she was too precious to waste any more time, and that if it helped, to think of what she would want *me* to do if the situation were reversed—then do it.

She agreed and thanked me once again for the motivation. But within a few days, she told me she felt like she was living in a nightmare and couldn't wake up from it.

"I'm not having any fun!" she whined.

I knew she was trying to stay lighthearted with her childlike murmurings, but I also knew something was keeping her terribly disempowered.

> **Me**: I feel so helpless and in such disbelief you're in this state. 😢 I wish having some laughs and fun would turn things around! Do you feel any hope about Matrix and vitamin C infusions? Or are you truly past feeling hopeful with how bad you feel?
>
> **Her**: I haven't given up hope, I promise. I just need something to go right for me. Oh wait, my house is clean. That's a good thing!
>
> **Me**: Well, I'm glad to hear that. Something HAS to go right for you and there are definitely lots of ways for that to happen! We'll figure it out somehow. You're NOT leaving us!!
>
> You enjoy your clean house and I'll talk to you later, ok?
>
> **Her**: Ok honey. I love you 😘
>
> **Me**: Love you too 😘

On Friday, August 14th, the day of her first Matrix session and a follow-up appointment with Jason, the recommended nurse practitioner close to home she'd begun seeing, I sent her an enthusiastic message in hopes it would miraculously find her feeling better.

> **Me**: Big day today! How are you? Did you sleep ok?
>
> **Her**: Another terrible night. I'm in a lot of pain and couldn't get comfortable. Ended up throwing up several times. Misery! 😖
>
> **Me**: Oh Little Bree! I'm just heartbroken over what you're going through. I can't stand that you're in pain and am so worried about you.

Though I had asked repeatedly if she wanted me to come out and she said no, I asked her again. Only this time, I didn't receive her standard no.

"Not yet, but pretty soon."

I paused to take her answer in. It implied that she thought her body was giving up on her, and I couldn't see how that could happen when we'd given her so many viable options for taking care of herself and been sending so much concentrated healing energy her way. Tears filled my eyes that I didn't want her to sense.

"Well, I'll come out whenever you want me to." I wiped my face. "You just *have* to be okay."

"I *want* to be okay. I'm desperate to feel better and have my life back. But with me throwing up a lot of what I eat, I'm only getting weaker." She paused. "I'm afraid I'm in serious trouble."

My throat was tight, but I managed to say, "I know . . . I'm sure you do feel that way. We've been so concerned about what's going on with you. But at least you have your appointments today, and there is *always* hope. People spontaneously heal all the time . . . you *will* get your life back. I'll be eager to hear what Jason might recommend to get some nutrients into you. And Matrix could be just the thing to help you otherwise."

"I sure hope so."

Not long after we hung up, I received this text:

Her: I just weighed myself and I'm 105.5 😿

Me: 105.5? Oh my gosh . . . you're so tiny. We HAVE to get to the heart of this and turn things around right away. Let's hope today is a first step toward that, ok? In the meantime, I'll keep doing some research for other options 🩶

Her: Thanks honey. You're the best daughter and friend ever! 🩶

I was hopeful for her appointments that day, but I also knew I was going to have to start being proactive for her, or I was going to lose her and always regret that I hadn't done more. For months I had struggled with where to draw the line between letting her manage her own health as she assured me she would and swooping in like a fairy godmother who wouldn't take "You don't need to come here" as an answer. Now, it was clear to me: I was going to have to pull out my magic wand [read: take over to some degree] and hope it's what she secretly wished for.

Right away, I got on the phone with the Santa Fe Soul Center, the place that offered the vitamin C infusions, and inquired about an appointment, or series of appointments, for my mom. I didn't have the contact information for the colonics practitioner or the acupuncturist my mom had mentioned to me, but I was determined to get her connected with them as soon as possible too.

When she called me after her sessions that day and told me that Jason had given her something for pain and nausea, and that "there wasn't much to talk about," I was happy I was following my intuition.

"I'm glad you have something for temporary relief. But wasn't he concerned about your weight loss, dehydration, and lack of nutrition? Seriously, who is this guy?"

"Well, I guess because we don't exactly know what's wrong with me, he's hesitant to make suggestions."

"What about your naturopath? Can you get in to see her?"

"She's been out of town. But I'll call her. Maybe she'll see me."

"Okay, please find out. In the meantime, I got you a tentative appointment at the Soul Center for the infusion. And you'll get to see their naturopath too. Maybe that will prove to be the new connection you need."

"Oh wow, honey . . . you called them for me?"

"I hope you don't mind."

"No, I appreciate it. I'll call to confirm."

"It's just that I can't stand not doing something concrete to help you. You're so weak . . . and . . ."

"And you're probably thinking I'm not doing enough to help myself."

Her tone was resigned and understanding of how I must be feeling, but still, I didn't want to put her down. "I just feel like you've waited too long. Something is clearly wrong if you're close to a hundred pounds and can't keep food down."

"I know," she said with sadness in her voice. "And I know I told you I couldn't leave my girls without a mommy. That's too heartbreaking for me to imagine."

"Then please," I pleaded, "do whatever it takes to make sure that doesn't happen,"

"I will, honey."

A bit later, she sent me this message:

You've awakened me! Love love love you 🌛

I only wish it had been soon enough.

∾

Keeping the Faith
(with a Little Help from Our Friends)

*A*round noon on September 5th, my mom told me that her right side was very tender and that she could feel a protrusion. She'd taken some pain pills that took the edge off, but when she called Jason to ask him for a stronger pain prescription, he refused and told her she needed to get to the hospital.

"I know none of us want you in the hospital, but I agree with him," I told her. "Please don't keep putting this off."

"I know. I'm just afraid they'll keep me there, and that could be it."

"Please don't say that." I tried to switch tacks. "Hopefully they'll find the cause and help get you back on track."

"But what if it's another blockage? I don't want to have to have another surgery."

"But if that's what you need . . ."

She sighed audibly.

"I'm coming out. I'll get a flight for tomorrow."

"Well, wait," she said. "If I'm going to be in the hospital, I don't even know if you could see me, with COVID and everything. I think I should find out what's going on first, and then we can make that decision. How does that sound?"

It didn't sound good in the least, but I agreed nonetheless.

Shortly after we hung up, she texted that Deb and their friend Kellie were taking her to the hospital.

Me: Okay, good. I'm glad they're there. It's going to be okay. Somehow, you'll end up on a healing path, ok? We just have to

answer this pain message from your body so you can move
forward and get well. YOU'LL BE OKAY 😘😘

I didn't hear anything from her for over six hours.
Finally, at 7:15, I received a chipper text:

Her: I just got my CT scan. A very nice Dr. Rosenberg is fetching
the results right now!

Me: Oh wonderful! That's fast. I hope it's just a little alien that
can be removed arthroscopically 👽

Her: You never know! 😝 I'll text you when I get the results.

Around 8:00, she said:

Well . . . they're keeping me. For how long, I don't know. Seems
there is a small blockage in my small intestine that Dr. Rosenberg
said could work its way out. So, they're going to hydrate me real
good, get my pain under control and my nausea too. I keep
throwing up! I'll text you again when I get settled in my room. I'm
fine. 🤍 🤍

I was relieved to hear her say she was fine and told her I was glad
they were helping her with the most pressing things, and that I believed
she would likely pass that little blockage. I asked her to call me as soon
as she was awake and up to talking the next day so that we could make a
plan. Then I added:

You might need some comic relief . . . and I'm a good candidate
😊 In the meantime, you can always harken back to our airport
bathroom incident . . . lol 😂

The next morning, my mom called and told me she'd had to stay all
night in emergency because there were no rooms, and that now she was
in an observation room with no bathroom or sink while she awaited an

actual room. She also told me they'd put a tube through her nose down into her stomach to drain the bile and keep her from throwing up, and that it was very uncomfortable but at least working to stop the vomiting.

"My friends have been so great taking shifts with me," she said. "They only allow one at a time, but that's been perfect. It's nice not to be all alone."

I was devastated to learn that she'd basically been marooned in the emergency room all night where she got no rest at all, and that she was now "parked" elsewhere. But I was glad she'd had her friends with her. I told her that to make things easier for now, I was coming by myself and had already booked my flight for tomorrow.

Me: I should be at the hospital by 5:00 p.m.

Her: Ok great . . . we have some serious decisions to make tomorrow. This is more dire than either of us thought. CeCe is with me now. I'm sure the girls won't mind picking you up honey. Please give Dayni my love.

I immediately felt as if a balloon of angst inflated inside me. *More dire than we thought?* The night before, her messages had indicated to me that her condition was manageable, and now she was saying we had serious decisions to make? I had encouraged her not long before to think about how she was going to write a new story of her life, how she was going to be this phenomenal story of healing that would be a huge inspiration to others. She had wanted that so much, ever since the days she'd had the supposed MS—the longing to be a beacon of light for other people who had possibly lost hope.

"That's the story you need to keep in mind, okay?" I'd encouraged. "Keep visualizing it . . . how that beautiful story is going to turn out."

She had agreed she would. And I knew nothing was impossible. But hearing this news deflated even perennially optimistic me. Suddenly, though I wanted to remain strong and positive, I couldn't keep my emotions in check.

Me: Oh no . . . no. 😢 I can't bear this. I want to just come and turn this ship around and sprinkle more fairy dust on you and see you write that new story. ✨

Can you tell me why it's more dire than we thought?

And Dayn still might come . . . she really wants to be there for both of us. 🖤

Her: I just got a pic line for nutritional supplement. I think we should talk about my reality tomorrow when you're here. 🖤

I put my phone down and took a deep breath. *It's never too late*, played over and over in my mind. And then an idea came to me so strongly that I couldn't ignore it. I knew how powerful energy was, and that a rush of positive energy could absolutely heal someone. This idea felt like the Divine speaking to me, telling me that my amazing circle of friends and clients would want to help me if they could—and there was a way I could let them do that.

I picked up my phone again, typed everyone's name who I knew would understand my plea into the "send to" field, and composed the following message:

My dear and treasured friends,

I'm sending this group message to make a deeply personal request for my sweet mom . . . 🙏

She was admitted to the hospital yesterday in horrible pain, after having spent the last weeks not being able to keep food down and generally feeling terrible. We just found out that her cancer has progressed further than we anticipated. We've spent the past year working so hard on her healing journey, and this is devastating news for all of us. 😢

Although I'm being told that she may not have much time, I also believe it's NEVER too late for a miracle . . .

As you are all so dear to me and understand the healing power of energy, I wonder, if you're willing and able, if you would join me in flooding my mom with healing light energy. I thought it would be powerful if we all came together at the same time energetically, and so if it's possible, please set your alarm for today at 12:30 PST / 1:30 MST / 2:30 CST / 3:30 EST (about 30 minutes from now), and just give one minute of your brand of love and light to my mom. Her name is Briana (Bree) King. Maybe together we can make a difference.

If you don't see this message or can't make that time, I sincerely appreciate any prayers and love energy you're willing to send at any time. 🙏

I'm flying to NM in the morning, hopeful this won't be our final time together. She's only 68 and has so much more life to live.

I've never asked for anything like this, and I can't thank you enough for being part of this with me if you're willing.

With so much gratitude and love, Stacey

Literally within seconds, text messages began flying in.

Jim: I will be there 🖤😊🙏

Terry: I'll be there also 🖤

Laura: I will be 🖤🙏 there too

Paul: I am there 🖤😊😊🙏🙏🙏 Bill, Jeff and myself

Mary: I'm so happy to share any healing I can. I'll be with you in spirit 🖤

Rebecca: [attachment of a beautiful audio message]

Lori: I will be there covering her. 🖤

Susan: Count me in. Starting early.

Jayme: Glenco and I will be standing with you.

Patty: Deeply sad to hear this! I will be there Stacey. Hugs to you. 🖤 🖤

Moshe: With you Stacey. All Amare to your mom and you.

Paul: I have trust and faith in the entities of light and love for a healing for Bree.

Laura: She is receiving our light, love, and prayers deep in her cells 🙏 Stacey, you are so loved by all of us. Thank you for letting us help at this very stressful time.

Jay: Your precious mother will be in my prayers. And yes, we do believe in miracles 🙏

Moshe: Sharing this beautiful healing song with the group [link attached]

Terry: I will continue to send love, light, and healing energy 🖤

Donna: Sending the love and light of healing energy to your beautiful mom. I am holding both of you in my heart and in my prayers. Let Divine love embrace Bree and Divine guidance lead her onward. 🖤🙏

Vicki: I am praying and will continue to pray for Bree. I am sending her so much beautiful and powerful healing energy. Please surround her with comfort and peace. 🙏🖤

Tori: Prayers, love, and healing light sent to both you and your mom during this difficult time. 🖤

The momentum and feeling of togetherness was evident in the flurry of "loves" people were attaching to each other's messages and my heartfelt professions of gratitude. I truly felt like George Bailey in *It's a Wonderful Life*, when everyone in town comes to his rescue when he needs it the most.

The clock was ticking toward the time I'd asked everyone to give my mom their brand of healing energy, and I couldn't help but wonder if my mom would feel it. But I also knew her spirits were down, so I thought a message of hope would buoy her and allow her to focus on what was coming her way.

> **Me**: I want you to be open to receiving a massive wave of healing energy in about 10 minutes. It is NEVER too late for a miracle, and I've called in all my angels to flood you with love and healing light. We're all coming together at 1:30 your time. Get ready to accept and believe in the power of love and energy healing you because it's going to be amazing! ✨
>
> **Her**: I'm ready!

After a few minutes had passed, I took screenshots of all the messages my friends had sent to me and asked her if she was ready to see what had just happened, that I was completely overcome by the outpouring of love and caring we had received. Then I sent them all to her, including the voice recording from Rebecca and the link to the beautiful song from Moshe.

I knew my mom was likely dealing with distractions from the staff coming in and out of the observation room she was in, but I finally received a response.

> **Her**: How precious that you brought your trusted angels together for me today! Boy, are you loved and well tended, and by extension so am I. I'm a believer!
>
> **Me**: It was truly the most magical span of time for me . . . and yes, by extension, for you, which was the whole point—to bring loving, healing energy to you. I am still overwhelmed by it all in the most remarkable way.
>
> Sorry about the deluge of screenshots, but I really wanted you to experience it all as close to the way I did as possible. It was so very

special hearing the sounds of all those messages pouring in. I wish you could have heard them.

I hope you feel your body doing its job to put you back in balance. No matter what, I'm going to be with you tomorrow. The girls will be together. 🤍🤍

Coming to Terms

A t the last minute, I decided I did want Dana to come to Santa Fe with me. We hadn't traveled anywhere together for four years because Dana had always stayed home with Shaia when I had a trip to take. But Shaia had left us at the end of May, and my intuition told me that Dana should be there to see my mom, and to be by my side. So I added a ticket to my itinerary only the night before, and we scrambled to get ready to leave early the next morning, on Monday, September 7th.

Right away, I was glad for that eleventh-hour decision.

Around 8:00 a.m., I texted my mom to see if she had a room yet, and to tell her Dana was coming with me after all. I was relieved to find out she had finally been moved to a private suite, and she was happy Dana was joining me. But then she casually delivered an unanticipated blow.

"I'll be going home tomorrow or Wednesday to hospice," she said.

Hospice. I took a deep breath and held it for several seconds. I told myself that maybe it was just a way for my mom to get care at home, which was much better than being in the hospital, especially since she was only allowed one visitor per day there now. After all, it might take a little time for everyone's healing energy from yesterday to fully sink in and perform the miracle I hoped for. If anyone was holding fast to the possibility that my mom would make a complete recovery—the one we would write that compelling story about—it was me.

But I also couldn't ignore what hospice typically signified: that it was to make one's end of life more comfortable, and that whatever was more dire than we thought meant there was nothing more they could do for my mom.

When I finally arrived at the hospital late that evening, it was not at all like the last time she'd been hospitalized and diagnosed with cancer, when I'd felt no fear or worry because I believed we were armed with knowledge and a wonderful plan. This time, the first sight of my fragile, hundred-pound mom broke me. Instead of the positivity I usually exuded, I immediately started sobbing. I turned my back so I wouldn't upset her too much, but it didn't seem to matter. When I faced her, even with tears pouring down my cheeks, she was embodied by an odd composure.

"It's okay, honey," she said. "I'm okay."

I wiped my face. "What do you mean you're okay?"

"I mean I've made peace with the fact that I'm dying."

I shook my head. "How can you be dying? You're too young. How do you know there's nothing left to do?"

"Because the doctor explained to me what's going on in my body," she said calmly, "and I've come to terms with it."

"Why can't they remove the blockage?"

"Because another surgery isn't feasible. It would just make things worse."

"Worse than you dying?"

She softened. "I know this is very upsetting, but honey, there's nothing left to do. The cancer has spread to my abdomen and one ovary. Dr. Rosenberg's going to come tomorrow and explain it all to you."

I turned my face away as the tears streamed down.

"But there's still so much I want to share with you in this lifetime. I can't imagine you not being here."

"I'm *so* sorry," she said sincerely.

I nodded, my throat too tight to respond.

"The woman who coordinates hospice is going to be back soon, and she'll explain all that to you too."

I nodded again, keeping my face turned. I realized I couldn't remember the last time my mom had seen me lose it emotionally to this extreme. I'd been so strong, so positive, for so long, and now it had all collapsed right before her eyes. I didn't want to make her feel bad, but I couldn't begin to conjure something funny or lighthearted to say like I usually did. Our lives together, in this particular lifetime we had shared in our special way, had shifted irrevocably and I knew it. Yes, I still believed in miracles, but I had the feeling my mom had given up on them at that point. And if her heart wasn't holding out hope anymore, and she was this resigned to move on to her soul's next journey, I wasn't sure it was appropriate for me to even suggest a possible path to the contrary.

"I'm okay, Doob," she repeated. "I really am. I've had time to think about it, and even though I know it's breaking your heart, which is killing me, I'm tired . . . I'm just really tired of trying to figure all this out. Even if there *were* something left to try, I just don't have it in me."

I thought about all the protocols and articles and healing modalities I'd suggested to her over the past six months that she'd ignored for too long. It wasn't until the prior week that she'd signed up for a couple of very promising programs I'd shared for reversing cancer that could very well have saved her life. Now, it was too late.

I hated acquiescing to the idea of my mom's physical life ending, but since she had just made it clear she wasn't going to try anything else to get better, it seemed the only choice I had was to be supportive, as awkward as that felt.

Suddenly, my mom drew in a quick breath. "Oh my gosh . . . Dayni's birthday you planned for her. I can't let that get ruined."

I put my hand on her leg. "That is the *least* of what you should be thinking about. Seriously. It's not even something to discuss in the midst of what you're going through."

But my mom knew this wasn't just any ordinary birthday.

I'd always enjoyed putting a lot of thought into celebrations, but for reasons I didn't yet understand, I'd gone completely overboard for this one—more even than I had for Dana's fortieth and fiftieth birthdays, and those were pretty special. And this one wasn't even a milestone.

The world was pretty much on lockdown from COVID, which meant that there was really nowhere to go to have any fun this year. So, I'd begun a full seven weeks early with granting her big wish: ordering a cake from Carlo's Bake Shop, the one featured on *Cake Boss*, even though we rarely ate refined sugar anymore and it would be a rare splurge. "Do it!" my mom had said when I told her I was considering it. And then that had grown into an idea for an at-home birthday fun day, which then grew into a full-blown extravaganza. Before I knew it, I was spending a ridiculous number of hours on the Internet, finding all kinds of gifts I knew Dana would love and not be expecting. I told her I was "building something" for her birthday in our loft closet (aka, my secret workshop), and she'd remained blissfully in the dark as I shuttled box after box upstairs every time another delivery came. I also delighted in ordering a variety of cards, wrapping papers, and notions from Etsy and Society6 to create the visual fantasy I'd hatched in my mind.

"I love that you're supporting independent artists," my mom had said. "And I love the sound of it . . . all those retro colors we love."

"I knew you would," I'd said. "I love that the three of us are such stationery and wrapping girls."

"I just wish I could be there, like a little bee buzzing around."

"You mean a little *Bree* buzzing around."

She'd laughed. "If only."

All three of us were such kids at heart together, which was why sharing parts of the planning and sending photos of different elements to my mom made it that much more fun for me. She agreed that having a bunch of presents to open would take the sting out of not being able to go anywhere. But because I'd wanted it to be more fun than just opening gifts, I'd come up with an ongoing activity to last the entire day. I even designed and made a special birthday banner. Never had I done so much or been so ahead of the game for a birthday in the twenty years Dana and I had been together, and my mom was as excited as I was for the surprises to be unveiled.

By September 5th, the day my mom was unexpectedly admitted to the hospital, I had masterminded every last detail, signed every card, wrapped every gift, written out the timing of every activity, and planned the placement of every element, so that on the night of the 17th, all I would have to do was bring everything downstairs and set it all up.

Now, sitting on my mom's bed in the hospital, with the news of this latest turn in her health weighing heavily on us both, I didn't want my mom to give the birthday another thought. Being who she was, though, she said, "Oh Doob . . . after everything you've done to plan this birthday for Dayni, there's no way I can keep it from happening."

I looked at her tenderly. "It's so sweet of you . . . and so like you . . . to care about that, but obviously it doesn't matter now. At some point down the road, when we can bring ourselves to celebrate, we'll have the party. All that matters now is *you*."

"I know, but . . ."

"But nothing. Dayn would *hate* to think it's something we're giving any importance to, or even talking about at all. Please don't give it another thought, okay?"

My mom gave me a look that said *okay* but that, as absurd as it seemed under the circumstances, she regretted her terrible timing.

"It would be awful if I died on Dayni's birthday," she said.

I caught my breath at the thought. "That would be heartbreaking . . . as if it isn't already."

My mom looked into my eyes. "I promise I won't leave you on her birthday. Before or after, but not on the 18th."

I nodded, feeling strangely comforted by her promise, as if anything could make her leaving less painful.

Just then, Jan from hospice came in to meet me and tell me how things would get set up at my mom's house when she was discharged. She was lovely and compassionate, but I was struggling to come to terms with the reality of what we were facing, and the whole conversation felt as surreal as the evening of my grandma's funeral twenty-four years prior, when I had thanked person after person for coming as if suspended in an opaque bubble of denial.

After she left, we didn't have much time before visiting hours were ending, and I was still immersed in a fog of disbelief when I hugged my mom goodbye. But my senses were fully awakened when she held me for the longest time, longer than I ever remember. "My baby," she said softly. Though I believed we still had several days ahead of us for hugs like this, I felt an overwhelming sense that my mom was holding tight to her little girl for the very last time.

The next day, while I was at the hospital with my mom until she was released in the late afternoon, Dr. Rosenberg came in as promised and explained where the new blockage was in my mom's upper intestine, why they couldn't operate, and why he believed they had run out of options.

"She doesn't have *months*," he said, "but possibly weeks. Especially if she takes in a little food and water every day, to tell the body it's not starving."

This was a revelation. "Weeks? I thought having hospice meant she was close . . . that she didn't have that much time."

"Not necessarily. Even having little bits of water will help prolong her life."

"But I thought she couldn't have any food or water. Couldn't that make her throw up?"

"It shouldn't," he assured us. "She'll have the nasogastric tube hooked up to a portable machine at home, similar to the one here, and that should keep her from vomiting. Again, the amounts have to be small. But it shouldn't be a problem. Whatever she takes in will be brought up the tube before it has any time to bother her stomach." He turned to my mom. "There's no reason at this point for you not to enjoy some food if you're craving it. No meat or anything hard to digest, of course, but broth, ice cream, a milkshake . . . things like that."

"That sounds good," my mom said with a smile. "I could go for a milkshake!"

I smiled too. "Then we'll get you one on the way home!"

I turned back to Dr. Rosenberg and offered him a heartfelt thank you. "I'm still devastated by all of this, but at least you've painted a better picture than I was imagining . . . about how much time we have."

"I know this is very difficult, and I wish I could offer more options, but what's important is having this time together."

My mom and I looked at each other and agreed.

After the doctor left, I said, "Do you feel more hopeful now? I know I do."

"I do. And this means you can get me settled, go home for Dayn's birthday, then come back afterward."

I made a face that needed no translation. "We're *not* letting the birthday be a factor, remember?"

"Well, we are if *I* say we are," she said in her little-girl sarcastic voice.

"How about, we'll see . . . after you're home and everything . . . how you feel."

"Okay. But it might all work out. Wouldn't that be wonderful?"

I shook my head, wondering if diverting her attention from this reality we were facing was some kind of tincture for her breaking heart. "What would be wonderful is if you didn't leave me for a long, long time."

❦

Going Home

Despite the circumstances, my mom was eager to get home that next day to the comfort of her own bedroom, surrounded by her kitties. I had no idea it would be the first of only eight more days we would have on this Earth together.

My mom had remarked multiple times how she couldn't wait to shower and wash her hair, which I'd planned to help her do that evening. But by the time she was settled, she was too tired to do either. Plus, the hospice "setup" took a lot out of her for more reasons than one.

Because my mom still required the portable drainage machine to keep from throwing up, the tube she had in the hospital was left in, and that had to be hooked up with a catheter to the machine. It sounds simple, but the nurse was at a loss for precisely how to do it.

"Not too many people have these in hospice care," he said, riffling through the bag of supplies.

My mom and I exchanged uneasy glances.

"Does that mean you don't know how to set it up?" I wanted to know.

"No, no . . . I can do it. I've just only done it one other time is all."

My mom rolled her eyes at me as he tinkered. I took in a calming breath.

Eventually, after multiple tries and resorting to rigging the tube with paper tape, he determined all should work fine. He showed me how to unhook the other end to rinse the bucket, which I should only need to do once a day, and he said my mom could be untethered from it for short periods, such as to use the bathroom or bathe. It *seemed* straightforward enough.

"So for your visitation schedule," he said turning to my mom, "you'll have a nurse come to help you twice a week with whatever you might need. Since today is Tuesday, your next visit will likely be on Friday."

"Not until Friday?" I said. "But I thought she'd have someone here every day."

He shook his head. "We really don't have the staffing for that unless a patient has no one to take care of them. Technically, you can request someone to come every day, but with COVID . . ."

"So you're saying we *can* request it, but that it wouldn't be fair to other patients who really need it," I said.

"Pretty much, yes," he confirmed. "How long are you planning to be here?"

Right away, I knew my mom's idea of me going home for a brief spell wasn't going to fly. With the machine, her needing someone to get her food and water, and Rick being willing to run to the pharmacy or to the store but not being cut out at all to be a caregiver, there was no way I could leave her, or *would* leave her. Plus, the idea of going home to have a celebration during my mom's final days was just wrong on every possible level.

"As long as I need to be," I told him.

"That's great," he said. "You're so lucky, Briana."

"I am," my mom said with a genuine smile. "But I didn't expect my daughter to be my full-time nurse."

I knew exactly what was going through my mom's mind. Ever since she was a little girl, she had felt like a burden to my grandma. She'd carried that wound so intensely that she'd actually told me she would *never* allow herself to be a burden to me, that if it ever came to that, "there was a bullet with her name on it." She didn't mean she'd literally shoot herself, but she did mean she'd take herself out before she'd put me in a position to have to care for her. She simply couldn't bear the thought of doing that to me. We'd kind of joked about it at the time, but I also knew she wasn't kidding.

"It's okay," I said lightheartedly. "I don't think there's anything we can't handle."

"Good. But if you need anything at all, we're on call 24/7, okay?"

"Great," I said, taking his card.

"And not for now," he added kindly, "but for when the time comes, what funeral home have you chosen?"

I looked at my mom with eyebrows raised.

"I haven't," she said.

"That's okay," he assured us, then gave us the names of the two local ones that were most highly regarded. "Either one is excellent." He turned to my mom. "Have you decided if you want to be buried or cremated?"

In the big scheme of life, I understood that a person making these choices for herself was ideal, and that I shouldn't feel uncomfortable with him asking. But still, the air of finality made my stomach contract.

"Cremated," she said.

"Okay. Well, like I said, both funeral homes are excellent. It's a good idea to decide now so that you can call ahead and make the plans." He patted my shoulder then picked up his bag. "You have a good night, Briana," he said, giving her foot a gentle squeeze before I walked him out.

Okay, I thought. *This part's done. We'll decide on the funeral home and get that out of the way. And then we can have our time together.* I had already imagined us planted in her living room while Rick was at work, watching all our favorite movies together on her big-screen TV, quoting lines and laughing, having our typical exchanges of witty banter, tiptoeing through my baby albums and keepsakes of my childhood, and maybe having a few deep conversations. Clearly, she wasn't up for any of that her first day home, but still it's what I foresaw us doing in the days to come. Sure, there was the need for periodic pain meds, this machine to deal with, and having to dump and clean its bucket along with the one in my mom's portable potty that hospice brought for her bedside. But compared to what a lot of people faced in caring for their parents, this was nothing.

Dana and I had booked an Airbnb near the hospital, about twenty-five minutes from my mom's house, since we didn't know how quickly she would be released. And now that she was home, it was logical that the two of us would simply "move in" to the office/guest room. Only there was a hitch: my mom's youngest kitty, Emeline, recently had surgery and had to be kept fairly immobile, which in this case meant she resided in a large soft-sided crate that took up the entire middle of "our" room. Breaking it down and moving it to the living room would be a huge task, so for the time being, we had to stay at the Airbnb.

That first night, though, I decided to sleep on the couch in the office with Emeline, just in case my mom needed me. She could give herself the liquid morphine she required at pretty steady intervals for pain, and she had a bottle of tiny anti-anxiety pills—which would take the edge off but also calm nausea—that were easy to swallow if she felt the need for one. And since she had taken to chewing on crushed ice in the hospital, which she'd never cared to do before but found oddly satisfying now, she thought having plenty of water and a couple big cups of ice chips was the only other thing she needed for the night. Still, she admitted she felt better having me there.

Between Emeline's stirrings and litter box activity, and my mom needing me a couple times, I didn't get much sleep. But I was glad I was there because the first time my mom called for me was to help with the meds, and the second was for disaster control: the paper tape holding the catheter to my mom's tube had soaked through and fallen off, which meant that the tube was leaking bile all over the place. Luckily, it wasn't so much on her as on the tile floor and area rug. But the real dilemma was how to fix it after I cleaned everything up so it wouldn't keep leaking. I resorted to using the paper tape again to hopefully get us through the night as we both let out our frustration with the ghetto-rigging the nurse had passed off as "fine."

"There's a little on your white top," I said, noticing as I smoothed the sheet. "That's going to stain. Here, let me get you a new top and I'll rinse this one."

My mom looked at me tenderly and whispered, "Honey, it doesn't matter. I'm going to shower tomorrow anyway. And the top . . ." She shook her head with a sweet smile that said everything.

She was never going to wear that top again.

September 9th

When my mom woke up around 9:00 a.m., she was perfectly herself, though tired from the rough night.

"Did you get any sleep at all, honey?" she wanted to know. "I can't believe I heard Rick go into your room to feed Emeline at 6:00 a.m."

I rolled my eyes. "I know. But in his defense, he didn't know I stayed here last night. I think I actually startled him! But yeah . . . I didn't get much sleep. I'm so glad I was here, though."

"I am too. But this sleeping arrangement is ridiculous. You girls should be able to stay here and fold out the couch bed."

"Well . . . do you think Rick could help me break down the crate and move Emeline, maybe to the dining room since no one's really eating there now anyway?"

"I'm sure he could. I know it will be a little tricky because you'll have to carefully corral Emeline so she can't get hurt, but the crate does collapse."

"Well, we've already paid for one more night at the Airbnb, so maybe we can do the move tonight or tomorrow."

"That sounds like a plan!"

I exhaled with a flourish. "So *today* . . . I know how much you want to shower, so just let me know when you want to do it so I can help you."

"Probably in a little while, honey," she said, adjusting her position.

"And what about the bank?"

"Maybe this afternoon."

The day before, eager to get home, my mom had passed on picking up a milkshake, as well as on the trip to the bank she'd wanted to take to sign her account over to me.

"Okay. How are you feeling? Are you in pain?"

"A little. I took some morphine around 5:00 a.m., so I can have some more now, I guess."

"If you need it, you should. The nurse said there was no reason not to have the regular doses every four hours."

She winced. "Yeah. It's time."

I hated seeing her in pain but was happy we had a way to manage it without knocking her out. I jotted the latest doses down in a journal the way I'd been instructed to keep track.

"Hey . . . you should use your CBD gummies for pain," I said. "That would be so much better than only using morphine, don't you think?"

"I *do* think," she said, perking up. "I have a decent amount, and Jen can always get me more."

I felt relieved. "Are you hungry at all?"

She shook her head. "Uh uh."

"Because I can get you the shake whenever you want."

She made a yummy sound. "Yes, that sounds good for later."

I looked at the rigged catheter. "It seems to be holding okay."

"Thank God," she said.

I realized how disheveled I must look. "Don't hate me because I'm beautiful," I joked.

"*You*? What about me?"

We both chuckled and agreed that appearances didn't count this week.

"But hey," she said, "I think I want to rest some more anyway, so why don't you go back to your Airbnb for a bit. I know you want to clean up and change clothes. Then maybe you and Dayn can run a couple of errands for me. I'll be fine until you get back."

"You're sure?"

She flipped her hand in a playful wave. "I'm totally sure. Can you just bring me some more ice before you do?"

"Oh, shoot. You're totally out! Yes. I'll be right back."

She eyed the porta-potty. "I'm gonna use this bad boy while you do that."

I ground the ice into small pieces with the NutriBullet and brought her three big cups full with a spoon. Then I pulled out the bucket from the potty and went into my mom's bathroom to dump and rinse it.

Okay, I thought. *We're finding a routine. I can totally do this, however long she needs me.*

When I got to our Airbnb, I was eager to see Dana and to get into the inviting, claw-footed tub and just relax for a little bit. I felt like I'd been in an emotional whirlwind for the last few days, and I was grateful to my mom for giving me a little time to decompress. But not five minutes after I sank into a mound of bubbles, I received this text:

Her: This damn thing is leaking again! I just don't know what to think! ✨

Me: Nooo!!! Crap!! I JUST got in the bathtub. Can you use a towel for now and I'll jump out and be back as soon as I can?

Her: Take your time honey, my leak and I aren't going anywhere. Do you think I should call hospice?

Me: I'm so sorry this is happening and I'm not there. 😟 I do think you should call them. It should NOT be leaking. Will you let me know if they can come out pretty quickly?

A few minutes later:

Her: Ok, I put in the call and a nurse should get back to me. I'm having Rick pick up some popsicles for me! Yum!

Me: Ok good! I'm going to grab a quick bite, throw myself together, and be back, ok?

Her: Ok honey, take your time. 🖤 I'm just resting. 😴

Shortly after, a nurse named Karen called and told me she'd be at the house within the hour, and that she was calling a tech to come too. I let my mom know that help was on the way and was happy when Karen arrived just after I did. The problem was, she knew even less about my mom's machine than the nurse the night before.

"What about the tech?" I asked. "I thought someone was going to meet you here."

"Unfortunately, no one was available. Let me call the company and see if there's someone who can walk me through it."

"Good, because it made a major mess in the night," I said. "This can't keep happening."

The tech on the phone told Karen to pull a new catheter from the ones in the supply bag, and then told her how to thread it with the tube. But the process was as clunky as it had been the night before.

"How about a stronger adhesive?" she suggested.

I found some electrical tape. "How about this?"

"That should do it!" she declared chipperly.

But after she wrapped it, I said, "That part might hold now, but the angle is such that when the tube backs up, it rushes out through here." I pointed to the hole in the backup valve. "I thought this was to keep the flow steady and to keep it from spilling out."

Karen shrugged with a grimace. "I would think so too. But again, I've never worked with this machine before."

"So, we're just supposed to hope for the best?" I said. "Because it looked like this last night, and it was a disaster."

"I understand. They just don't have anyone they can send out now, but I'll give you the number for the company."

I couldn't believe it—and neither could my mom. Karen was very nice, but her not being familiar with the machine was incredibly frustrating. We were talking about smelly, sticky black bile surging and spilling out everywhere. It wasn't something we could live with and "hope for the best" for another day and night.

After Karen left, I told my mom I wasn't so sure a trip to the bank was viable and she agreed.

"Are you wanting to shower now?" I asked.

"I do . . . but maybe later."

"Okay, well . . . do you want to watch a movie or something?"

She winced and put her hand over the little bulge where the blockage was. "Not really."

I grimaced. "You're in pain?"

"Not too bad. How long till my next dose?"

I looked at my watch. "About thirty minutes."

She nodded.

"Is there anything you want to do? Or want me to do? You mentioned at the hospital you wanted to go through your clothes with me to show me what you thought we should consign."

She made a face. "I don't think I'm up for that right now." She looked around. "But we could go through my jewelry. Can you bring me that box on the dresser? I want to sort out what's valuable for you."

I retrieved it and sat back in the chair next to her bed. She opened the box and started pulling out certain pieces and setting them aside. As she did, she expressed no sentiment about them or made any comments; instead, she went through them more like it was a task that needed to get checked off "the list."

"Is this weird for you?" I asked.

"No," she said matter-of-factly. "Is it for you?"

"I don't know. I guess it's nice to have this time together for you to give me what's important to you. But it *is* kind of weird. I feel like I'm here waiting to collect booty or something."

"Oh," she laughed in her playful way. "Don't feel like that. I know you're not here for the booty."

The awkward fog lifted a little from the room and soon enough, she had made a small pile and told me the rest was costume, and just to donate what I didn't want.

As I replaced the box on the dresser and put the valuables in a baggie, I wondered what my mom was really feeling. She loved all her beautiful, unique pieces of jewelry—pieces she knew weren't my style at all —and she was never going to wear them again. What did it feel like to touch these items for the last time? To suddenly face that their life with her had come to an abrupt end, and they would be moving on to a life with someone else? She had gone through everything in such a utilitarian way, as if no memories were attached to them. But I knew that couldn't be true. Was it too painful to think about? Or had she already reached a place inside where they truly didn't matter anymore?

I noticed her ice had mostly melted and took her cups into the kitchen, ground up enough ice to fill them both, and brought them back to her.

"Thanks, honey." She scooped some chips into her mouth. "I'm sorry about this. It must drive you crazy."

"Drive me crazy?"

"The sound of the ice crunching," she said between chomps.

I laughed. "Not at all. It doesn't bother me."

"Really? I've always hated when people chewed ice like this. Now here I am doing it. For some reason, it just tastes so good, not that it tastes like anything. It's just satisfying somehow."

"I get it. It's like eating and drinking at the same time."

"I guess."

I looked at her stomach. "How's the pain?"

"It's never really gone. But it's manageable. The gummies really help."

Once again, the idea that my mom was in pain crushed me, but I had to be grateful that it appeared tolerable. "Good," I sighed. "I'm so glad you have those." I paused, scanning my mind for the next right caregiver question. "Is there anything I can get you?"

"No, I can't think of anything."

"Okay . . . did you maybe want to try to shower now?"

Once again, she pushed it off until "later."

"I think I just want to rest for a bit. Do you have work you need to do?"

"I do have a couple things."

"Why don't you do that, and I'll call you if I need anything."

"Okay. I'll just be in the living room."

She smiled. "Okay, honey."

I opened my mom's laptop and brought up a book file I was pol-
ishing. When we were at Hope4Cancer, it felt perfectly normal to be
away for a few hours and work while my mom was doing her therapies, because I knew she was getting better every day. Now, there were
no therapies left to do, and I was having a hard time swallowing that.
Nonetheless, I switched gears for a few hours until my mom woke up.

"Doob?" she called.

I jumped up. "I'm coming!"

She laughed. "Look at you at the ready."

I curtsied. "What can I get for you, your highness?"

"Ooh, I'm royalty now. Well, I just wondered if maybe I could have
something. I'm actually feeling hungry."

"You are? Okay . . . um . . . how about some broth? There's some
nice organic soup in the pantry that I could drain the vegetables out of."

She made a yummy sound. "That sounds good."

When I returned with it, I fed her a warm spoonful, then waited a
beat. "Okay so far?" I wanted to know.

"So far, so good," she said with a chipper tone.

I kept feeding her like a baby until she'd had enough.

"That was really good," she said. "Thank you. What about you?
Have you eaten anything? There's plenty of Daily Harvest stuff in the
freezer."

"Yeah. I had a snack earlier."

"Good. What time is it?"

I glanced at my watch. "Almost five."

Her face brightened. "I have an idea. Why don't you pick up food
and go back to your place to have a nice dinner with Dayni."

"And just leave you?"

"I'm fine. And the machine's still fine, right?"

The bucket was fairly empty and nothing much was floating in the
tube. "It looks like it."

"Then what do you think? I want to call a few friends anyway. And
Rick should be home soon if I'm in a real bind."

"But what about your shower?"

"We can do it tomorrow."

"Really? You want to wait another day?"

"Yeah . . . it's fine. But tomorrow for sure. I can barely stand myself at this point. I *so* need to wash my hair."

She'd had her chin-length bob covered with a crocheted cloche since I'd arrived. "I'm kind of scared to see what's under that hat," I teased.

"You and me both, sister!"

The truth was, my mom was still hopelessly cute, despite the lack of recent grooming.

"Well, if you're sure about me having dinner with Dayn . . . that would be nice. And then I'll come right back afterward."

My mom smiled. "Okay, honey. No rush."

I dumped her potty bucket, replaced her ice supply, and called in an order to a favorite nearby restaurant that had a few organic options.

When I called Dana to tell her I was coming home for dinner, she was elated. "Just be careful driving in the rain," she said.

At that point, visibility was fine, so I didn't think much of it until the rain suddenly became torrential and electrified branches of lightning cracked across the broad Santa Fe sky. In an instant, the rain was pelting down so hard that I couldn't see, so I pulled over, hoping to wait it out.

As I sat there with my blinking hazard lights and the cacophony of rain turning to hailstones beating down on the car, reality hit me hard. *I was going to pick up dinner, like it was nothing, while my mom was never going to have a real meal again. The ice, some broth, maybe a milkshake . . . it was all just prolonging the inevitable: that I was going to essentially allow, and watch, my beautiful mom starve to death.*

Tears welled up and began streaming down my face, mirroring the weather outside. *How did this happen? How can I let her starve?* The whole idea squeezed my heart like a vice. We were still bantering in our way, but the truth was, *my mom had come home to die.* It's not that I didn't know that, but we weren't having maudlin conversations, or feeling the need that other families did to forgive grudges or rough times we'd had over the years. There was no question of our love for each other; we had always said "I love you" before we hung up from every single phone call. My whole family did. And my mom didn't just say it in a perfunctory way. She often said "I love you *very* much" with her whole heart. We had talked so openly for so many years about every topic under the sun that I couldn't think of any bridge we hadn't crossed. The main thing was what she desired after the fact, and she'd already told me that. And because people couldn't gather in the normal way because COVID was still a thing, she wanted me to wait to plan a celebration of her life until everyone could be together without restriction, possibly the following summer. Besides that, she'd had her will done the previous fall, just before we left for Hope4Cancer; everything that was hers, including her half of the house, went to me. It seemed there wasn't anything complicated to figure out. And because we had always had this open, outwardly loving relationship, it felt like there was nothing left to do in the days ahead but to just keep on being *us*.

But I also couldn't help but question what I might regret *not* doing while my mom was still here. *Is there anything I want to ask her?* I wondered. *Anything I want to know that maybe I've forgotten or that I want to talk about one more time?* Of course I wanted her last days to be as light and sweet and normal as possible. But if I only had a few weeks, how could I make the best of them? Already, she wasn't feeling up to watching our favorite movies. *What if she never was? What would I want us to share? What would I want to do for her, knowing I had the gift of this finite time?*

I believed so strongly in the power of perspective and seeing the bigger picture. Einstein said, "There are only two ways to live your life. One is as though nothing is a miracle. The other is as though everything is a miracle." I preferred the latter, which meant that my mom's leaving at this time must have some divinity in it, and it was up to me to find it, as much as my heart was breaking in the physical world.

I asked myself: *If I had the choice of how to lose my mom, what would it look like?* Of all the scenarios—sudden death in an accident or during a surgery, her not remembering me, a drawn-out, painful illness, to name a few of the worst—the way it was playing out was actually the most gentle, graceful, and humane way it could happen. She was home; we had the luxury of being together, her lucidity and ability to manage pain, her decision-making capability, my flexibility with work and the most understanding clients in the world, the list went on. *Yes,* I decided. *If in some fantasy world, the Divine had given me a menu of options for how I would say goodbye to my mom, this is what I would choose.* And for that wish being granted to be my reality, I recognized what a gift it was and felt supremely grateful.

My mind was swirling with these thoughts as the hail morphed back into rain and let up enough for me to drive again. I wiped my face and pulled back out onto the highway, deciding I'd have to just listen to my intuition for how to make this time together count as the days faded one into the next.

After dinner, Dana and I had been watching TV when she roused me gently. "Hey . . . don't you have to get back?"

I jolted awake. "Crap!" I grabbed my phone and texted my mom.

Me: Oh gosh . . . I drifted off!! Are you okay?

Her: Into a ditch???
Yes, I'm ok. In pain, but ok.

Me: No, no ditch. But I did get caught in a torrential lightning storm! We were just watching TV and I dozed off. 😬
Crap . . . you're in pain? Have you had morphine or a gummie lately?

Her: No, no helpers. Just woke up. Gummie next!
Do you want to stay in town?

Me: Oh gosh . . . only if you think you'll be okay. I think with the machine working, you should be fine. But do you have ice and water? Would Rick be able to get you some?

Her: Rick is fast asleep!
The only thing is that my bucket may overflow. I still have some ice. Your call. 🖤

Me: Hmm . . . well, there wasn't much in there when I left. But I would hate for it to overflow in the night. 😬

Her: It's not going to overflow. Just stay!

Me: Oh man . . . are you sure? ONLY if you're okay. I hate to take you up on staying, but I'm just so dang tired . . . and it's still raining pretty hard. 🥺

Her: Sit . . . stay!

Me: Yes, master. 😌
It would be great for me to get some rest tonight. Thank you!! I'll be back in the morning then, ok? 😘😘

Her: Ok, see you tomorrow morning 🖤🖤😘😘

Me: 🖤🖤🙏😘😘🙏

September 10th

*A*t 6:13 a.m., I awoke to the sound of my phone and bolted across the room.

Her: Please come back soon. The bucket leaked and I'm covered in it. I can't do this by myself! 🖤🖤

Me: Oh no! Ok. Damn. I'm sorry!! The text woke me so I'll be there shortly!

Her: Thanks honey 😊

After finally getting a decent night's sleep, I felt immediate guilt for it. If I'd been at my mom's house like we'd originally planned, she wouldn't be lying in bile right now, waiting a good half hour before I could get there.

When I arrived, it looked like a monster had thrown up all over my mom's bedroom floor. Luckily her being "covered in it" wasn't true. Only a little had actually gotten on her clothes and she'd dabbed off the rest.

"I'm so sorry," I said frantically. "I feel so bad. I shouldn't have left you last night."

"Nooo, it's okay, honey," she said. "I just don't know what we're going to do about this."

"I don't know either. I have to get someone from the company out here. This is ridiculous."

I dampened a washcloth with some soap to clean the small spots on her top and the sheet, then I peeled off long strips of paper towels to wipe up the goo. It took a good twenty minutes to clean up the floor, the rug, and the bucket. Then I re-rigged the tube with fresh electrical tape. "At least less got on you than I expected," I said, relieved.

She nodded and shrugged with a frown.

"Are you okay?"

She paused. "Not really."

"No? Are you in pain?"

"No," she said with a heavy sigh.

"Did something happen with Rick?"

"No. I just can't believe this is happening to me."

Yesterday, my mom was tired and rested a lot, but she was mostly still herself. Today, she already seemed different. I could hear it in her voice and see it in her body language.

"I know," I said with compassion. "This must just feel surreal to you."

"It does. And for you too."

I nodded, trying to keep my emotion in check. "Yeah."

We looked into each other's eyes, and I saw fear in her for the first time.

"Are you scared?" I asked.

"I am. I wasn't before, but now I kinda am."

"Do you want to talk about it?"

"I just don't know what to expect. I really don't want to die."

I put my hand over hers. "I know. I don't want you to die either." I took a deep breath. "Do you feel like this isn't your time? Like you still want to try something? Because if you do, you have those programs you were going to do. Maybe it's not too late."

"I don't know. Maybe."

"You mean, maybe you still want to try to recover?"

"I don't know. I'm just so tired. I don't know if I have the strength now to do anything. I'm wasting away."

My eyes filled with tears. "I know. And it's breaking my heart. But if you don't feel like this is your time, and there's still a chance to have a re-markable healing story, I'll get on it now and get you whatever you need."

She smiled meekly. "I know you will."

"So should I? Look into the cannabis program? Or the Chris Wark protocol?"

She seemed unsure of whether to say yes or no. Finally she said, "I guess if you want to."

She wasn't very convincing, but she also hadn't had much nutrition in the last three days since they pulled her alimentary tube at the hospital, so maybe her brain wasn't working at full capacity. Or maybe she needed me to take the reins again and simply do it.

"Okay, I will. I'll see what we'd need to do."

She nodded slightly and asked for ice.

I ground up two cups full and spooned a few chips into her mouth.

"That tastes so good," she said.

"Do you want more?"

She nodded and I obliged.

"You seem really tired," I told her.

"I am."

"Do you need anything else right now?"

She shook her head.

"Okay. I'm going to call Karen and see about getting the machine company to send a tech out. You rest, all right?"

She managed a whispered "okay" before I got up and went into the living room.

Karen didn't answer, so I left her a voicemail. Then I started looking into the two programs, wanting so much for one of them to be the answer, yet at the same time fearing my mom really didn't have it in her to do either one. She was already so weak. I would be forcing her at this point. *Is that what I should do? Or am I grasping at straws? But she said she didn't want to die and was scared. How could I not help her if she didn't believe it was her time? How could I live with myself if I didn't do everything I could to turn things around?*

In that moment, I wished strongly for one specific thing: to talk to Susan, my dear friend who was a gifted intuitive. But she had just been through a major dental surgery, and she'd told me herself that she wasn't doing any readings for clients for a while because she needed all of her energy to heal herself. I completely respected that and didn't want to assert myself into her space, so I didn't reach out to her, as much as every fiber of my being wanted to.

About thirty minutes later, I magically received this text:

Susan: You ok?

Me: Oh honey . . . Not really. 😢

I wish I could talk to you. Thank you for checking in. 🙏

Susan: I don't want to overstep . . . I believe I had a visit from Bree a little over an hour ago so I had to reach out. I'm here for you. xo

Me: Oh honey . . . you could NEVER overstep. I've wanted to talk to you so badly, but I didn't want to impose on your energy, knowing you need it for your own recovery.

You think you had a visit from her? I wish I could know more. We've been struggling over this really being the end, or if there's something I could still do to help her. I don't know how you feel about tuning in to her energy and reading that, but if you're open and willing, we would both welcome knowing what you see or feel.

Your love and support mean the world to me. Thank you so much for being there. 🙏 🖤

Susan: Your situation FAR outweighs my bubble right now. I have an appt from 1-2 my time. I can talk now and/or after if you have time.

Me: You are such an angel. I would be so grateful to talk to you now. Bree is sleeping. I'm going to go where I won't disturb her and call you. 🖤

I went into the gym on the other side of the house where I could be out of earshot in conversation but still hear my mom if she called me. When Susan picked up, she right away told me that until she'd heard back from me, she thought my mom might have already left her physical body completely, and that was why she texted to see if I was okay.

"Really?" I said. "I can't imagine the encounter you had that made you think she might have already transitioned."

"Well, I had decided to stay in bed later than normal this morning, and suddenly, there she was. Even though I've only talked to her and have never seen her, I knew it was Bree."

"You did?"

"Uh huh. She was floating face up, with chiffon-like cloth hanging down, as if someone was levitating her. She said, 'Don't snap me out of my revelry. I'm figuring out plan B.' I could sense right away that I'd better write it all down for you, so I grabbed a notebook and pen."

"That's amazing. But how do you 'see' the vision and write at the same time?"

"It's hard to explain, but it's like I can do both and be fully present. My Spirit Guides are communicating to me, like telepathically, and I'm aware of the vision too."

"How fascinating. Not that I doubt you, just that it amazes me."

"I know. It amazes me too."

"So you have notes?"

"I do. I had to write quickly, so some of it is my shorthand, but this is what I heard and saw."

"I'm ready." I sat with my own journal, poised to take notes.

"Okay. I was aware that Bree hears and gets called back easily, meaning her soul leaves her body for a time but she's aware of the physical world. Like if you walk in or wake her, she gets pulled back quickly from wherever she is. Then Bree said, 'Do you think I want to be in this predicament? No! It's the cards I was dealt.' She was a bit annoyed and fully cognizant. She said, 'This is different. I'm the same—whole, thoughtful, full faculties—only somewhere different, slightly elevated, on another plane, right across the veil. I think in my own voice. I hear myself without using words. It's rather cool and expanded. I have to come up with a plan before it's too long away. I didn't think it would come to this. I fully expected to be a helper there. Now I realize the possibility of working from an expanded space. So much possibility—only not many can appreciate this perspective. They're so set on remaining. I must reconfigure."

"Wow," I said, struggling to keep up getting it all down on paper. "This sounds like her . . . wanting to be a helper here, but now seeing the possibility of an expanded space to work from."

"Then she said, 'I'm the mist that hovers just beyond your reach, much lower than the clouds but above your head. I gather and swirl around you. I'm still here, just invisible to the seeing eye. I promise it's me. I can tell you now while I'm still near and closest to you in flesh. I want to stay if only I could capture this expansiveness and keep its wisdom on your plane. What joy I can spread knowing what I have here! Now I have to figure out how to use it from another angle. Best to do it now while I'm still partly there.'

"And then she directed these words to you:

'I so appreciate your presence. You feel the life-force rising and falling through my hand. You witness the coming and going through my flesh. It is real. I hover here able to distinguish the levels. It really happens. I am separating from the flesh yet nothing has changed. The ability to communicate remains. It is the human level that does not know that yet. Some do, and wonder what it is.'

"And then suddenly," Susan continued, "she spoke directly to me. She said, 'Hi Susan . . . you're trying to hide by stepping back to give reverence to us. Why? You hear me . . . don't play humble when you're privy to what's happening.'"

"She did?"

"Yes, and she was playful and almost sarcastic about it, like, *Don't try acting like you're not there when I know you are.*" She laughed.

I laughed too. "I can see her doing that."

"And then she said, 'Tell Stacey that I'm reconfiguring—same life to live but now to plan B or maybe C. I'm working it out. It's going to be grand, just you wait and see.'"

I took in a breath and felt a rush of hope fill my insides, as if her moving on to the next soul chapter was right and that she was getting ready for it with some degree of awe and excitement.

"Last," Susan added, "she said this directly to you:

'I'm sorry to leave but it's not in vain. We did good, you and me. What a team in such an unconventional way. Thank you for being my girl. I love you beyond.'"

My eyes welled in a rush and I brought my hand to my heart.

"And then what happened was really something," Susan said. "My pen actually stopped writing, ink stopped coming out, as I wrote down the last part. She said: "You did great . . . and you've done all you could.""

The tears spilled down my cheeks. "That's what she said? I did great and I've done all I could?"

"Yep. At the word 'great' the ink ran out, but I can see the impression in the paper from what I wrote after that."

I exhaled audibly and wiped my face. "And then what happened?"

"I tried and tried to make the pen work, but it was completely dry. Then the image of her and the voice was gone and I was back."

"Oh wow," I whispered. "I'm speechless."

The idea that my mom didn't like what was happening to her, but that she was seeing where she could "work from" in a higher realm and spread joy there made my heart swell. She would love that idea, I knew. She had such aspirations of being a beacon of light for people on Earth with her healing story, and if that wasn't going to happen the way she envisioned, then knowing this option was before her was perfect.

"Oh, Suz . . . you've just given me a tremendous amount of comfort. I don't know how to thank you for this."

"I'm so glad. But I was just a conduit," Susan reminded me. "Bree wanted you to know what she's been experiencing in the dreamtime, and she knew if she came to me I'd get the message to you."

"That's so remarkable. And the timing . . . I've been in such turmoil over whether to keep trying to heal her or to let her go. Now I feel like I have my answer . . . that there's nothing left to do except to be with her until she moves to the next plane."

"Yes. And I feel very strongly that she's not going to be far from you. She's only going to be in a different form, but still your Bree and still there, very close to you."

"I love that."

Susan paused. "Are you okay?"

"I am. I'm actually more okay than I've been in days. It sounds weird to say, but I feel more equipped to let her go now, as hard as it is, because she feels excited about where she'll be and what she'll have the ability to do . . . that trying to get her on some protocol at this stage is pointless. I'm still completely heartbroken over the thought of losing her, but I feel like I can see the divinity in it. I'll have to get used to life without her physically, but I love the idea of her spiritual presence in the way you described. I actually feel like I can breathe, and that every-thing will be okay." We shared a few moments of silent understanding. "I truly don't know how to thank you enough."

"You're welcome. I'm always here for you."

"I know. I just hope you know how much it means."

"I do. And there's something else."

"What?"

"About half an hour after the vision, I picked up the pen and tried it, and it wrote perfectly fine."

"Whoa."

"The ink running out was her saying, 'That's all for now.'"

"That's mind-blowing to me."

"To me too."

I took that in for a moment, marveling at the magic of it.

"And Stace . . . I also received her asking if going to Mexico, to the clinic, was the right thing to do. If she should have saved the money be-cause it didn't ultimately work."

I took in a silent breath. "And . . . ?"

"And I received strongly that it was absolutely the right thing. Her time there allowed her to remain a 'real person' for this past year. She would have been embarrassed and horrified by what happened to her if she'd gone the conventional treatment route. The money was worth it."

I exhaled. "I've totally believed it was too. But I'm so glad to hear you say that. I know there are people who wonder if it was some kind of scam."

"Nooo . . . not a scam at all. You chose that place because you knew it was legitimate. And it was the right choice. Just know that."

"So . . . what do you think about me sharing this with her? All of what you told me? I feel like it would give her comfort and hope . . . or maybe she's already aware of having an encounter with you on a soul level."

"I don't know. She might be. It's hard to say."

"The problem is, I really couldn't keep up with writing everything you told me. Is there any way you could take a photo of your notes and send them to me?"

"Sure. I don't know if you'll be able to read some of my abbreviations, but if not, just call me and I'll decipher them."

"That would be perfect." I sighed audibly. "This is the best gift, Suz. It really is."

"Well, you should probably thank Bree. She's the one who knew you were struggling and needed to hear this. And she couldn't express it in her physical form. She's clearly in between planes right now."

Almost to myself, I said, "And of course she'd find a way to tell me."

After my mom woke up, I restocked her ice and got her the gummie she asked for.

"Are you up for hearing something miraculous?" I asked her.

"Miraculous?"

"Yes. I talked to Susan earlier . . . and she told me she had a soul encounter with you. Do you remember visiting her?"

"No."

"She said you might not. But she took notes and screenshot them for me, and I have them right here. Can I read them to you?"

"Sure," she said in a meek but interested voice.

I proceeded to read her the entire exchange she'd had with Susan. My voice was animated and enthusiastic until I reached the end: "We did good, you and me." My throat caught. "Thank you for being my girl. I love you beyond. You did great . . . and you've done all you could."

I looked up from my phone and grabbed a tissue, adding about how Susan's pen had stopped writing at the end when Bree was done talking.

"Isn't this amazing?" I said.

"It *is*."

"And you have no memory of this, like maybe in a dream?"

"Uh uh. But it sure is fascinating."

"What do you think about what you told her? About the joy you can spread on the other side, and about the possibility of working from an expanded space?"

"I like that idea."

"Does it give you any peace? I know you said you were feeling scared. Maybe this will help you not to feel that way anymore."

She nodded slightly, considering it. "How does it make *you* feel?" she wanted to know.

"Honestly . . . the idea of losing you is still unbelievable to me. But hearing all this has given me comfort. And a lot of hope, really. I hope it gives you that too for the next part of your soul's journey. You actually said, 'It's going to be grand, just you wait and see.' That must give you some sense of encouragement for what you're moving on to."

"It does."

Part of me wondered if she truly felt that way, because I could still sense a bit of unsettledness in her. But I also knew she was feeling over-whelmed.

"I know it's a lot to take in. But just think, you knew I needed to hear from you in a way you couldn't communicate with me in the here and now. And how wonderful that we have Susan and that you were able to seek her out and tell me these things. Don't you think that's pretty magical?"

"I do," she said sincerely. "I just don't know how long I'm supposed to be here if I've decided to move on to the next plane. I don't want to prolong this."

I had a flash of her asking me to megadose her with morphine to assist her dying and freaked a little. I also wondered if by giving her little bits of food, we were encouraging her body to linger, which I knew she didn't want. "Do you think you want to talk to Susan on the phone? She said she'd gladly talk to you if you wanted clarity on anything. Or if you'd find it comforting."

"Maybe. I'll think about it. I keep getting messages from people who want to come see me or talk to me on the phone. I could only handle a couple of calls yesterday . . . and right now, I'm just so tired. I think I just want to sleep some more."

"Okay. I'll let you rest."

"I'll go find Susan and chat with her."

We both giggled. "You do that," I said with a smile. Then I remembered the additional note I'd written in the journal I was holding. "Wait, there was one more thing." I opened the journal and told her what Susan had said about Mexico being the absolute right thing to do.

She closed her eyes and smiled in a way that told me every cell of her being was relieved. Then she nodded and whispered, "Thank you."

I squeezed her hand. "We did good."

I felt heartened with tremendous relief by what Susan had shared; at the same time, I couldn't help but feel overwhelmed watching my mom diminish a little more each day. *Was* giving her food the right thing to do? It seemed that on a soul level, she was working out her next "chapter," but on a physical level, she wasn't so certain. It was already becoming clear that none of the things I'd imagined us doing together were going to happen. It was day three of her being home, and she still hadn't made the effort to shower or wash her hair, as much as she kept saying she wanted to. She was still strong enough to get up and use the porta-potty on her own, and she could pop her gummies, spoon ice chips, and drink water with a straw. But it had become easier for me to squirt the liquid morphine into her mouth than it was for her, and she hadn't felt like doing much of anything. Even her beloved kitty, Roxy, who was my mom's baby and was often in her bed, was becoming an annoyance for her. When Roxy would knead near or on her, my mom would gently push her away, which she rarely did. We would chat a bit when she wasn't resting, but I was suspecting, after only a few days, that my mom wasn't going to be here for *weeks*, at least I couldn't imagine she would be, not with the rapid pace she was deflating before my eyes.

When I asked Susan about it, she said:

> While she still has her wits about her and unless she warrants mega doses or asks for it, don't do anything to speed up the process. She will decide. Her plan is not complete yet. I sense confusion. A lot still on this plane. She will feel better with a burst of energy. Give her those moments "as if."

I of course had no intention of giving my mom higher doses of pain meds without her asking for them. But I did appreciate that she was in a state right now that was between veils, which I felt immensely grateful to be present for, but also compassion for too, because when she was awake, she had no recollection of what her soul was working to figure out during the dreamtime. I also had to keep reminding myself to be in the moment, to not project ahead, because these moments were going to be gone before I knew it, and I didn't want to have any regrets if I could help it.

At some point that afternoon, Karen got back to me and agreed to come out again for the machine and to check on my mom. But she still had no solutions for the frequent leaks I was having to clean up.

That evening, Rick helped me break down and move Emeline's crate to the dining room so I could fold out the bed to stay there that night, then pick up Dana the next day to move in altogether. When I checked on my mom afterward, the tube was leaking yet again, and both my mom and I had had it.

"I'm calling again," I said. "They have to come out here and fix this once and for all."

"You go, girl," my mom managed.

Though they finally did promise to send someone out right away, it was after 10:00 p.m. before two guys arrived. They took a look at the machine, did a suction test with the bucket and some water to make sure it was working properly, then examined the catheter and the hookup to the tubing.

"Well, the machine is working fine," one said, "but this is the wrong size catheter. Where's your supply bag?" I handed it to him and he went through it until he found the correct gauge. "This is the size you need. The one in there now is too small . . . that's why it's leaking. It's not creating a complete closure in the tube."

My shoulders slumped. "I didn't even know there *were* different gauges . . . and neither did the two nurses who've been here. I can't believe that's all it was and no one knew it."

He nodded but didn't move.

"So . . . good," I said with an expectant lilt. "You can go ahead and fix it now."

The main guy shook his head. "I'm afraid I can't do that."

"What do you mean? If you know how to fix it, isn't that why you're here?"

"We do know how. But because there's contact with the tube, it's considered a medical procedure, and we're not authorized to do that."

I glanced at my mom in frustration, then back to the guy. "But the part you'd be touching isn't where it goes into my mom. How can it be called a medical procedure?"

He shrugged. "It just is."

"Well then, can you show *me* how to do it? You can't be liable if I'm the one who actually does it, right?"

Again, he shook his head. "I can't do that either."

At this point, I truly wanted to lose it. "So why did you come all the way here if there was nothing you could do?"

"We came out to verify the machine was working. And we did that. But we can't do anything else."

My mom remained uncharacteristically silent during this verbal tennis match, likely wondering how Aurora Greenway I might get as I picked up the package that held the catheter he'd said was the right size. "Well, it can't be that difficult. The catheter gets threaded into the tube until it's tight, then gets hooked into the machine, right?"

He hesitated. "In theory, yes."

"All right, fine. I'll just do what makes sense to me and you guys won't have to worry about liability."

"If that's what you want to do."

"Just tell me one thing before you go: this backup valve is basically horizontal because of how it goes from my mom to the machine. So it's been leaking too. Shouldn't it be vertical to prevent that?"

As I wondered what line I'd crossed with *this* question, the main guy said, "You might want to secure it to the machine in a vertical position, like with heavy tape. That might help."

I was grateful he'd given me this "unauthorized" medical advice, but this, too, was a source of frustration. "So there's a major flaw in the design. If I secure it like that, I'll have just enough tubing to give my mom only a little room to move around without tugging the tube. I don't want it hurting her."

Again, I was entering disallowed territory and could see it in their body language.

"You know what," I said, "thank you for coming out. But I think I've got it from here since there's nothing else you're able to do."

With that, they wished us both well and left. And I set to work on doing what amounted to the simplest, most common-sense connection of the now correct-size catheter, then maneuvered that damn valve into a vertical position and taped it to the machine like a hostage.

Kissing my mom good-night, I said, "If that doesn't hold tonight, I'm out."

"Ditto to that, sister," she joked.

September 11th

I'll just put it this way: that machine was the bane of our existence. Even with the valve vertical, it bubbled up and leaked in the night, greeting me with yet another slimy mess in the morning. And, bonus! Now the bile was suddenly green.

"I wonder what that means," I wondered out loud. "Why would it change color?"

"I don't know," my mom said in her fatigued voice. "Maybe from green gummies?"

I welcomed a flicker of her humor. "That's it!" Then I volleyed back in hopes she'd play. "Just how many green gummies have you had without my knowledge?"

"Not that many," she said coyly, averting her eyes.

"Well, I might have to monitor you from now on. You have alien bile now."

"Cool!" she mused, albeit meekly.

I laughed as I pulled yet another long strip of paper towels from the roll and began wiping. "You seem better today. Did you sleep pretty well?"

"Not too bad."

"How's the pain?"

"No pain right now."

I grabbed the journal and pen. "That's great! When did you take your last pain med?"

"The dose you gave me last night."

"You mean you didn't need any pain relief during the night?"

"No."

For a moment, with my mom's mood being a little lighter and finding out she hadn't been in pain all night, I actually entertained the notion that perhaps all of this had merely been a temporary setback, that she'd changed her mind about living her expansive existence on the other side of the veil and decided to stay here with me.

"Did you have a spontaneous healing during the night?" I asked excitedly.

She placed a hand on her intestinal bump. "I don't think so. Lumpy's still there."

I deflated like a sad clown. "Well, maybe it just hasn't fully gone away yet. But the rest of you is healed!"

"I like that," she said.

Feeling buoyed by our banter, I took care of the usual: grinding and replacing the ice cups, and rinsing and replacing both buckets.

"So today you *must* finally want to shower," I teased.

"I *do*. And I think I want that shake today too. Can you get one for me when you go pick up Dayni and get all your stuff?"

"You betcha. Did you want anything to eat now?"

"No, I'll just look forward to my shake. And maybe you can pop in to the bank too and see what I can do without going in . . . maybe you can pick up paperwork to sign."

Suddenly, the spark that my mom wasn't going anywhere after all dimmed a bit. But I remained lighthearted. "Okay. I'll do that."

It was early, not much past 8:00, but I planned to get to the Airbnb, finish packing, do the errands, and get back to my mom as soon as possible. It was also going to be the first time Dana would get to see her since we'd been there, which Dana felt some anxiety about. She was worried she'd crumble emotionally seeing my mom in this state, and I understood because the same thing had happened to me in the hospital. But she also *wanted* to see her. My mom had been Dana's unconditionally loving mother since the day they met over twenty years ago, and the hour was finally approaching for them to have some time together. So we made haste with all the errands and thought we were doing well on time when I received this text:

Her: Major leak for you to come to. Huge mess! 😰

Me: Shit!!! I'm so sorry! Help is on the way!

Like I said, that machine was the bane of our existence. Only two hours away from it and it was mocking me like a bully that wouldn't give me a break.

When we arrived at my mom's with her long-awaited vanilla shake, I thought Dana should be the shiny delivery person. But first, I braced myself for yet another slimefest to clean up.

"I'm so sorry!" I said as I scurried around the hall corner. But when I got into her room, there was nothing on the floor. "I thought you said there was a major mess."

"There isn't?" she said, perplexed.

"Uh uh." I looked at the bucket, which now had a decent amount in it. "I think what you heard was it draining into the bucket, and you thought it was spilling onto the floor."

"Oh," she said, biting her lips together and looking away in her childlike way. "Sorry."

"That's okay. I'm just so glad it wasn't really leaking. I couldn't believe it when you texted me."

Again she apologized.

"You know," I said, half joking, "if this thing wasn't keeping you from throwing up, I'd seriously want to hurl it out the window."

"You and me both," she said.

"But I can't even *imagine* you dealing with throwing up, or even the feeling that you might, so my fantasy is off the table. Not to mention you're stuck with that NG tube."

She rolled her eyes. "Lovely, isn't it?"

"Actually, I do have something lovely for you."

She clapped her hands gently. "Is it my Dayni?"

"Yep."

Right on cue, Dana appeared in the hallway with the shake in her hand. "Look what I haaave," she said playfully.

"Oh boy!" my mom mustered in the most enthusiastic little voice she could, referring to both gifts coming toward her.

Immediately, Dana was overcome and the tears came quickly.

"Come here, honey," my mom said, holding out her arms.

I took the shake and the two of them shared a heartfelt embrace. When Dana pulled away, my mom nodded and said to her sincerely, "It's okay."

I knew what Dana wanted to say in reply. *No, it's not.* But instead she just shook her head, trying to manage her emotion. Finally, she said, "I can't believe how tiny you are."

"I know. I'm just a little featherweight."

"But," I chimed in, "look what you get!"

I presented the shake to her ceremonially and she drew a sip through the straw. "Oh wow . . . that is *sweet.*"

"Uh oh. Too sweet?"

"Well, let's just say it will be good in small doses. But it's wonderful. Thank you, girls."

"Good. You're welcome. Though we were mortified going through the drive-thru. We felt so weird at a fast food restaurant."

"I'm sure you did. What's it been? About ten years since you've eaten that frankenfood?"

"Close, yeah."

Dana said, "I wanted to say, 'This isn't for us. It's for someone else!'"

Bree chuckled. "Normally I'd feel the same way, but at this point, I don't have to worry about it." She said it in a lighthearted way, but still.

Noting the discomfort on our faces, she switched tacks.

"What did the bank say?"

"Oh." I hesitated. "Well . . . there's no paperwork you can sign without being there. They said I won't be able to do anything until . . ."

My mom waited for me to finish the sentence, but the words stuck in my throat. Finally, I said, "until after."

"Okay," my mom said, nodding. "Well, as long as my account can get transferred to you."

"I'll do what I can."

After the three of us spent a little time together, Dana and I put the groceries away that we'd picked up, then went out to the garage to bring our luggage in from the car.

"I can't believe how weak and frail Mommie Bree is," Dana said, her emotion grabbing hold of her again.

"I know," I sighed. "She's becoming less of herself every day. But then this morning, when she was bantering a little with me, it was almost like a glimmer of her miraculously bouncing back. But now her voice is weak and scratchy again. It's breaking my heart."

Through tears, Dana said, "I can't even fathom what this is really doing to you. I know you're strong on the outside, but . . ."

I took in a breath. "Yeah. I guess I just feel like I need to stay present and not get too far ahead of myself. I don't want to squander our time with me picturing the worse-case scenario and going to that place, you know?"

"I know. And that's good. But it's hard not to."

I nodded and she followed me inside with our suitcases in tow. As we turned the hall corner, my mom said, "I'm glad you're both here now. That's how it should be."

I agreed. No more running back and forth to the Airbnb to freshen up and change or to bring Dana a meal she didn't have to cook herself. No more texting updates as things transpired, and no more being apart. Because truth be told, I felt more and more each day that I could use the support of Dana's constant presence.

That afternoon, I got a bee in my bonnet to organize the fridge and freezer again while my mom was resting. As Dana and I were making use of our categorizing skills in the kitchen, we suddenly heard my mom's familiar, little-girl voice call out, "What you are girls doing?"

We looked at each other wide-eyed, as if we'd just heard the sweetest sound. In that moment, my mom didn't sound weak, or tired, or like she was diminishing at all. She sounded exactly like herself.

"Just playing!" Dana called out.

As if hearing our new baby wake up and being giddy to retrieve her from her crib, we scurried into my mom's room where we found her with a smile on her face.

"Hey," I said. "Look at you all chipper."

"I know, huh?" was her familiar childlike response.

"Can I get you anything?"

"No. I just like hearing the sounds of you girls puttering around. It's good for a mommie."

And just like that, so bent toward optimism that I was, I once again entertained the idea that maybe she'd still come back, that wherever she'd been while she slept, pondering her Plan B or Plan C, she'd decided to stick with Plan A, which was to stay with her girls and miraculously get well.

That night, Dana got to witness firsthand what a joy that suction machine was, and how even electrical tape would get soggy from the back-up valve leakage and loosen the adhesive, creating an endless loop for me of cleaning, re-taping, and cursing that necessary but maddening heap of vexation. Karen had eased my mind about the bile turning green, saying that the body would do that as it went through its natural stages, and it had once again turned to black. No matter, though. Black, green, clear . . . more of it ended up on the floor than it ever did in the bucket. But my mom couldn't manage without it, so I reminded myself that our situation as a whole could be much worse and simply sucked it up (pun intended).

Besides, my bigger concern was that my mom had returned to feeling drained and her voice had become weak and scratchy again. And the shower she'd so desperately wanted to take on Tuesday? As we tumbled into Saturday, it seemed less and less likely she'd ever have that pleasure again.

September 12th

𝓑y this time, our caregiving routine was pretty solid—and pretty simple: grind and feed her ice, help her sip cold water through a straw, check the nasogastric tubing and clean up machine output and spillage, log and give her pain meds, dump and rinse her potty bucket. In between those things, I'd been able to have *some* time with her, but it was increasingly brief and not at all sentimental, nothing like what I'd imagined. What's more, the radiant sparkle of my mom I'd gotten the day before had already been eclipsed, nearly in the blink of an eye, by a sullen mist that settled over her and pulled her away from me, leaving me to wonder if that burst of aliveness she'd emitted when Dana and I were in the kitchen was the one people often experienced just before the end. She was still able to get up and use her portable potty on her own, which surprised both Dana and me, but other than that, she could barely speak or keep her eyes open more than a few seconds. She was definitely fading before our eyes, so much so that I messaged Susan to see if there was anything she could tell me. I could actually sense that my mom was detaching from her physical body, and I was terrified that she would linger, which she had been adamant about not letting happen.

I was also caught in a dilemma over something else: my mom's brother had been calling and texting about wanting to come out, as had two of her close cousins, but she'd been waffling the last couple days about seeing or even talking to anyone, and she had asked me to put them off until she could decide. She hadn't even wanted her circle of best girlfriends to see her in this state, and she had told me not to let them in no matter what. She felt terrible about keeping her brother, in particular, at bay, but her waffling had turned into her having no decision-making capacity at all, which left it up to me.

The truth was, keeping anyone dear to her from seeing her one last time felt completely insensitive and wrong. At the same time, allowing anyone to see her one last time at this point went against what she would be comfortable with, and my allegiance had to be to her. I *knew* my mom. She was in no condition to have a "final" much of anything with anyone now, and the last time I'd broached that topic, I could tell it simply no longer mattered to her. It wasn't that she didn't love these friends or family members, because she did; it was that she didn't crave the exchange or need the closure, even if the other person did. The only thing she asked of me was not to let her die alone, to be with her when the time came. And I had promised her I would be. This was partly why I'd reached out to Susan: to know if the end was near so that I'd know not to leave my mom's side.

It was nearly 7:00 p.m. before I heard back from Susan, and she asked if I wanted to call. I told her I'd love to talk to her, but I was worried that even though I was right next door to my mom's room, I didn't know if I should be absorbed in conversation, just in case.

"She's not ready to leave yet," Susan assured me. "She's still working things out in the dreamtime."

So, Dana offered to periodically check on my mom, and I ended up on the phone for nearly two hours, during which Susan shared all kinds of things, including that she was clearly seeing my mom on a magic carpet, and also driving around with glee in an electric child's car, a yellow one.

"That's so bizarre," I said. "I had a little yellow car that was electric when I was four. But I don't remember her ever saying she had one." I paused. "But she did drive a yellow Datsun 240Z when I was little. We have such fun memories of that car."

"I don't know," Susan said. "Maybe it was a combo of yours and hers. I just know it was like she was a little girl again, and so carefree."

"I love that. I'm going to hold on to that image." I choked up. "With the way she's been today, so out of it, I don't think I'll ever see her be animated again."

Susan did her best to soothe my concerns. "She might still surprise you," she said.

Just then, Dana came in and told me my mom was awake.

I rushed off the phone to find my mom in yet another energy burst.

"I have to pee," she said. "Can you get me some more ice?"

I left her alone for a few minutes, then returned with the cups. "Are you in pain?"

"I'll take a dose," she said.

After the squirt, I asked, "Do you feel like you've been on a magic carpet ride?"

She was intrigued. "I don't think so. Why?"

"Because I've been on the phone with Susan, and she said you were on one."

"Cool," she said.

"And did you have a little car when you were young?"

She smiled. "I did."

"Well, apparently, you've been driving around having a lot of fun in that too."

"Oh good," she whispered.

And, just like that, I could see that the window that had been thrown open for me for five minutes, allowing our fun, abbreviated conversation, was already sliding toward the sill, as if its ability to stay open was limited by the weight of gravity.

My mom closed her eyes, and I left her once again to sleep through the night without calling me for pain meds even once.

September 13th

*A*fter another day much like the one before, where my mom in-frequently awoke from a deep dream state with varying levels of coherence and confusion, but still insistent on using her potty, I held fast to the brief moments we were still able to connect and stayed near her as much as I could.

At some point, after yet another machine leak, my mom's beautiful area rug was beginning to hold a stench from all the spills, despite my rigorous scrubbing, so Dana rolled it up and took it to the garage. But a voice told me to replace it with something, not to just leave the tile floor bare. My mom had preferred being barefoot, so my initial thought was that I didn't want her having to stand on tile to use the potty. But it was actually more than that.

The truth was, she was making me nervous whenever she got up. I was glad she could maintain the dignity of managing this one endeavor on her own, not that she would have minded me helping her. But now, she was so weak that it took her several tries to stand up, even holding the handles of the potty chair.

"Why don't you call me when you need the bathroom?" I'd im-plored.

But for whatever reason, this task was where she'd held on to her autonomy.

In the office, there was a large padded mat, about two inches thick, that was folded behind the door. I'd never seen my mom use it, and with the room so small, I had wished there was another place for it. But now, its presence felt like the greatest gift: if it hadn't been right in front of me, I might not have unearthed it so quickly. And in fact, it couldn't have fit more perfectly in the space next to my mom's bed.

"I don't need padding," my mom said, confused.

"I know. But just to make it more comfortable for you."

But the mat didn't feel like enough. I had always been obsessed with creating "cozy" everywhere, for our kitties, for us, and this was no different. So, I covered the pad with a plushy blanket. If my mom refused to call for me and God forbid ended up losing her balance, I believed there would be enough cushion on the tile to keep her from getting hurt. Dana and I both kept pretty vigilant during the day while she was resting, as well as at night. But if we happened not to hear her, it made me feel slightly better to know a protective layer was underneath her.

I had no idea just how much I would appreciate that foresight.

∞

September 14th

The early hours of the 14th were the worst yet. Hearing her moving around, Dana woke me sometime around 1:30 a.m. and I got up to find my mom in a state of intense confusion.

"It's stuck," she was saying over and over, gently pulling on the tube taped to her nostril. She was in such a childlike state that I instinctively responded to her like a caring parent would.

"No, honey," I said in a compassionate voice. "Don't pull on it. I don't want you to hurt yourself. It's not stuck. It's supposed to be there."

"It's stuck," she insisted. "Get it out."

I tenderly took her hand away. "No, sweetie. It's not stuck. I know it probably feels that way. But it's there to keep you from throwing up, so it has to stay, okay?"

"Get it out," she repeated. "Get it out."

I sighed and held her hand, worried she'd yank it out herself if I didn't give her an alternative. "Okay. But *we* can't take it out. A nurse has to do it so you don't get hurt. I'll call first thing in the morning, okay? And I'll have her come and take it out for you. Is that okay?"

"Okay," she said, calming a bit.

"Don't worry. We'll have the nurse take it out."

She nodded. "Okay."

She relaxed and closed her eyes, and I realized we had turned a distinct corner.

My mom was no longer my mom.

Since the 8th, I could count on one hand the sum of what she had eaten: seven spoonfuls of broth; three sips of vanilla milkshake; and three popsicles, none of which she liked and therefore barely ate. From lack of nutrition, and her soul coming and going from her physical body, she had moved into a whole other state of consciousness.

Within two hours, I heard her rustling again and went back in her room to find her maneuvering herself to the edge of the bed. Then she brought her hand to her mouth, as if she was holding a cup.

"Did you want some water?" I asked. "You don't have a cup. But I can get it for you."

"Okay."

I put the straw in her mouth and asked her if she could drink some. She did, then I asked if she wanted ice.

"No."

Just when I thought she might be calming for a while again, she looked right at me. "I'm dying. I can't do this anymore."

I caught my breath, searching my mind at lightning speed for how to respond. "I know," I said softheartedly. "I'm so sorry this is happening to you." I didn't know if crying would upset her, or if she'd even be aware that I was, but I tried my best to hold it in. I also knew how often people held on because they were worried about who they would leave behind, so although it was breaking me to think of letting her go willingly, I said, "If you're ready to leave . . . you don't have to hold on for my sake. I'll be okay."

She paused, then repeated, "I'm dying."

I gave her a dose of morphine to calm her, then I held her hand and sat in the chair next to her bed, where I stayed by her side until daybreak.

When I woke up, my mom was still here and seemed to be in a deep, restful sleep. I got up quietly and went into our room, where Dana was lying awake.

"You're up already?" I whispered.

"I have been for hours."

I sighed. "Really? I'm sorry you didn't get much sleep either."

"It's okay. I can't really sleep being so worried about you and

Mommie Bree." She paused. "I actually thought she'd left at about 1:15."

"You did?" I sat on the bed. "Why?"

"Because I was lying here, wide awake, and I totally sensed Bree's spirit between planes. It was so strong, I really thought she had completely transitioned. I was sure of it."

"Really?"

"Yeah. I was just lying there thinking and interpreting the energy of the house, and I suddenly felt as if Bree was telepathically communicating with me. I heard her thoughts and words as clear as a bell. I *so* felt I was having this conversation with her."

"Oh my gosh. What did she say?"

"She said that she left, at this particular time, to protect us for what's ahead, and not to fear."

"Like Susan said, that she was going to be just on the other side of the veil. Not completely elsewhere yet."

"Right. And then Bree pointed out that *this* is part of my gift, that I have the capability of sensing energies and can be an intuitive. That I was *meant* to be here, helping you. She knew that my fear was keeping me away at first, but that I was meant to have this experience. She also said we will be blessed. I wasn't sure exactly what it meant, but I had the feeling she meant financially."

"Wow."

"I also sensed the energy of the house was different. It actually made me smile slightly. She said it was because she's not burdened anymore."

I was mesmerized. "And you really felt it was her talking to you, not something in your mind?"

"It was definitely her. It was a brief conversation, but I knew it was her. I had such clarity . . . it just flowed, you know? And I knew it was real. I don't know how else to explain it."

"That's so amazing. I love that she came to you like that."

"Me too. And then it faded. I knew it was over and I was back to my own thoughts."

"So . . . I have to ask . . . if you thought she'd left, why didn't you wake me?"

"I don't know. The experience was so powerful. I'd never had an experience like that before, and it was like something sacred had happened. It was like my mind thought she was gone, because the energy had shifted and it really felt like she'd transitioned, but then I think I had an inner knowing that she was still here physically but had met me on another plane, the way she did with Susan. I don't know. Our conversation was so brief, and I was just taking it in when it ended, wondering if it really *did* happen because it was such a surreal experience. And then a few minutes later, I heard her make a noise. I was actually shocked she was still with us because I was so convinced she had left."

"That's when you woke me to go check on her."

"Yeah."

"That's really something . . . that she gave you that experience. And that she told you you had intuitive capability . . . that that's part of your gift."

"I know. I'm still so blown away by it."

"And that she's leaving now to protect us for what's ahead and not to fear."

"I know."

"It's like she's working overtime on a soul level to let us know that. First with Suz, now with you."

She nodded and grew reflective again. "It just all seemed to happen in this little pocket of time. I can't really explain it. It was like she was gone and talking right to me, and then she was back in her bed."

I wanted to stay in the space of Dana's supernatural encounter with my mom, but I was also concerned about how Bree had been during the night.

"I don't want to change the subject, but I have to tell you . . . Bree is so confused. She doesn't seem to know what's real and what's not anymore."

"I know. I pretty much heard everything when you guys were awake."

"So you know I told her I'd call the nurse today to have the tube taken out?"

"Yeah. Are you really going to?"

"I am. I'll call closer to 8:00, though. It's not even 7:00 yet."

Dana and I talked a bit more before my mom stirred and I went in to check on her.

"What's happening to me?" she asked me. "Am I dying?"

I honestly didn't know how to respond. Saying yes to her felt incredibly cold and insensitive, and saying no felt like a deception I couldn't bear. From somewhere divine, I said tenderly, "Your soul is figuring things out right now. You're going on a grand adventure."

She wasn't coherent enough to fully take that in, but she also didn't contradict it or press me on it.

I looked at her tiny body, lying there on her back, partially sitting up against her pillows, with her thin, shapely legs swimming in her extra-small black Athleta pants she wore home from the hospital, with her sweet white top that had the little stain on it, and that adorable lime green cloche that still concealed her blonde bob. In that moment, I saw so vividly the little girl Bree, my little girl, and my mom at the same time.

As soon as she closed her eyes, I quietly but fiercely wept.

Later that morning, after I'd texted Susan with an update, and she had confirmed that Dana's encounter with my mom was indeed real, I secured a visit from the nurse on duty that afternoon, then went into the gym to make an important call.

Shortly afterward, Dana called out, "Bree fell!"

I dashed off the phone to find my mom on the floor of her room, her head flush with the tile and the nasogastric tube pulled clean out of her, lying on the floor.

"Help me," she said weakly.

"We're here," I said. "You're okay." I wasn't actually sure of that at the time, but I said it nonetheless.

"Oh my God . . . did she hit her head?" I asked Dana.

"I don't know," Dana said, frantic. "I was just coming around the corner when I saw the motion of her falling. It happened so fast . . . I couldn't get there to keep it from happening."

"It's not your fault. She must have been trying to use the potty again. Here, help me get her up."

Though my mom weighed less than a hundred pounds at that point, the dead weight of her was a lot, even for the two of us. Once we carefully hoisted her onto the bed, I checked her head for an injury and didn't find evidence of any.

"I'm *so* grateful I put that pad on the floor with the blanket," I said.

Dana agreed it had been timely.

Then I realized my mom had wet herself in the fall. "I need to clean her up. Can you help me get her back against the pillows?"

It was a struggle, but we maneuvered her into her normal position, and then Dana left to give us privacy.

"Does your head hurt?" I asked.

"No," she said.

"Okay, good." I sighed with relief. "You're safe in your bed. And I'm right here."

At that, she closed her eyes and I was certain she nodded off.

I warmed a washcloth and gingerly cleaned her up as gently but efficiently as I could.

Suddenly, she caught me off guard. "What are you doing?" she wanted to know, her words coming out at a snail's pace yet startling me.

"You had a little accident, and I'm just cleaning you up, okay? Don't worry about it."

"Okay," she managed.

I wriggled her into fresh underwear and pajama pants, then realized I should have added a maxi pad to the equation so she wouldn't have to worry about the potty anymore. As I worked to put it in place, she once again asked me in her labored cadence what I was doing. I admit, I felt like I'd been caught doing something inappropriate. Even in her less-than-coherent state, she wanted to know why my hand was in her pants, and in her crotch, no less. From the outside, I was certain it looked odd, and the humor of it actually struck me.

"I'm sorry," I said. "I'm just giving you a pad so you don't have to pee in the potty anymore. This will make it easier for you if you have to go."

"Oh," she murmured, then drifted off again.

In the moment, I didn't consider that trying to change and clean her up if she used the pad was going to be more labor intensive, but I also couldn't imagine her trying to stand up again to use that portable potty. She was so weak that she couldn't hold herself up at all. Bless her heart, I thought, for trying so hard to maintain her humanness as she was pulling further away from it each day.

As unnerved as I was that she fell, it felt serendipitous that the NG tube had gotten yanked out, and I actually wondered if my mom had somehow orchestrated it of her own volition. She seemed to have no pain from the incident, and she'd begged me to pull it out the night before anyway. It didn't seem likely that now, with her not ingesting anything but occasional ice and water, she could possibly feel the urge to throw up. And if that was the case, I could bid a welcome and fond goodbye to the machine that had given us both so much grief.

I peeled the tape carefully from my mom's nose, then dabbed off the adhesive with coconut oil. Then I unhooked all the tubing and put the machine in the corner, where I was grateful it no longer served as an element of a lifeline to my mom—and that she had granted her own wish of being rid of it.

When the nurse came that afternoon, she was someone new, and I immediately loved her air of compassion and quiet manner. The other two nurses, while very nice people, always spoke loudly, which never felt appropriate to me. It's not that I didn't appreciate their upbeat tone of positivity, but there was something off-putting about it. This nurse, on the other hand, carried almost a sense of reverence for my mom and me, and her tone—and her words—reflected her empathy and understanding of what we were facing.

She quietly took my mom's vitals, then she whispered to me, "She's getting close. It probably won't be more than a day or two now."

I nodded and thanked her for her honesty and kind manner.

"I know how difficult this must be for you," she said. "Are you and your mom close?"

I choked back tears. "Very."

She put her hand on my arm. "I'm so sorry for what you're going through. I know it's very painful. But just so you know, she's not in any pain. She seems quite comfortable."

"That's good to know. She hasn't asked for pain medication for a couple days now."

She smiled tenderly.

"But she's confused a lot."

"That's normal at this stage," she assured me.

I didn't know what her spiritual beliefs might be, so I didn't broach the topic of my mom's soul moving in and out of her body as a likely source of that confusion. Instead, I simply nodded.

"Well, if you need anything at all, please don't hesitate to call, okay?"

"Okay. Thank you."

I walked the nurse out and returned to my mom. She woke up again with her eyes empty looking and unfocused. "What's happening to me?" she asked. "Am I dying?"

Heartbroken, I relied on my previous answer and delicate delivery. "You're getting ready for a grand adventure," I told her.

She blinked and asked me slowly, "Where am I going?"

I thought for a moment. "I'm not completely sure, but I know you're looking forward to what you'll be able to do there. You told Susan to tell me you were reconfiguring and that it was going to be grand." Then I added, "And you and I will always be together, so don't worry about that."

She seemed to contemplate that as I wondered if any of it made sense to her. Even in her awakened presence she was mostly absent, yet she still had the wherewithal to ask me what was happening to her.

She quickly drifted off yet again, and I couldn't help but wish she had a recollection of her time in the higher realm, the one from which she talked to Susan and Dana. It was clear she was regularly moving between here and there, much like a person does during a high fever, when it's nearly impossible to know what's "real" and what's a dream. I was also concerned about her being scared, and her questions weren't assuaging that concern.

For the rest of the day, I mostly stayed in my mom's room. A few more times, she insisted on needing the bathroom, no matter how much I tried to convince her otherwise. I'd have to go through the motions of sitting her up before she'd finally change her mind and tell me she had to lie down. Once I got her back on the pillows, she'd conk out for another spell. Each time, I'd imagine her on her magic carpet, or driving the little yellow car around, gleeful like a child with no awareness of her body slowly saying goodbye.

∞

September 15th

Late the night before, Dana assured me she'd keep an ear out for my mom to let me get a little rest, and that she'd check on her periodically. I didn't like not being in the room with my mom in case she spiraled quickly without my knowledge, but Susan had told me I'd know instinctively when to be with her, so I reluctantly agreed on the condition that we take shifts.

I never intended to fall into a deep sleep, but it wasn't until 4:00 a.m. that Dana woke me.

I rushed into my mom's room to find her agitated.

"I need to sit up," she said.

"Okay. Do you want more pillows behind your head? Because you're already kind of sitting up." I grabbed another pillow, but it wasn't what she wanted.

Instead, she looked at me with a bit of panic. "I don't want to die."

My heart sped up. "I don't want you to die either."

"Something's wrong," she insisted. "We have to do something."

In that moment, I actually thought my mom had spent more than enough time on the other side and had once and for all decided that she didn't like Plan B or C, that it wasn't going to be a grand adventure after all, and that she was done being sick and on the verge of dying. In other words, she wanted me to save her.

"Okay . . . what do you want to do?" I asked.

"Help me."

Help you. What can I do? I looked around. With no other option in sight, I asked, "Do you want some ice?"

"Okay."

I fed her a few chips, not expecting it to be a remedy, but it satisfied her enough to drift off temporarily. I was afraid to leave her, so I sat in the chair next to her and laid my head on the bed. That way, if I dozed off, I'd be right there if she needed me.

Several more times that night, she woke up restless and upset, even after I gave her a dose of morphine and an anti-anxiety pill. She kept saying things like, "Why is this happening?" "Don't let me die." "Help me." "I'm so scared."

I flashed to the day I arrived at the hospital when she hadn't even shed a tear, telling me she was okay, that she was ready and fine with dying. I had found that difficult to swallow, but I respected and even admired that she seemed so resolved and peaceful about it. But now, at the eleventh hour, when she'd been without food for days, when we'd abandoned the idea of starting yet another protocol because her message through Susan had been so encouraging about what she saw herself doing on the other side, she was telling me to help her, to not let her die.

I was beside myself in turmoil and took her hand. "If you want to live, ask the Universe to heal you . . . and I will too."

She nodded. "Okay."

After a few minutes, she said to me, "It's not working."

My heart cracked in two. "It might take a little more time," I encouraged. "Don't give up."

"I don't want to die," she repeated.

The nurse had told me yesterday that if my mom became agitated, I could give her extra morphine, that I couldn't overdose her and it wouldn't hurt her, only calm her down. So, I went with my intuition and filled the dropper with three doses, hopeful it would relieve the fear that gripped her. The last thing I wanted was for her to be scared, and I couldn't believe that after everything she'd been through, fear could be the final emotion she left the Earth feeling.

In the dim illumination of the ceiling fixture, I put my hands on her abdomen and closed my eyes, asking silently for white healing light to come through me into her, visualizing the black cancer dissipating and leaving a completely healthy space. I did this earnestly for quite a while, but at a certain point I stopped, wondering if I was trying to make something happen that wasn't meant to be.

From what Susan experienced with her, my mom had full under-standing of her next chapter and her higher purpose. Her telepathic conversation with Dana conveyed the same understanding. It seemed to me that her soul got the next phase of her evolution, but her mind and body were *not* on board. Even when I told her she was being elevated and was going to be protecting us, I could tell she had no cognizance of it. Everything she said to me screamed, I DO NOT WANT TO GO. And worse, she was scared about it.

I instantly felt responsible to save her somehow, like she was count-ing on me to figure it all out. How could I let her slip away when she clearly and verbally didn't want to? I would much rather she lived too. But how? I couldn't feed her because there was a blockage, unless it really was disappearing from all the visualizing. I felt like I was letting her waste away and it was killing me. I simply didn't know what to do.

At long last, the triple dose of morphine kicked in and she fell into a sound sleep for a few hours. But by the time my mom woke up, I knew in my heart there was no going back.

The flicker of hope I'd felt only hours ago was stomped out in a flash. My mom was having spurts of recognition, but her eyes were empty and unfocused. She was no longer responding to me at all, as if she was unaware I was even there. This hadn't happened with any of my grandparents in their final days, so I was completely unprepared for what my mom was experiencing.

Suddenly, she opened her eyes again and cried out, "Oh, God."

I so wanted to help her, but I didn't know what to do. Instinctively, I took her hand and said softly, "You're okay. I'm right here and I'm not leaving you."

Within seconds, she calmed and faded back into sleep.

Desperate for understanding, I reached out to Susan. In response to all I shared, she said:

Let her be the guide now. Just be with her and let her know you are there. Her free will has been overridden by spirit calling. Ease her worries. Know you did all you could, lovingly and respectfully. She knows. It's her last attachments to Earth that cause the crying out. She is not in pain.

After being afraid of not doing enough, Susan's words were a tremendous balm to my soul.

For the next twelve hours, I remained at my mom's bedside. I placed my phone on the table next to us and played the beautiful suite from *Enchanted April* over and over that we both loved so much. Then, thinking how my mom would enjoy hearing her favorite songs, the idea came to me to open the playlists on her phone. True to her eclectic nature, she had everything from Bobby Caldwell to The Bee Gees, Al Jarreau to Ed Sheeran, The Beatles to Bruno Mars, Carly Simon to Justin Timberlake, Todd Rundgren to Flunk, Tom Jones to Pharrell Williams, our staples of Earth, Wind, and Fire and the Doobie Brothers, and more, including several artists she loved from *The Voice*.

I played a medley of these songs she loved, and many that I loved too, for hours, hoping to provide a soundtrack to which she could take flight and feel nothing but lightness and joy.

Though she barely moved, and she never spoke another word, I felt a degree of peace in my heart that she was calm, that we were together, and that I knew she could hear the music, no matter where her soul was traveling.

Later that evening, I felt instinctively to stop playing the music and to let my mom's soul find its way without possibly feeling tethered to the physical world.

Around 11:00 that night, my mom's breathing changed, and it suddenly sounded as if her lungs were filling with fluid.

"Please don't breathe like that," I begged, finding it too much to bear to imagine the idea of her drowning. I placed my hand on her heart and held it there, feeling every beat resonate from her into me. And then, at 11:20, as if her guardian angel embraced her with a final gentle reminder that she and I would always find each other from here to eternity, I heard the sound of what I knew was my beautiful mom's final breath, and the slow but rhythmic pulse beneath my hand fell silent.

The After

It is a profound experience to be present for a person's last breath. I had been holding the hand of both my grandma and grandpa Hays when they took theirs, and now I had been there for my mom's.

In the pocket of heartbreak and grace that surrounded me in the dim light of the room, I fell lightly onto the bed next to my mom and sobbed, grateful she was now free, yet in a state of disbelief that our physical time here together had ended. I imagined her hovering near me and heard her voice telling me she was okay, but nothing could stop the dam-break of emotion that flowed through me.

Hearing my weeping, Dana came in and immediately enveloped me, her intense emotion flowing with mine. After a long while of being in that sacred space that held my mom's and my last moments, Dana rose and went to wake Rick to tell him my mom had passed, and I went into our room where I collapsed onto our bed and cried harder than I knew was possible to cry.

In that space of the most potent anguish I'd felt since I lost my grandma, a film reel of specific childhood memories ran vividly through my mind: my second birthday party, in the blue dotted-Swiss dress with the white pinafore my mom made for me; her doing my hair for my dance recital when I was seven; her buying me the eighth birthday dress I wanted so much; receiving Natasha for Christmas. Her laugh. Her sparkle. Gratitude. So much gratitude.

An hour passed before I was able to bring myself to call hospice, followed by the call to the funeral home. They didn't arrive until close to 1:30 a.m., and by the time I did the paperwork, properly disposed of all the medications, and they took my mom away, it was nearly 3:00.

Dana and I didn't fall asleep for another hour, but we were up at 8:00 and at the funeral home by 10:00. After the surreal task of filling out all the paperwork and making the arrangements, we returned to the house, where my mom's empty room brought me to my knees once more. Only hours before, I had been sitting by her side, playing her favorite songs as she found her way to her next grand adventure, and now she was actually on it. How mysterious the Universe was. How nearly unfathomable it seemed for a physical being to be here in one moment, and on a whole other plane in the next. Though I knew the essence of my mom would never truly be gone, and I felt a great deal of comfort in having been privy to so much encouraging information from the other side to help me cope, the sting of her absence was still like someone poking a fresh wound. Even in my numbness, I recoiled.

Out of respect for my mom, I felt a strong sense that I didn't want to leave her room in the state it was in. So I stripped the bed and put fresh linens on it so it wouldn't feel so stark, finished it with her sweet pale pink comforter and pillows, then tidied the night table. Last, I gathered everything for hospice to pick up into the foyer.

When Rick came home that afternoon, I told him I'd booked our flight home for tomorrow, and that we were taking my mom's car and leaving it in long-term parking until we could come back in a week or so for at least five days. The air between us was awkward but he conceded to that plan. I felt the best thing for Dana and me to do was leave, get our bearings at home, and then come back sooner than later to face the days of sorting through the closets and drawers and boxes and keepsakes that were what was left materially of my mom.

It also hadn't escaped me that my mom, in her last gift to us, had kept her promise: that she wouldn't leave us on Dana's birthday.

Joy in the Mi(d)st

Traveling back to Washington on September 17th was a day-long event, and by the time we arrived at our house on the island, it was 9:00 p.m. Dana had remained adamant that after losing my mom, having even the smallest celebration for her birthday was something she couldn't fathom, or even want. And when my mom was in the hospital and Dana's birthday had come up, it seemed unthinkable to me, too, to do anything resembling fun so close to losing my mom. But now, strange as it might sound under the circumstances, that celebration waiting for us at home felt like the most amazing gift in the midst of our grief that I ever could have asked for.

As we tumbled through our front door with our luggage in tow and rolled it into our room, Dana was exhausted.

"Honey, seriously," she said, "you must just want to collapse. I can't believe you actually want to decorate tonight."

"But I *want* to do it. I really do. It's the one thing making me feel happy right now. Plus, I know Mommie Bree is as excited about it as I am."

Dana looked at me tenderly.

"She *is*. I know it. I know I keep saying it, but I just can't get over the timing. She didn't want to linger, and she really wanted this party to happen if it could. I know it seems so unimportant in the big scheme of things, and maybe even shallow, but I also can't ignore that somehow, in her magical way, she left on the *precise* day this could all happen. If she'd left even a day later, we couldn't have come home for your birthday." I softened. "I believe this was her gift to us . . . not just the party, but the opportunity to feel joy during the worst time of our lives. Don't you think so too?"

Dana sighed. "I hear what you're saying. I just don't want you pushing yourself to do something for me right now when you're hurting."

"But that's just it. *This*, everything I planned for you, is somehow taking the hurt away right now. Any other time, we would have come home to an empty house and all our grief. But instead, we came home to a fully planned celebration. I know it sounds weird, but I can't help but see the divinity in it. Don't you? That's why I did everything so far in advance without knowing precisely why . . . the buying, the wrapping, everything. It was so it would be here waiting for us after Mommie Bree left us."

"I guess," Dana conceded, still concerned about me.

"So please, just let me have this. Let *us* have this. I can hear Bree so clear in my mind saying, 'Yes! Do it! And I get to be there!'"

Dana's eyes welled.

"I shared so much about your party with her. We would have given her the play by play like always on the phone the next day, but imagine how now, she gets to be part of it. She even told me she wished she could be like a little bee buzzing around to see it all . . . and now she can be."

Dana shook her head. "I just can't believe all the serendipity you're able to see right now."

"How could I *not*? Look at the circumstances, the timing. It would be sad not to recognize and enjoy it."

"Okay," Dana granted. "If your heart is really set on it."

"Good," I said, practically pushing her out of the living room. "Now make sure you have water and whatever else you need, because you won't be able to come out here until morning."

"How long are you going to be?"

"Probably two hours."

"*Two hours?*"

"I have a lot to do. Now you go."

After Dana disappeared into our room, I went upstairs to the loft, opened the closet door, and flipped on the light. The site of all Dana's presents arranged just the way I'd left them, the way they were going to be set up on the dining room table, greeted me like a giant smile, and my heart instantly swelled. I made multiple trips bringing everything down carefully. Then I strung up the banner, hung the ribbon decor in its pre-planned spots, and placed all the cards for the scavenger hunt game throughout the house. I had a few more things on my list to set up, and then I surveyed the space.

"Well, Mommie Bree . . . what do you think?" I said softly.

"It looks perfect," I heard her say in my mind. "Just perfect."

Then I flashed on the one item that had started this whole birthday extravaganza rolling: the cake from Carlo's Bake Shop.

When I felt certain we weren't going to be home by the 17th, which was the day the cake was being delivered because of our previous plans for that week, I had canceled it on the last day possible. But then, when I realized on the 16th that we'd be coming home after all, I went back online to see if there was any way of getting it by Dana's birthday, thinking it could be our one small way of celebrating. In yet another shimmer of serendipity, I was just in time to get it on the 18th if I paid for overnight shipping. *This will be even better,* I'd thought, *for it to arrive on the actual day. No matter what time it comes, it will be a wonderful surprise.*

With everything in place, I turned off the lights and ambled into our room with an impish grin.

"You're done?" Dana said.

"Yep."

"And you still have this much energy after such a long day?"

"Well . . . I'm starting to feel it, but yeah." I smiled. Then I copped to what I could read in Dana's face.

"Maybe I'm in denial . . . or still in shock. Probably both . . . but that's okay. All I know is, I just had so much fun setting everything up, and it was like Mommie Bree was with me doing it for you. I could sense she'd *want* me to enjoy this time . . . even though."

"Of course she would."

"And I know it seems weird for me to be this happy right now, but I really can feel her with me so strongly. It's like she's cheering that I recognize this is a gift to accept and cherish, not to waste any time wondering if it's okay to feel this way in the midst of losing her."

Dana nodded. "It *is* really something."

"It is. So let's enjoy every moment, okay?"

As I got ready for bed, I continued to marvel at the timing of my mom's departure from this plane, and how she would be with us on her new one tomorrow.

I looked up and whispered "thank you," then climbed into bed.

When morning arrived and my eyes popped open, I couldn't believe what met them: a heavy white mist blanketed the trees outside our windows. Tiptoeing into the living room, I saw that the mist was so prevalent that it also obscured the water, the other side of the island, and the Olympic Mountains beyond.

Now, mist wasn't unusual on Whidbey Island, and we'd witnessed this kind of weather many times since moving there. What was special about it was that it was Dana's absolute favorite weather, and that's precisely what settled on our little hamlet for her birthday morning.

"I *love* when it's like this," Dana remarked. "I only wish it would last all day."

The truth was, the weather was the perfect backdrop to this day. Not only was it Dana's favorite, but it felt like the right atmosphere: cozy outside, and warm and festive inside. Mist like this usually burned off by mid-morning, though, so we relished it for as long as it would last.

I kicked off the day with the first surprise: a personalized Captain Zoom birthday song. When I was six years old, my aunt gave me one made for Stacey that my mom would play for me on my birthday morning. It was this flimsy vinyl disc that came in a paper sleeve, and both my mom and I had marveled at how, with all the times I'd moved, that record stayed with me—and continued to play flawlessly for all these decades. Dana had never heard it when we met, and she got the biggest kick out of it. So, each year on my birthday, she'd play it first thing for me just like my mom had when I was little, and she loved it so much, she'd have me play it on her birthday too, even though the singer said my name, not hers. Until this year, I hadn't been able to find a Dana version, and I was elated to discover the company had been rebooted and that they recreated that original song almost to the tee, which was now available to order on a CD. When I told my mom, she was as delighted about it for Dana as I was.

Having it queued in the computer, I hit play, scurried downstairs to walk Dana into the living room with her eyes closed, and the song started playing. Only instead of my name in the opening, which Dana expected, it said:

This is space command to Zoom
All messages are go for your message to Dana

Then the song started playing as Dana's eyes grew large. "What??!! How? What??!!"

I was giddy and imagined my mom was too as the song went on:

Hey, Dana, it's your birthday!
I'm in charge of the stars and I'm here to say,
Hey, Dana! You're the big star, to-day!

It continued playing as Dana took in the table full of gifts, the decorations, the banner, with her mouth hanging open and tears in her eyes. She even spied a few cards I had "hidden."

"Oh my God, look what you've done."

All I could do was smile from ear to ear and bounce with delight.

After the song ended, before we launched into the festivities, Dana said, "Wait, maybe we should have some music playing."

I grinned. "How about we do the first one, and then we'll figure that out."

She agreed, did the quiz that led her to find the card, then opened the gift that went with the card.

"What?!" she exclaimed as she unwrapped it.

I laughed. "I was a step ahead of you."

In her hands was a TimeLife set of CDs called The Best of Soft Rock, which was a collection of all kinds of popular songs we both loved from the '70s and early '80s. She had recently seen an infomercial for it and told me how fun she thought it would be to have.

"I ordered this right after you told me about it," I said. "I thought it would be our perfect soundtrack for the day. And it has 150 songs." I chuckled as I went up to the loft. "That oughta last us till tonight, huh?"

I slid the first disc into the Crosley. The notes of "Lowdown" by Boz Scaggs filled the air—a song my mom had always loved—and the party truly felt like it had gotten started.

I had set up the scavenger hunt for every half hour, which was signaled by "Happy Birthday" playing as my alarm tone. Dana would continue to do quizzes that would lead her to find each card, then open the gift that went with the card. With fifteen gifts, I expected the fun to last for nearly eight hours with little gaps in between. But with Dana, there were no gaps because she made it even more fun and special by relishing every card, every bit of wrapping, and every gift, just the way she always did. My mom had always appreciated and lingered over these details too, and I imagined her doing that right along with us. Dana even photographed every component, which meant that the half hour allotted for each gift sometimes turned into forty-five minutes, which stretched our blissful day out even further, not to mention she created a wonderful photo journal of the whole thing. And with each disc I swapped out throughout the day, songs my mom had loved, or that we had both sung to when I was growing up, kept peppering the day's soundtrack. When they did, I could so clearly see her making her groovy face and bobbing her neck the way she used to while she gyrated her upper body, her hands swiveling at the wrist and dipping to the beat.

But that wasn't the only way my mom's presence illuminated that already glossy day.

In the midst of our celebration, Dana and I both continued to notice that as each hour passed, the mist outside hadn't yet burned off. Never, in the four years we'd lived on Whidbey, had mist remained so thick and low to the ground without fading, even when the sun never came out. But on this day, it had sometimes morphed into an artistic display over the water, and other times enveloped the house and hugged the trees, but it never fully lifted. Suddenly, I remembered what Susan had told me my mom said during their spirit encounter: *I'm the mist that hovers just beyond your reach, much lower than the clouds but above your head. I gather and swirl around you. I'm still here, just invisible to the seeing eye. I promise it's me.*

"Oh my gosh," I said to Dana. "It's Mommie Bree. *She's* the mist. It's her way of showing us she's here."

"Yeah?" Dana said, a bit skeptically.

I knew that was a huge thing to take on faith, but still I held no room for skepticism. In my heart, my mom had the power to create mist outside on Dana's birthday, mist that would last hour after hour, and nothing could make me believe otherwise.

As evening was rolling in, we were both getting hungry. On the way home from the airport the day before, we had picked up a delicious spread of organic Indian food from our favorite restaurant in Seattle, just like I had originally planned, and all we had to do was heat it up. It was around 6:30 at that point, so we put the gifts on hiatus and Dana went into the kitchen to do her thing.

A few minutes later, I saw a UPS truck go down our street to the one below, then make its way back up to our driveway. I knew it was the cake, and I had planned to give Dana a specific card, then have her open the door to find the cake on our porch. But instead of distracting her in the kitchen for that to happen, I missed my opportunity.

"There's a delivery guy walking up our driveway!" Dana said. Then, "Oh my God, are you kidding?! It's from Carlo's Bakery!"

I thought the box would be plain, but I dashed in just in time to see it for myself: the "Carlo's Bake Shop" logo in red was clearly visible on the side that faced us. For an instant, I was disappointed that my plan didn't turn out the way I anticipated, but then I realized it worked out even better. For Dana to see that box coming toward our porch could not have been more perfect, and I once again silently thanked my mom for making it happen.

"Really?" Dana squealed as I brought the box in.

"Yep! You got your Carlo's birthday cake!"

"No way!" She lifted the frozen cannoli cake carefully from the box. The instructions said it needed to sit out or be refrigerated for a good hour at least, and I marveled at yet another component that worked out ideally that day. By the time we ate and were ready for our uncharacteristic sugar splurge, the cake would be just right.

After dinner and dessert, and the last box on the table had been opened, there was a secret one left that I'd hidden. Though Dana hadn't been a doll person like my grandma, my mom, and I were, she nonetheless had told me that she'd one day love to have a special boy doll, because she'd always wanted a little boy. I'd searched from time to time over the last few years, but I'd never found one I loved for her. For this birthday, however, when I went searching, I found not only the most adorable, realistic baby boy doll from Ashton Drake, but his name was Oliver, a name Dana adored for sentimental reasons. He even had Dana's brown eyes. My mom had been in on the acquisition of this little guy, and I'd even made a clandestine unboxing video for her in the loft closet. Her excitement over Dana getting Oliver was as heartfelt as mine, and knowing she would be there to witness it was the true cherry on the day's sundae.

As I was getting ready to unveil this last, unexpected piece of Dana's birthday, which would lead her to where I'd placed Oliver's wrapped box, an idea came strongly to me and I abruptly changed my plan.

I said I had to use the bathroom and disappeared into our room, where my mom's phone was. From around the hall corner, I could see

Dana's reflection in our living room windows and that she was near her phone. I opened my mom's text app and sent this message to Dana from her, in the words so like my mom would say:

I've been so thrilled to share this special day with you, my darling girl. 👵 What a celebration it's been . . . and so well deserved. 💕

Now go open the coat closet for one last gift from Doob and me. 🎁

I love you more than you know. 🖤 Mommie Bree

I watched Dana's reaction in the reflection as she picked up her phone. "*What?*" she said. Then I saw the tears come.

I came into the living room and wrapped her in my arms.

"How?" Dana said, crying.

"I'm sorry. I didn't mean to upset you. I just felt so strongly to send that message to you from her. I really believe I heard her voice in my mind telling me what she'd want to say." I smiled and brought her a tissue. "I hope I didn't freak you out too much."

Dana wiped her eyes. "Well, it *was* weird to see her name pop up on my screen. And it sounded *just* like what she would say. But honey . . . what do you mean there's still something else?"

"You'll just have to go where Mommie Bree sent you and find out."

Dana slowly opened the coat closet door. Her mouth dropped open and she gingerly pulled the box out. Attached to the front was a personalized card, and there was a gift card inside from Mommie Bree.

"You'll know what that's for after you open the box," I said.

We sat on the couch together, and Dana took photos like she had of everything else. Then she carefully unwrapped the box and pulled off the lid. In that moment, I was two distinct joy-filled people—eight-year-old me receiving Natasha on Christmas morning, *and* my mom who had the delight of gifting her to me—as I watched Dana fold open the tissue and see Oliver for the first time.

"Oh. My. Gosh," she said. "You got me a doll?"

I nodded and smiled.

"I *love* him," she gushed. "He's so perfect!"

I helped her untie all the ribbons that held him in place, then gently picked him up and presented him to her.

"Mommie Bree knew about this?" she said.

"She did. And she was so thrilled to be part of it. The gift card is so you can have fun buying him real baby clothes."

The entire day, I had been conscious of being completely present in the moment, of being immersed in the happiness every part of our day had given to us for hours on end. And now, as it was winding down, this pocket of time could not have been sweeter, where my soul mate got her little boy, just like I had gotten my little girl from Bree so long ago. I decided then and there that for every birthday and Christmas to come, I would find a meaningful gift to give to Dana that would be something special from Mommie Bree.

For the rest of the night, we listened to music and replayed the day we both declared one of the most joyful and memorable we had ever spent in our lives.

My mom had not only sprinkled the entire day with her stardust, but in the amazing way she could be now was there for every minute of it, beautifully communicating to me that the celebration hadn't only been for Dana, it had also been a celebration for my mom—and a perfect way of showing me that our soul connection would never end.

Salt in the Wound

*A*fter Dana's magical birthday, we remained enveloped in its pixie dust for several days, which somehow kept grief from sweeping me into those dark recesses of the heart where the physical absence of my mom still seemed impossible.

But within a week, it was as if we were pulled into a tornado, one in which nothing in the wake of my mom's passing happened as we expected.

In an unforeseen twist of the law, the house that my mom had invested so much in, had sacrificed so much emotional and physical well-being to stay in, and had held on to so tightly so that she could one day leave half of it to Dana and me, went entirely to Rick.

Out of deep love and respect for my mom, I will not discuss the details of how this news was delivered to me and carried out, but suffice it to say that all of my mom's hopes and dreams of passing on the legacy to us that meant so much to her were dashed in an instant.

We were informed that Rick was already taking the steps to put the house on the market, so we had to quickly jump on a plane to Santa Fe. We were grateful my mom's car was at the airport, and that we wouldn't have to arrange for a ride. But the whole way there, the numbness I'd still been residing in had been replaced by a churning in my stomach of anger, resentment, hurt, disappointment, and disconsolation, as if someone had forced me to drink a toxic cocktail. Instead of the five to seven days we should have had to go through my mom's things, Dana and I were told that we'd be given less than half a day. In other words, we had to cram about fifty hours into a mere ten.

To decide the fate of the sum of my mom's lifetime of material possessions in so little time was akin to the Queen of Hearts spouting the phrase I despised—"Off with her head!"—cold, unfeeling, and with no regard or compassion. This forced limitation meant that I would not only be unable to go through and make thoughtful decisions about all that belonged to my mom, but I'd only be able to keep relatively little of what was hers. It wasn't that I was materialistic; it was that I was hopelessly sentimental. So it was disquieting to me that I would I have no choice but to toss or donate whatever I couldn't keep while we were in Santa Fe, all the while worried that I'd give something away out of haste that I'd later come to regret.

Desperate for a solution that would give me some level of peace amidst the despair I felt, I was relieved to find a wonderful store that sold gently used and higher-end items, all in support of the Santa Fe Animal Shelter and its programs. If I had to give virtually every lovely item of my mom's away, at least it would go to a place that supported the welfare of animals. I called about scheduling a sizable pickup on short notice and luckily got one.

Rick and I had never been close, but up to my mom's death, Dana and I had always maintained a cordial relationship with him. Fifteen years prior, we had helped the two of them move into their new home by taking three road trips from LA to Santa Fe with Rick's van filled to the brim with their things, just the two of us. We had visited and stayed at their house several times. We had even given him some thoughtful gifts over the years he seemed to genuinely appreciate. Then, like a lightning strike, we became, with no explanation, the enemy. We had arrived to discover that Rick had changed the locks, required us to be at the house supervised, and that we were not allowed to stay the night there. The unwarranted cruelty of this, on the heels of losing my beloved mom, felt as if he had physically assaulted me, yet worse because it went deeper than that, permeating every cell of my being.

On the morning we were let into the house, Dana and I were launched into a veritable race against the clock. Dana took right to packing the collectible dishes in the dining room cabinet, and I dragged a stack of large boxes down the hall and into my mom's room. Under any other circumstance, simply entering that space where I'd had to let my mom go, I would have wept and been cloaked in sentimentality, but there was no time for that. The clothes she'd had every intention of sorting and donating were just as I'd left them a year ago.

I slid open one side of my mom's closet, the side with the double bar of blouses, and hurriedly started sliding them off the hangers. When I had about ten, I laid them on the bed and folded each one quickly but neatly, then placed them in a stack in one of the boxes, which would hold four tall columns. I kept a handful of smaller blouses that suited both Dana and me, but the rest I had no choice but to detach from without much thought.

That side of the closet alone took me over three hours, as there were a good three hundred items to pull and fold. Then I moved on to the other side, which held around seventy-five beautiful jackets. After that, I had all her sweaters, layering tops, pajamas, scarves, hats, handbags, socks, shoes, and boots, almost all of which were practically brand new or only gently worn, to go through. Again, I saved only a few items that particularly spoke to Dana or me; the rest I couldn't stop to think about. It was grab, fold, box. Grab, fold, box. Hour upon hour at lightning speed.

In one aspect, I was lucky: my mom's plethora of adorable, high-end clothes looked great on her, but almost none of them were my style, and the majority were the size she had been before losing all the weight, so thankfully, they were too big for Dana and me. Even her shoes were a size too big. The normal me would have agonized over every piece going into those boxes, partly because I would have loved the idea of wearing some of her clothes for sentimental reasons. Had I allowed myself to fully take in that I was giving away thousands of dollars of my mom's cherished garments as if I didn't care in the least, which of course wasn't true at all, I would have lost it. But again, I didn't have the luxury of time for sentimentality or emotion.

Once we finished with that first phase, I still had my mom's long dresser to go through, along with other family heirlooms and treasures in her closet to unearth, now that all the clothes were gone. One of the first things I discovered was the journal I'd made for her for Mother's Day in 2014, the one with all the inspiring quotes that was meant to be a place for her to write down her daily list of goals so she could feel a sense of accomplishment for tending well to herself. I took a moment to open it, hoping to see some of the things she had documented. The letter I'd written to her was on the first page, and the first quote I penned a few pages later. But when I flipped through it, other than my writing, the entire journal was empty. My heart sank. I reasoned that she simply wasn't a journal person, but I also wondered if the words of encouragement I'd taken such care to write had had any impact at all.

Once again, I couldn't spend time thinking about the sad turn my mom's life had taken in the previous years. I was already distressed that I hadn't even begun to dig through the garage, where I knew there were several more boxes of collectible dishes, family china, photos, and other items that belonged to my mom. When I'd asked her about the garage soon after she came home with hospice, she'd said most of the things in there were Rick's, and that her boxes were on the right-hand side. When I'd gone out to assess what was hers, I was in complete overwhelm. Not only would I have to move a lot out of the way to get to her boxes, but I could tell that there were at least fifteen, and likely more. Originally, I had figured the garage would take a day on its own, which was partly why we'd originally planned to come for the better part of a week. Now, I had no idea how I'd be able to get to any of it.

Left with no other option but to arrange for shipping of everything we couldn't go through or fit into the car, Dana and I stood in the muted light of the twilight-tinted sky that seeped into the garage.

"We'll never come back here again," Dana said.

Seeing my mom's handwriting on her boxes made my throat catch. "I guess there'd be no reason to, would there?"

We were both quiet for a moment.

"It seems kind of weird to think of never coming back to Santa Fe." I felt tears well. "But Rick's already selling the house, so it's not going to be Mommie Bree's anymore anyway."

"Oh, honey," Dana said, taking me in her arms.

I clung to her and blinked the tears down my cheeks. "I just can't believe she's gone," I whispered.

"I can't either."

"She told me last year she was afraid it might be her last Christmas . . . I never thought it really would be."

Dana held me tighter and whispered, "I know."

When I finally pulled away, Dana's emotion mirrored mine.

"We've been through such a tornado these last days. I just feel wrung out, you know?"

"I know," Dana said. "I feel that way too." Then her face registered a peeved shift as she shook her head. "I just can't fucking believe how you've been treated. It was unthinkable. There was *no* reason for that. My heart breaks for what you've been through."

"I just never imagined I'd have to give her things away like that, in such a frenzy. It felt so disrespectful, as if I didn't care."

"Mommie Bree *knows* that wasn't the case. She *knows* you cared. You didn't have a choice."

I knew she was right but felt plagued by all of it nonetheless.

"I just don't want you to be immersed in all the negative energy these last few days have put us in. It's not good for you."

I sighed. "I know."

"Maybe for these next days driving home, we can just focus on enjoying the road trip and not think about what's still ahead."

I shuddered inside. "There *is* still a lot of stuff I'm going to have to deal with."

"I know . . . but for now, we really *should* try to let go of this ugliness. We're going to be driving through places we've never seen before, and we don't want to miss it because we're still holding on to the stress we've been feeling."

I nodded.

Then Dana tipped her head and asked tenderly, "Are you okay?"

I took in the garage one more time. As I did, I thought about how my mom had seemed trapped in a rabbit hole while she lived in this house, and how I felt some sense of satisfaction that I had freed her from it. Though it was frenetic and heartless how I'd had to go about it, at least I was able to do that for her, to some degree anyway. But there was still so much I'd been robbed of.

"I just don't like the feeling of Mommie Bree being erased . . . of all her things just being gone. I mean, I know I kept certain things that are meaningful to me, but it just feels so wrong that no one else is ever going to meet her, or see her smile, or hear her voice."

Tears flooded my eyes again and Dana held me.

After several moments, we parted and she softly said, "We should probably go."

I wiped my face and nodded. As we walked toward the car, we stopped and took one last look at the house, remembering all the good times we'd had there in years past, before things had become so laden with acrimony and sadness. Then we got into the car and crunched through the gravel driveway for the last time to start for home.

∞

Heeding My Heart

W e ended up spending six days on the road, where we took in the beautiful fall scenery and the serenity of so much gorgeous landscape that proved to be therapeutic in the wake of all we'd been through, staying in lovely suites and stopping when we felt like it, instead of rushing our way anywhere.

When we finally arrived home, the air of Dana's birthday took us in like a hug as we walked in. We had left some of the decorations up, and they instantly conjured the pure delight of that day, that veritable gift from the Universe and from Mommie Bree.

The next day, I went up to the loft and sat at my desk. My mom had given me the most adorable card for my birthday in 2017, and I had loved the illustration and the words so much that I'd always kept it sitting out, where I could see it every day. Like anything that has a home somewhere long enough, it had become part of my decor, and I hadn't read it in some time. Though I knew seeing her handwriting would tug on my heart, I reached over and picked it up. The front read:

A daughter is a story whose words you know by heart.

I opened it.

I love the beautiful story of you.
Happy Birthday

Underneath, my mom wrote:

The story of you makes my heart sing. I'm so very proud of you.
I love you,
Bree

I held the card for a moment, then brought it gently to my heart. How perfect that she had found that card, with me being a writer, referring to the story of me.

But there was another story: the one of *us*.

In that moment, I felt as if a magnet was drawing me toward writing that story. It was so powerful that there was no room for doubt, or hesitation, or even the notion of someday. Yes, I had—and was still—dealing with the consequences of my mom's unsavory marriage to someone who held no compassion for me, but I refused, no matter how difficult it was some days, to allow that to take up too much space in the heaven-kissed story of my mom and me.

I looked out at the soft current of Puget Sound, with the muted rays of the sun making it shimmer like fish dancing at the surface, and at the snow-capped mountains that watched over that playful scene in the distance. Though it had only been six weeks since my mom took her last breath, and I was still numb over losing her and all that had transpired afterward, a smile spread across my face as I thought of my wacky and wonderful young mother and the things she had done that we'd cracked up over through the years. Her trying to get me to swear as a toddler. Her begging me to stay home from school and play with her. The Mean Mothers Association. The Big Black Button. Those hilarious yet tender memories morphed into all the ways we had been the best of friends, how much we'd made each other laugh, and how even though we'd been apart during some of the crucial years, never was her love anything but unconditional, and how as an adult, I'd always been able to count on her. I also thought of how Susan had told me, shortly after my mom left, that she was in a place where she was being shown all the good she had done. I hoped with all my heart that being my mom was one of those things.

❧

Maybe on the surface, my mom doesn't seem so remarkable. She didn't invent anything, or make great strides in a particular field, or even find her way to healing the deep emotional wounds that plagued her so that she could become the resplendent recovery story and pillar of hope she had so wanted to be for others. But even without achieving that, she made a lasting, luminous impression on everyone who knew her. She lit up the room with her effervescent personality, her witty sense of humor, her genuine warmth, her heartfelt compassion. Even the majority of boyfriends she once loved but who hadn't worked out remained friends with her. She treated everyone in service positions with respect and kindness, and she used endearments with strangers and friends alike. When a nearby family—people she didn't even know—lost their home in a fire, she jumped to buy clothes and necessities for both the parents and the children. For years, she bought a cart full of baby dolls that she donated to Toys for Tots because she believed "every little girl should have a dolly to open and love on Christmas morning." That was the heart of my mom. But perhaps most striking is how that childlike girl with the bubble hairdo and braces on her teeth, who got pregnant just shy of sixteen, became a mother who so naturally and strongly believed in acceptance and freedom and allowing her daughter to be her authentic self, she infused her, infused *me*, with more than she could have imagined. And to me, if only for that, she was indeed remarkable.

Though I always relished being her only child, and protecting what was uniquely ours, I continued to be pulled toward the idea of immortalizing our story in book form. And as I was, I couldn't help but think that maybe others might be inspired, or moved, or even simply entertained by our particular brand of mother-daughter, daughter-mother-ness that shaped us both over the five decades we shared in this lifetime.

And so, hopeful that I was right, with my beautiful Bree in my heart and with her stardust surrounding me, I put my fingers to the keyboard and began to write.

Afterword

On the precise day I finished writing this manuscript, completely unbeknownst to Susan, she told me that my mom had sent me a message through her—and that she wanted it to go in the book.

By now, after making this journey with us, that probably doesn't strike you as terribly odd, but even for me, I was rendered speechless.

"She wants it in there verbatim?" I asked Susan, still a bit blown away and wanting to be certain.

"Yep. That's what she said. She called it a 'foreword,' but it would be more understood after the journey. As you honored her, she wants to honor you in her own words."

And so, with deep gratitude in my heart, I give the last words of this memoir to my mom.

What makes me qualified to write the [afterword] to this book? I am the expert at being the mother of Stacey. I may not have done things perfectly, but everything was done with love. That in itself makes my love for my daughter—PERFECT.

Our bond can never be broken. Although I am no longer visible on the physical plane (to most), I live on in these pages and, most importantly, I live on in your heart.

My dearest Stacey, thank you for capturing our life together. You make me laugh. You make me smile. You make every day a time to cherish no matter what. I am always with you—just on the other side of the veil. Dare you be still enough to hear me whisper? Feel my breath on your cheek . . . I breathe life into you always.

I am so proud of you, my angel.

With eternal love, Bree

∞

Photo Gallery

I chose the following photos to allow you to "grow up" with my mom and me, starting with her young years, leading up to my parents' brief relationship, then the two of us both separate and together, to reflect the people, events, and stories within the pages of this book. I hope you enjoy them.

Baby Cynthia, later Bree, age two

(top)
Three-year-old Bree holding new baby brother, Randall (note the large infant photo of my mom on the TV that was always prevalently displayed in my grandparents' house).

(left)
One of my favorite photos of my mom as a toddler – I love how it captures her personality so perfectly.

One of the few photos of my mom and grandma together when my mom was a little girl. A true treasure.

A rare photo of my mom around the age of ten, holding one of the first of her many beloved kitties, in the backyard of her house.

This is the photo of my parents that was snapped when my mom visited my dad at the base shortly after finding out she was pregnant. Despite what they were both experiencing, I love how happy and cute they look together.

My parents' church wedding day, October 13, 1968.
(I'm behind the bouquet)
All four of my grandparents are pictured below with the
smiling couple.

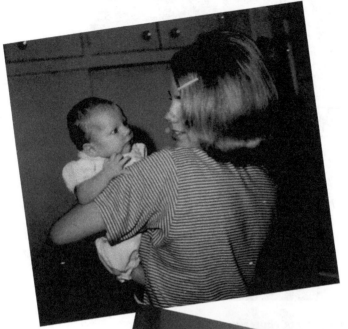

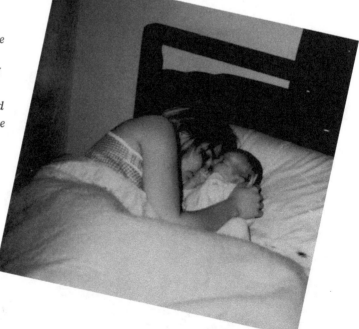

My mom and me in our first bonding days. I love how she's holding my hand as she sleeps. She finally had a biological connection to cling to.

My mom and me on my first Christmas, where she's already looking lighter in her mommyhood.

My mom, just shy of seventeen, on her first Mother's Day, and us together. I just love her youthful, happy glow.

(above) The photo session we had when I turned three and my mom was nineteen.

(below) The dining table we had in our first apartment, where my mom finally started to sprout wings.

Me in total delight receiving my Thumbelina baby doll on my fourth birthday, as my mom looks on in equal delight. I named her Sally, and I still have her, wearing her original pale yellow outfit.

(above)
My mom and Bobby, the first serious boyfriend she had when I was a little girl.

(left)
My mom in our famous orange and yellow kitchen in the Gundry house.

Me in my costume the day of my cherished starring role in my first and only ballet recital, age seven.

(below)
One of my mom's favorite photos of me, age six.

Me in the treasured dress my mom bought for me for my eighth birthday party.
Next to me is my friend, Lisa, and on the far right is my childhood best friend, Christi.

A couple of shots from our many trips to Cherry Avenue Park together. I'm wearing a dress my mom made for me in the photo to the left.

(To this day, I've never outgrown my love of Mary Jane shoes.)

Two sweet surviving heirlooms:

Above: one of the famous
"Guess What Color" tees, in lime ;-)

Left: a romper my mom made me
with her signature tag

(right)
The glorious
Christmas
morning I
received my
beloved Natasha.

(above)
My memorable ninth birthday in Santa Cruz, when my grandparents surprised me. This is one of my favorite photos of my grandma and me, dancing to a song from Saturday Night Fever.

(left)
Us blondies on my mom's 26th birthday.

Christmas, 1978. I had to include both because I love that my grandma is kissing my mom in the photo above, and I also love the one of just the two of us.

Us girls being playful, which was the hallmark of our growing up together.

(below)
A rare Hays family photo of my grandparents, my Uncle Randy, my mom, and me, around 1979.

The happy day of my mom's wedding to Danny, August 1, 1982.

A sweet moment captured of my mom and grandma.

This photo, around 1982, really shows why my mom and I were so often taken for sisters.

The night of Homecoming when I was crowned Sophomore Kitten, October, 1984.

The portrait we had done in 1984. My mom always referred to it as her "June Cleaver" photo.

Both of us growing up but always so close.

Our famous (often mocked by us) 1989 photo session framed in my grandparents' den. My mom was thirty-six; I was twenty.

My mom and me with Audrey Meadows, on the completely surreal night we met on the set of the Uncle Buck show taping at Universal Studios, September 28, 1991.

Aletha, my mom's birth mother. It amazes me to see the resemblance between them. I only wish Aletha had met her remarkable daughter.

*My Scripps
College
three-day
graduation
weekend.*

*(right)
My mom and me
on the day of my
Phi Beta Kappa
induction.*

*After cracking me up, my
mom snapped this of me on
my award convocation day.*

*The long-awaited, happy day
of my graduation,
May 14, 2000.*

*It was never hard to
find glamorous shots
of my mom . . .
these are a few
wonderful ones.*

*My two angels.
I couldn't have been loved
more by these two very
different, yet equally big-
hearted women.*

Two of my very favorite pics of my mom, around the year
2000, in her beloved Nantucket house. She was the picture of
health, and her radiance reflects her happiness with her life.
Below was her Christmas card photo with her fur babies.

My mom with her girls, her two daughters, Dana and me. Left and bottom are at her home in Santa Fe. Below is at my grandparents' house during one of her visits.

I love this playful pic of my mom in 2015. No matter what she went through, she always had this fun little girl side that was a total delight.

(below)
My mom with Dr. Tony Jimenez, the founder of Hope4Cancer, reflecting the glow of health after weeks of immune-boosting therapies at the clinic in Mexico.

My mom during her only visit to Whidbey Island for
her birthday week, June 14, 2017.

This photo so perfectly captured my mom's genuine
heart . . . it's the one I kept open on my desktop as
inspiration during the writing of this memoir.

I miss her every day,
but know in my heart she is never far away.

Acknowledgments

I offer my profound gratitude for the following angel people, places, and things:

First, to my remarkable mom, Briana King, who was the best friend a girl could have from the moment I came out of her womb. Thank you for giving me so much freedom, for always allowing me to be myself, for having so much respect for me as a human being, and for treating me as your equal from my earliest days. Though we suffered through some periods of being apart, I adored our unconventional relationship, and I never wanted you to be anyone other than who you were as a mother. I loved our signature wackiness, our movie line speak, our "us-ness" that nobody had but you and me (and Lorelai and Rory Gilmore). Thank you for being there for me so steadily as an adult, and for letting me be a touchstone for you. If not for you, I never would have made it through that dark night of the soul that lasted so many dark nights. Thank you for keeping the letters I wrote you in those early years of being apart, and for saving other keepsakes that made their way into this book. Thank you for never resenting my relationship with Grandma when you so easily could have. You always had the sense to take the high road when it came to me, and I have always loved you so much for that. Thank you for every gift you ever gave me, but especially the ones I know were an enormous sacrifice for you during the lean years. Thank you for always being genuinely interested in my passions and my career, for delighting in my every accomplishment, and for supporting every dream. Thank you for being the one to take me to Scripps and to tell me I belonged there, and thank you for giving Dana a safe space to land and for embracing her so wholeheartedly as your daughter. I know you regretted not being there more when I was a baby and toddler, but know this: *you really did do so good for being a young mother.* How you managed, I'll never know. All I know is, I had an amazing childhood in so many ways, and you were a huge reason why. I've also been incredibly blessed as an adult, and you were a huge part of that too. I will miss your voice and physical presence for the rest of my days here on Earth, but I feel your energy so strongly with me and take comfort in knowing that we made a pact many moons ago to always find each other from here to eternity. I feel enormously blessed that in this particular lifetime, I was able to immortalize you in this memoir. What a gift it has been.

To my cherished soul sisters:

Lori Stillman, for being my steadfast accountability partner during the writing of this memoir, for never ceasing to be a well of encouragement, for being my daily gratitude partner for over a year now, and for being an early trusted reader—twice! Thank you for always seeing the golden side of everything, for joining me in envisioning my highest aspirations, for making me laugh, and for your ability to say just what I need to hear, when I need to hear it. I adore you.

Susan Bova, for being my angel and for blessing me with your profound intuitive gifts. There aren't enough words to thank you for all of the readings you have done so graciously for me, Dana, and Bree, and for all the insights and magical connections you've revealed about our lives. Thank you for not only being one of my cherished and trusted early readers of this book, but for all of the honest, deeply appreciated input you gave to me that made the book so much better. Most of all, thank you for being there for me like a lighthouse in a storm during my mom's last days and beyond. Your soul encounter with her gave us both so much peace when our hearts were breaking in two. You being a conduit for us, then *and* now, is a gift beyond measure, as is your friendship. I love you to the moon.

Patty Bear, for being an ebullient cheerleader and deeply appreciated supporter of this book. Your profound sensitivity, awareness of others' feelings, fun-loving sense of humor, and special brand of insightfulness are gifts I count myself fortunate to receive from you on a regular basis.

Thank you for being such a willing and eager early reader, and for all of your honest, loving feedback. I treasure our sisterhood, our mutual trust, and you.

Mary Odgers, for knowing my heart so well and for being such a precious friend. Thank you for letting me step into your soul space in crafting your remarkable memoir, and for being willing to step into mine as an early reader with so much love and sincere caring for my experience. Your heartfelt feedback and suggestions were a true gift, and I'm so grateful for the bond we share. I love you dearly.

To Hope4Cancer, for being a beacon of light and healing for people with cancer. Though my mom didn't ultimately make it to the other side of her dis-ease, which many factors contributed to, our time together at the clinic was special and will always be a wonderful memory for me. May you continue to offer cutting-edge treatments, educate Western countries on your amazing protocols, and be found by people from all over the world.

To my iPhone, for holding thousands of texts between my mom and me. Though I was reluctant to revisit them after her transition back to stardust, they became a source of immense help and joy during the writing of this book, as well as meaningful additions in just the right places. I'm beyond grateful to have them as a record of so many conversations, both poignant and humorous, that my mom and I shared over many years.

To Amy Sherman-Palladino for giving life to characters that in so many astonishing ways reflect my mom's and my rare, wacky, and wonderful relationship. *Gilmore Girls* will forever be my favorite show because of its heart and brilliance, but also for all its uncanny parallels of the special brand of us-ness my mom and I shared.

To Sharon Bially and Lauren Hathaway of BookSavvy PR, for taking my story into your hearts and making it possible for others to take it into theirs. You're not only top-notch publicists, but true mensches with beautiful souls. Working with you both was a tremendous joy and privilege in every way, and my gratitude is more far-reaching than you know.

To my dad, Ralph Hill, for being the best young father a little girl could have asked for, for giving me such an exceptional childhood with you, and for taking on the teen years without reservation. You've always been my dad and my friend, and I've always loved you for that, and so much more.

To my late paternal grandmother, Georgia Hill, for sparking my craft gene during our time together when I was a child, for so generously providing a place to call home when I most needed it, and for being a wonderful source of support during my academic years. You were a much more admirable woman than you ever gave yourself credit for.

To my late maternal grandparents, Lucille and Darrell Hays, for showing me by beautiful example what unconditional love means, and for being there for me unfailingly, generously, and gladly my entire life. I may have been an unexpected arrival in your lives, but you never made me feel anything but wanted and adored. My gratitude for that, and for the countless ways you both stepped up to support me, no matter the situation, will live in my heart forever.

Last, to my soul mate and playmate of twenty-one years, Dana Chalamet, who not only was my rock during my mom's final days, but let me immerse myself after she left us in writing this book and not a whole lot else for two months straight. Thank you for being our health guru and for taking amazing care of me every day so that I can do what I love. Your insightful feedback on the book was unparalleled and allowed me to make certain parts so much better. I am deeply grateful for your honesty. I hope you how much I appreciate your understanding of what writing this book meant to me, and how much I love you and our life together.

Look out . . . our story may be next.

Book Discussion Questions

1. In what ways did you view Bree as remarkable?

2. What did you make of Stacey's young years? How was your childhood similar or different in terms of freedom and having a voice?

3. In what ways did Bree's choices as a mother shock you? In what ways did you admire them?

4. What was your reaction to the open-minded, unconditional acceptance of Stacey by her family members?

5. Why do you think Bree didn't object to Stacey's decision to live with her dad when she was nine?

6. What did you make of the odd similarities between Aletha and Audrey Meadows, and of the roles they played in Bree's and Stacey's lives?

7. How did the many mystical connections and events shared in the book impact you? Did they change how you see the Divine?

8. Do you believe in past lives? If so, how does this influence your life?

9. Why do you think it was important to Stacey to live with her mom during the years they did?

10. Have you seen *Gilmore Girls*? If so, what parallels did you draw between Bree and Stacey, and Lorelai and Rory?

11. What was your reaction to Bree standing firm in her choice of healing protocols for both MS and cancer?

12. How have you witnessed people's toxic relationships and environments affecting their health?

13. Why do you think it was important to Bree to marry so many times? What do you think she was seeking? Why do you think she stayed in her fourth marriage?

14. What was your reaction to Stacey being drawn to Judaism and later finding out from her DNA results that she had Jewish ancestry? Have you ever experienced a strong inner knowing that was later corroborated?

15. How did Bree's adoption saga affect you? Do you think all adoptive children have a right to meet their birth parents?

16. What did you make of Aletha never meeting Bree after seventeen years of having a long-distance relationship?

17. Why do you think Stacey was able to find so much joy, during a decidedly devastating time, in the celebration of Dana's birthday? Discuss the mystical occurrences surrounding that event.

18. Do you believe that our ancestors who have passed watch over us and guide us? How have you experienced otherworldly guidance?

A Conversation *with*
Stacey Aaronson

YOU SAY YOU BELIEVE WE CHOOSE OUR PARENTS. WHY DO YOU THINK YOU CHOSE YOUR MOM, IN PARTICULAR?

I see the divinity in the influences of my entire family, but with regard to my mom, I definitely believe we have traveled together through many lifetimes, each time having a unique and evolutionary soul experience, such as when we were twins. This time, besides the special connection and all the fun I knew we would have, I believe it was her turn to be the mother and mine to be the daughter, but in a way that allowed her to be nurtured by me in the absence of her own mothers' nurturing. I believe our ongoing soul journey explains how harmoniously we fit together, even though we were also very different, and how natural my mother role was in her life as her daughter.

HOW DO YOU THINK YOUR LIFE WOULD HAVE BEEN DIFFERENT WITHOUT THE STABILIZING EFFECT OF YOUR FATHER?

I always had the stability of my grandparents, but I can definitely say that I would have missed out on an incredible amount of grounding, practicality, and a specific brand of fun without my dad in my life. He was truly the best young father I could have asked for, and in significant ways, he was a wonderful role model.

YOU GREW UP WITH WITH A RADICAL LEVEL OF ACCEPTANCE AND HAVING A VOICE AS A CHILD. HOW DID THIS SHAPE WHO YOU BECAME?

Though I was never an arrogant or spoiled child, I did expect to be treated well and with respect by everyone—and it was natural for me to offer that in return because that was my example. I had no tolerance for people who were judgmental—particularly because of race, gender, or sexual preference—and I was deeply offended by witnessing mistreatment or silencing of children. My opinions were always welcome and considered, and that made me a co-creator of my life, not a puppet manipulated by adults. I also came early to despise labels; in fact, I reject the label of "gay," and I don't believe anyone should have to "come out." The radical acceptance of my family showed me from the earliest age that everyone should be able to pursue their own passions, embrace their own beliefs, and love whomever they choose, without requiring parental or societal approval. This enabled me to stand firmly, and unapologetically, in my choice of spiritual path, my name, my life partner, to list a few, without seeking "permission," and fully expecting my family to stand by me, which they so beautifully have. I sincerely hope this book has been a testament to that, and a way of honoring the superb human beings who helped me become who I am with such love.

YOUR CHILDHOOD SEEMED SO CAREFREE, YET YOU'RE A SELF-PROFESSED PERFECTIONIST. WHY DO YOU THINK THAT IS?

I honestly believe I was just born that way. From the earliest age, I held myself to ridiculously high expectations, and I was always self-driven to excel. My family not only *didn't* put pressure on me, but they constantly encouraged me to give myself a break. Bless their hearts . . . it never worked! But in the past decade, though I still strive for as close to perfection as possible as a book production professional, I've become more dedicated to excellence than perfection.

YOU TALK ABOUT PAST-LIFE UNDERSTANDINGS, MYSTICAL CONCEPTS, AND ALTERNATIVE HEALING IN THE BOOK. WAS THIS SOMETHING ENCOURAGED IN YOUR ENVIRONMENT, OR DOES IT JUST COME NATURALLY TO YOU?

Because my mom was always open to all of these things, I naturally followed that openness as a child, and it carried through into my adulthood. Though I never really discussed those topics with the rest of my family, I've always been fascinated by the mystical aspects of life and have become more and more aware of my divine connection and appreciative of the miracles that surround us everywhere. I will say that having that openness in common with my mom was a truly wonderful thing, as it lent to intriguing conversations and allowed us to have an even deeper bond.

I truly believe that my grandma suffered from undiagnosed depression
after having a hysterectomy at twenty-six, and having no emotional or
physical support afterward. I think this clouded her ability to be a
more connected mother, though it does break my heart that my mom
had to suffer the consequences of that. I know that my grandma deeply
loved my mom, but they simply didn't have the same connection that
my grandma and I did, which happens so often in families. I also
believe that by the time I was born, my grandma's heart was able to be
more open, and while she did lavish enormous love and attention on
me, she was also very generous with my mom, in the way she could be.
I did come to understand at some point that my mom had every right
to feel whatever disconnect she did, and that I couldn't expect her to
miraculously feel the closeness with my grandma that I had. The fact
that my mom appreciated my grandma's and my connection with no
resentment was a gift I never took lightly.

A LOT OF DECIDEDLY MIRACULOUS AND MYSTICAL EVENTS AND
CONNECTIONS HAVE OCCURRED IN YOUR LIFE. WHY DO YOU THINK
YOU'VE BEEN SO FORTUNATE TO EXPERIENCE THESE?

I do feel like an old soul who has been blessed with heightened
awareness of and openness to the Divine. And while I truly believe I'm
no more special or deserving than anyone else, I also believe that the
more we are open to and recognize Divine occurrences and offer
genuine appreciation for them to the Universe—and also for the
everyday miracles that may not seem so impactful but are no less
miraculous and beautiful—the more we are given to appreciate. I am
grateful every day for countless big and little things, and I feel like that
gratitude invites more magic to come into my life.

YOUR FATHER HAD MORE CHILDREN AND YOU WERE OKAY WITH THAT. WHY WAS IT SO IMPORTANT TO YOU TO ALWAYS BE YOUR MOTHER'S ONLY CHILD?

I know I dwell a lot in the mystical, but from the beginning, I had an inner knowing that my mom and I were always going to be each other's one and only. Her having another child seemed inconceivable to me, probably because on some level, I knew it wasn't meant to be that way. On a human level, though, perhaps it was because in growing up together, our bond was so singular that it seemed impossible for another child to step into it—or possibly to take away from it. Though my mom had thought she'd one day have more children, she conceded early on that she was glad I was her only child; she, too, couldn't imagine how a sibling would have fit into our distinct dynamic, and she treasured our uncommon brand of closeness as much as I did.

YOUR MOM STAYED WITH RICK FOR MANY YEARS WHEN THE MARRIAGE WAS CLEARLY DISTANCED. WHY WAS THAT HOUSE SO IMPORTANT TO HER?

My mom had never been content to stay in one place for too long, but when she bought her first house, it was a huge milestone for her in terms of reflecting her feeling of success. And once she had that, it meant a great deal to her to follow in my grandparents' generous footsteps and one day leave that house to me, so selling it involved a lot of mixed emotions for her, even though she was happy it had been Dana's and my safe haven for ten years. Leaving me her house was so important to my mom that it was almost an obsession. I can't say she stayed in her unhealthy marriage strictly to leave me her half of the house if she passed on first, because I know it was more complicated than that. But it was undeniably heartbreaking to be informed I had no stake in it, after my mom had made so many sacrifices to hold on to it.

IT WAS CLEAR YOU EXPERIENCED TURMOIL TOWARD THE END OF YOUR MOM'S LIFE WITH REGARD TO HOW MUCH TO DO TO TRY TO SAVE HER. DO YOU ULTIMATELY FEEL YOU DID ALL YOU COULD? OR DO YOU STILL FEEL TORN ABOUT YOUR DECISIONS?

I definitely struggled a lot with that, because I certainly didn't want to have any regrets about what I'd done or not done for her. That final year after the initial cancer diagnosis, I was committed to helping her in any way I could, knowing it had to be my mom's decision which protocols to try or follow. But that final week, each time she seemed more coherent, I entertained the idea that she might come back and wondered if I was being called to make that happen somehow. I strove to listen to my intuition, but I believe my emotions made it challenging. This was why receiving the intuitive gifts from Susan was such a balm to my soul—so few people get that level of insight into someone's process of transitioning. Had I not had that, I'm sure I would have always wondered if I could have, or should have, done something to try to save my mom when she told me she didn't want to die. Having an understanding of her higher purpose and grander path, however, gave me peace that she was going to be okay, and that with her ongoing spiritual presence, so would I.

WHY DO YOU THINK YOUR MOTHER'S SOUL CHOSE THIS AGE TO DIE?

We are witnessing a lot of upheaval in today's world as we enter the Age of Aquarius and see the crumbling of so many old and corrupt institutions. This is extremely unsettling for some and exciting for others, and it of course won't all happen overnight. I think that my mom, as resilient as she was throughout her life, would have landed in the unsettled camp when she was already so unsettled in certain parts of her life. And so, when she received the gift of seeing what she could do on a soul level—rather than on a human level—during this time we're in, it felt more right to her to ascend than to remain, in part to continue having a special influence on mine and Dana's lives, albeit from beyond.

WHAT WOULD YOU TELL A PREGNANT TEEN OR HER PARTNER?

This would actually be for any parent: You won't have a manual for parenting, and this book is certainly not meant to be one; however, I do believe you can glean a lot of gems from my enormously loving upbringing. I would say that coming from a place of unconditional love and acceptance, not thinking your place is to control your child but rather to foster their unique gifts with enthusiasm and support, and allowing your child to always have a voice and stand in their own beliefs will take you far in raising a valued, independent, and authentic human being. Create meaningful rituals that are grounding, but allow plenty of space and time for freedom, play, and exploring your child's creative ideas and passions. Take pleasure in being silly together and nurturing a special connection, and make sure to have lots of fun in every way you can. For teens in particular, remember that your child will absorb everything you say and do and take it as a reflection on them, so you'll need to step into a more mature place than you may be now to be conscious of those decisions and actions, knowing they are shaping your child, likely for their entire life. You can read books and articles, and get advice from others, but also go with your heart. You will do things you may look back on with some degree of embarrassment or regret, just like my mom did, but as she said in the Afterword: *I may not have done things perfectly, but everything was done with love. That in itself makes my love for my daughter—PERFECT.*

About the Author

Stacey Aaronson is the product of an exceptionally loving, accepting, and big-hearted family, who have always encouraged her to be no one but her authentic self. It took a while, but she finally uncovered her gifts and soul's calling in 2011 as a writer, ghostwriter, editor, book and website designer, graphics creator, and publishing partner, and has since been gleefully and gratefully involved in the full or partial production of over two hundred books. She delights in working with authors of multiple genres within her business, The Book Doctor Is In, and as a layout artist for She Writes Press.

She currently lives on Whidbey Island in Washington state with her soul mate and playmate of twenty-one years, Dana; their rescued Maine Coon kitty, Sienna Skye; and the many deer, squirrels, and birds that frequent their property.

This memoir is her first solo publication.

Visit Stacey's author website at www.staceyaaronson.com or her business website at www.thebookdoctorisin.com

CPSIA information can be obtained
at www.ICGtesting.com
Printed in the USA
LVHW091104010621
688707LV00023B/298/J

9 781736 460504